Do Young People Know ASEAN?

The **ASEAN Studies Centre** of ISEAS – Yusof Ishak Institute in Singapore is devoted to working on issues that pertain to the Association of Southeast Asian Nations as an institution and a process, as distinct from the broader concerns of the Institute with respect to Southeast Asia.

ISEAS – Yusof Ishak Institute (formerly the Institute of Southeast Asian Studies) was established as an autonomous organization in 1968. It is a regional centre dedicated to the study of socio-political, security and economic trends and developments in Southeast Asia and its wider geostrategic and economic environment. The Institute's research programmes are the Regional Economic Studies (RES, including ASEAN and APEC), Regional Strategic and Political Studies (RSPS), and Regional Social and Cultural Studies (RSCS).

    ISEAS Publishing, an established academic press, has issued more than 2,000 books and journals. It is the largest scholarly publisher of research about Southeast Asia from within the region. ISEAS Publishing works with many other academic and trade publishers and distributors to disseminate important research and analyses from and about Southeast Asia to the rest of the world.

Do Young People Know ASEAN?

Update of a Ten-nation Survey

ERIC C. THOMPSON
CHULANEE THIANTHAI
MOE THUZAR

ISEAS YUSOF ISHAK
INSTITUTE

First published in Singapore in 2016 by
ISEAS Publishing
30 Heng Mui Keng Terrace
Singapore 119614

E-mail: publish@iseas.edu.sg
Website: bookshop.iseas.edu.sg

The responsibility for facts and opinions in this publication rests exclusively with the authors and their interpretations do not necessarily reflect the views or the policy of the publisher or its supporters.

ISEAS Library Cataloguing-in-Publication Data

Thompson, Eric C.
  Do Young People Know ASEAN? Update of a Ten-nation
  Survey / by Eric Thompson, Chulanee Thianthai and Moe Thuzar.
  (Report / ASEAN Studies Centre ; no. 15)
  1. ASEAN.
  2. Regionalism (International organization)
  3. International agencies—Southeast Asia.
  I.   Chulanee Thianthai.
  II. Moe Thuzar.
  III. ISEAS – Yusof Ishak Institute. ASEAN Studies Centre.
  IV. Title.
  V.   Series: Report (ISEAS – Yusof Ishak Institute. ASEAN Studies Centre) ;
       no. 15.
JZ5333.5 A9A85 no. 15   December 2015

ISBN 978-981-4695-64-0 (soft cover)
ISBN 978-981-4695-62-6 (E-book PDF)

Typeset by International Typesetters Pte Ltd
Printed in Singapore by Markono Print Media Pte Ltd

CONTENTS

LIST OF TABLES

ACKNOWLEDGEMENTS

This updated report of attitudes and awareness towards ASEAN among young university students is made possible thanks to the commitment of the ASEAN Foundation to support a follow-up survey to the initial one undertaken in 2007, also with its support. The shared aspiration of ASEAN members to promote ASEAN awareness and a regional identity among young people of the region provides the overarching framework for our work. Through the good offices of the ASEAN Foundation, the Governments of the Republic of Korea and the Republic of the Philippines funded the 2007 and 2014 surveys, respectively. The ASEAN Foundation and the ASEAN Studies Centre of the ISEAS – Yusof Ishak Institute also supported the presentation of the surveys' key findings to a broad readership in an accessible way. Following the practice in 2007, findings of the 2014 survey were shared publicly twice: the preliminary findings on 29 April 2015 at a forum organized in Kuala Lumpur on the sidelines of the 26th ASEAN Summit; and the full findings on 24 August 2015 at a seminar organized by the ISEAS – Yusof Ishak Institute, in conjunction with the 48th ASEAN Day celebrations in Singapore.

We wish to express our deep appreciation to Ms Elaine Tan, Executive Director of the ASEAN Foundation, who continued the commitment to support and encourage initiatives aimed at promoting awareness and understanding of ASEAN regional cooperation among wider audiences in the various nations. Thanks and appreciation are also due to the Institute of

Southeast Asian Studies (ISEAS), which was recently renamed as ISEAS – Yusof Ishak Institute and its ASEAN Studies Centre. ISEAS Director Mr Tan Chin Tiong and ASEAN Studies Centre Head Mr Rodolfo C. Severino (who retired in August 2015) provided valuable advice and support in the preparation of the survey update's expanded scope, and in sharing the report findings. Mr Tan graced the launch of the survey's full findings at the August 2015 seminar in Singapore.

Our sincere thanks and appreciation go to all the students in the twenty-two universities across the region who participated enthusiastically in this survey update: Universiti Brunei Darussalam; Royal University of Phnom Penh; Universitas Indonesia; Universitas Syiah Kuala at Banda Aceh, Indonesia; Universitas Nusa Cendana at Kupang, West Timor, Indonesia; National University of Laos; University of Malaya; Universiti Tunku Abdul Rahman; Universiti Malaysia Sarawak; University of Yangon; University of Mandalay; University of the Philippines Diliman; University of the Philippines Visayas; Mindanao State University; National University of Singapore; Singapore Polytechnic; Chulalongkorn University; Khon Kaen University; Walailak University; Saint John's University at Bangkok; Vietnam National University, Hanoi; and Vietnam National University, Ho Chi Minh City.

The research would have been impossible without the support of local research partners who worked tirelessly in reaching out to the students and coordinating data collection: Dr Rommel Curaming, Mr Men Prachvuthy, Dr Stefani Nugroho, Mr Bounnhot Boupha, Dr Seyed Yasin Yazdi, Dr Chou Wen Loong, Mr Kuan Chee Wah, Dr Nurul Huda bt Marwan, Mr Ye Myat Thu, Dr Manuel Sapitula, Dr Cristabel Parcon, Dr Acram Latiph, Mr Nattapon Meekaew, Mr Manawat Promrat, Mr Dinh

Quang Hung, and Dr Truong Thu Thi Hang. We also owe special thanks to the student researchers participating in the Undergraduate Research Opportunity Programme (UROP) at the National University of Singapore's Faculty of Arts and Social Sciences: Ms Kung Xin Ni, Ms Ong Lin Hui, Ms Poon Yee Suan, Ms Sylvia Oh, and Ms Teshura Nair; to additional research assistance from Ms Sakunika Wewalaarichchi, Mr Raymund Vitorio, Ms Rachel Howard, and Ms Catherine James; and finally special thanks to the efforts of our research officer Ms Pham Thi Phuong Thao of the ASEAN Studies Centre at ISEAS – Yusof Ishak Institute. The dedicated effort and participation of these important stakeholders made all the difference to our work.

1
INTRODUCTION

ASEAN is on the eve of announcing a single integrated community in 2015, comprising three main spheres of cooperation: political security, economic, and sociocultural. Since its establishment in 1967, ASEAN has grown from a relatively limited diplomatic forum into an organization and concept that encompasses a wide range of cultural, economic, and political goals aimed at regional integration and international cooperation. The ASEAN "brand" has also gained wider attention and attraction over the years. ASEAN maintains a central convening role for gatherings of leaders from its members and dialogue partners: Australia, China, India, Japan, the Republic of Korea, New Zealand, Russia, the United States, the European Union and the United Nations.

ASEAN member states have carried out a wide range of activities, individually and collectively, to promote greater awareness and understanding of ASEAN, especially its aims, achievements, and workings. Yet, there still remains a perception that ASEAN is an elite, diplomatic forum far removed from the everyday lives of the citizens of its member states. ASEAN awareness activities are also concentrated more in the central metropolitan areas of each member state's administrative and/ or commercial hubs.

In an effort to gauge the extent to which attitudes and awareness towards ASEAN have changed from an initial survey conducted among university undergraduate students in the ten ASEAN members in 2007, the project investigators undertook an update in 2014.

As an update to the earlier survey, the 2014 survey replicates most of the questions of the 2007 survey, but adds two questions aimed at gauging how the students across the region think about ASEAN and its members, and their perceptions of similarities and differences amongst ASEAN countries. The 2014 survey also expanded the scope of investigation to twelve additional universities across the region, to represent regional, ethnic, and socio-economic diversity within the nations.

The survey thus continued to measure: (1) attitudes toward ASEAN; (2) knowledge about the region and the Association; (3) orientation towards the region and countries; (4) sources of information about the region; and (5) aspirations for integration and action. As with the 2007 survey, the one in 2014 targeted undergraduate students in the universities surveyed. It was undertaken from June 2014 to May 2015, and involved 4,623 students from twenty-two universities in the ten ASEAN member states.

Key findings of the current update, which are summarized in Chapter 2, show several similarities with the 2007 survey. The survey methodology, including the two additional questions, are explained in Chapter 3. Despite data collection challenges (which we detail in Chapter 3), the survey update found that there is a strong trend in commonality of responses and overall positive attitudes towards ASEAN throughout the region. ASEAN-positive attitudes have remained generally consistent, while awareness and knowledge of ASEAN show some increase. Main differences from the 2007 findings are found in the responses from Myanmar (more positive) and Thailand (more ambivalent), and in the ranking of aspirations for integration. These are further explained in detail in Chapter 4, with in-depth analysis of national findings summarized in Chapter 5.

The 2014 survey report added two questions to the original questionnaire. One of the two additional questions asked was to give a one-word description of ASEAN and each of its ten members, among others. Overall, words describing ASEAN primarily related to regionalism and cooperation. Many associate ASEAN with their own nation, and also mention diversity and culture. The country-by-country analysis of the one-word descriptions are explained in Chapter 6.

Chapter 7 examines at length the final additional question which asked students to judge the similarities and differences among the ASEAN members based on a triad-test. The results indicate a strong national framing of perceptions of the region. Three broad, transnational patterns of thinking about the region are also identified: "Malay-Muslim", "Mainland-Maritime", and "Singapore exceptionalism".

The 2014 survey thus provides a baseline for understanding how much recently educated citizens in each country know about ASEAN, its aims, objectives, and dynamic evolution. Dr Eric C. Thompson of the National University of Singapore, supported by Dr Chulanee Thianthai of Chulalongkorn University, Thailand, led the survey investigations for 2014 in the same manner as the 2007 survey. Ms Moe Thuzar of the ASEAN Studies Centre at the ISEAS – Yusof Ishak Institute joined as project investigator for the 2014 survey. A summary of the key findings was launched at a public seminar on

24 August 2015, and this report compiles the full findings of the 2014 survey. We have added a concluding section to highlight policy-relevant findings from the survey, which may provide useful inputs in deciding the future content and quality of efforts in making ASEAN awareness more widespread among citizens of the Association's members.

2
SUMMARY OF KEY FINDINGS

In this chapter, we summarize the key findings from our 2014 survey of 4,623 university students across twenty-two universities in the ten ASEAN member states. More details supporting these summarized findings are found in subsequent chapters. The 2014 survey included returning to survey students at ten primary national universities, replicating our 2007 ASEAN Awareness Survey and expanding it to twelve additional universities in selected nations across the region. The twelve additional universities were purposefully sampled in order to test for regional, socio-economic and/or ethno-religious differences in particular nations. These results give us specific insights into variations or similarities within particular nations as well as indications of the extent to which we generally find, or do not find, significant within-nation and across-nation variation. In other words, they give us insights into whether our findings appear to be particular to specific groups within nations, are nationally framed, or are more generally shared across the region.

The most general finding from comparing within-nation samples is that there tend to be strong national frames-of-reference with regard to the university students' attitudes toward and awareness of ASEAN and its member states. However, there are some exceptions on particular points, where students from universities within nations differ. The largest overall difference within nations is in Malaysia, between the majority Malay students at University of Malaya (UM) and largely Chinese-Malaysian students at Universiti Tunku Abdul Rahman (UTAR). On multiple measures, there is evidence that these students do not share a very similar perspective on ASEAN and Southeast Asia, despite all being Malaysian citizens. Results from a third university in Malaysia, Universiti Malaysia Sarawak (Unimas), where we purposefully sampled indigenous (*Bumiputera*) but non-Malay students from East Malaysia, show that those students' responses are mostly aligned with their Malay counterparts at UM (and differ from the Chinese-Malaysian UTAR students).

Elsewhere, despite some differences regionally, ethnically, or socio-economically among the students, these were largely subsumed within broad national similarities on how students view ASEAN. There were some minor variations, such as between Muslim-minority students from Mindanao and their counterparts in the northern and central Philippines and between Christian-minority students from eastern Indonesia and their counterparts in Jakarta and Aceh in the far west of the archipelago. But these, and several other within-nation variations, were not nearly as pronounced as that found in Malaysia. And even the variation within Malaysia should not be overstated, as in many respects, it reflected degrees of difference (such as how positive students were toward ASEAN) rather than absolute difference (e.g. between positive and sceptical students).

As with our 2007 survey report, we summarize the findings in terms of five general categories: **attitudes** toward the region and Association; **knowledge** about the Association; **orientation** toward countries within the region; **sources** of information about the region and the Association; and ***aspirations*** for the region and the Association. We also summarize the findings from two additional questions of our 2014 survey which were not included in the 2007 survey. In 2014, we asked the students to provide one-word descriptions or associations with ASEAN and member states. These give us a glimpse of how students describe the region and its countries in their own words. Finally, we conducted a triad-test of similarities and differences, the analysis of which allows us to produce and compare "cognitive maps" of the region across our twenty-two university samples.

ATTITUDES

In 2007, we found a strong sense of ASEAN citizenship almost everywhere in the region. In the 2014 survey, this sense of ASEAN citizenship has remained strong and increased among the universities where we repeated the survey. The main exception was at Chulalongkorn University, our primary university in Thailand, where attitudes and sense of ASEAN citizenship remained generally positive, but showed some decline compared to the previous survey. Another important shift, in the opposite direction, was found in Myanmar. Despite some difficulties with data collection (both in 2007 and 2014; for details see our methodology section), the results of our 2014 survey show a disappearance of a degree of ASEAN scepticism, which appeared in the earlier survey. The results from Myanmar in 2014 show a profile of generally positive attitudes toward ASEAN, which are the norm regionally.

In most places, we found that senses of ASEAN citizenship tended to be as strong or stronger among our additional university samples as compared to the primary universities within the same nation. The main exception was in Malaysia, where UM students showed greater affinity for ASEAN as compared to UTAR students. Benefits of ASEAN membership, both to one's country and oneself personally, remained high everywhere, with the main shifts being a decline in Thailand and a rise in Myanmar.

There is a general tendency, from both the 2007 and 2014 surveys, to see ASEAN members as culturally similar but economically and politically different. However, there are some substantial differences from nation to nation on these measures. The patterns of thinking about similarity and difference on these dimensions, when we compare university samples within and across nations, tend to support a view that these attitudes are largely shaped by national frames-of-reference. On the whole, Singaporean students tend to see the greatest dissimilarity amongst ASEAN members, while the greatest overall similarities across all three dimensions are found in Indonesia, Vietnam, and in the current survey, Myanmar (which represents a substantial shift from our 2007 findings).

KNOWLEDGE

In the 2014 survey, we found a modest decrease in self-reported familiarity with ASEAN, but a general trend of equal or increased objective knowledge about the Association as compared to the 2007 survey. We speculate that this reflects students being in fact more aware and knowledgeable about the Association, particularly where attention has been given in the run-up to the ASEAN Economic Community (AEC) in recent years; but with this, students are more aware of how much they *do not* know about the region, and thus have decreased self-reported familiarity. Further, detailed investigations might allow researchers to confirm or disconfirm that explanation. The clearest measure of an increase in objective knowledge about the region was a greater recognition of the ASEAN flag almost everywhere we conducted the survey. Other objective measures (knowing the year of founding and identifying ASEAN members) generally remained the same or rose modestly between the two surveys.

In 2014, as in 2007, the lowest objective knowledge about ASEAN was found among students in the Philippines, followed by those in Singapore. Myanmar students, who had been the least objectively knowledgeable about ASEAN in 2007 (along with Filipino students), displayed knowledge in 2014 that was more in line with averages across the region. Greatest objective knowledge varied by question. Vietnamese students were best at identifying the date of ASEAN's founding. Thai and Bruneian students were best at identifying ASEAN countries on a map. Recognition of the ASEAN flag was over 90 per cent in Brunei, Indonesia, Thailand, and Vietnam.

ORIENTATION

In addition to knowledge about ASEAN and the region, our survey measured students' orientation toward other countries in the region. In the 2014 survey, we again found the general Maritime-Mainland divide in salience that was reported for the 2007 survey. Students from Mainland nations (Cambodia, Laos, Myanmar, Thailand, and Vietnam) are generally more cognizant of other Mainland countries and similarly those from Maritime nations (Brunei, Indonesia, Malaysia, the Philippines, and Singapore) are generally more cognizant of other countries in the Maritime grouping. In some instances, students from the Mainland group exhibited greater awareness of Singapore and Malaysia than of other countries in their own subregion. Thailand often had greater salience than Brunei among students from the

Maritime group. Thailand and secondarily Malaysia remained the most salient countries generally for students across ASEAN as a whole. Brunei remained the least salient country to students across the region.

In the 2007 survey, Singapore dominated the imagination of university students as a destination for both travel and work, with Thailand and Malaysia as second and third choices. Singapore, across ASEAN generally, was the overwhelming choice as a destination for work, with Malaysia rating a distant second followed by Thailand. In terms of travel, Singapore registered as a strong though less overwhelming favourite, followed by Thailand and Malaysia.

In the 2014 survey, Singapore again emerged as the most desirable destination for travel among students across the region, though its popularity as a travel destination over Thailand was less clear-cut. Whereas Singapore was the top travel destination everywhere except for Laos in 2007, in 2014, Thailand emerged as the top travel destination in Brunei, Indonesia, and Malaysia. Interest in travel to Malaysia slipped somewhat between the two surveys. Rather than a clear-cut third choice, the popularity of Malaysia was much closer to that of Vietnam (the fourth overall choice for travel) in the 2014 survey. Singapore remained the overwhelming choice of destination for work in the 2014 survey. Thailand replaced Malaysia as the second most popular destination for work overall.

In extending our survey to additional universities, we found some within-nation variations with respect to travel and work destinations. The greatest within-nation consistency was observed in Singapore and Vietnam, while results from Indonesia, Malaysia, the Philippines, and Thailand showed some variations based on co-ethnic or regional factors. In Indonesia, for example, Brunei was a strong secondary destination for travel and work among predominately Muslim students at Unsyiah (Universitas Syiah Kuala) in Aceh, but did not rate as a destination for either from among predominantly Christian students from Undana (Universitas Nusa Cendana) in Kupang (West Timor). Muslim-minority students from both Walailak University (WU) in Thailand and Mindanao State University (MSU) in the Philippines rated Malaysia as a desirable work destination to a much greater degree than their national counterparts at other universities.

Interest in learning about other ASEAN countries remained high in 2014 as it had been in 2007. The same pattern of ASEAN enthusiasm held, with the greatest interest coming from Cambodia, Laos, and Vietnam. Also, the evidence of ASEAN scepticism from Myanmar, where a quarter of respondents said they were not interested in learning about other countries in 2007, disappeared in the 2014 survey. This time, Myanmar students exhibited the same generally positive to enthusiastic interest as students elsewhere in the region. We also observed that interest in learning about ASEAN tended to be generally higher in the additional surveys we sampled in 2014 as compared to the primary "flagship" universities sampled in both the 2007 and 2014 surveys.

SOURCES

We asked respondents to indicate their sources of information about ASEAN from a list of fourteen possible sources of information. The results were largely similar to those in the 2007 survey with some small but notable exceptions. The most obvious change between 2007 and 2014 was the increasing importance of the Internet as a source of information and a decreasing significance of the radio.

Television and school remained the first and second most important sources of information. One of these was the most important source of information in every nation with the exception of Myanmar. They were similarly first and second among primary university students in five out of the ten nations, and both were among the top four sources of information everywhere except Myanmar. In Myanmar (among our Mandalay University sample), Internet and newspaper were the first and second sources of information, followed by television. Books were fourth and school fifth.

Newspapers and books remained among the most important sources of information, but in the 2014 survey for the region as a whole, these were ranked alongside the Internet, which emerged as the third most important source of information after television and school, and ahead of newspapers and books. The Internet ranked as third or fourth in almost all nations, second in Brunei and Malaysia and first as mentioned in Myanmar. In the earlier survey, the Internet and radio had come across as secondary sources of information regionally, after television, schools, newspapers, and books. This also reflected a varied media environment in which the Internet was more important in certain nations while the radio remained popular in others. In 2014, the Internet had gained popularity everywhere.

Conversely, in 2014 the importance of the radio had dropped, particularly in places like Cambodia. This is a good indication of the shifting, and to some extent, homogenizing of the media environment, at least in terms of the media of communication. In 2014, radio rated as a middling source of information, along with friends, advertising, and sports. Sports dropped modestly in 2014, which may be attributable to it being an off-year for the popular biennial SEA Games (as compared to 2007 when the games were being held). The importance of friends as a source of information rose modestly; again we speculate that this may be attributable to the rise of social media and the expansion of networks and definitions of friends (e.g. "Facebook friends"). Family, travel, movies, music, and work experience remained the least important sources of information about ASEAN.

ASPIRATIONS

In 2014, as in 2007, there was a strong positive attitude across all nations when asked to indicate agreement or disagreement on the importance of eight aspects of integration and cooperation: Cultural Exchanges, Economic Cooperation, Development Assistance, Educational Exchanges, Security and Military Cooperation, Political Cooperation, Sports Competitions, and Tourism.

The most noticeable shift between the two surveys was Economic Cooperation, which fell from first to third most important aspect of integration across the region. Tourism and Development Assistance, which ranked second and third in 2007, moved to first and second most important in the 2014 survey. As we have argued above, particularly for Thailand but perhaps for the region more generally, focus on the launching of the ASEAN Economic Community (AEC) in 2015, may well have highlighted the drawbacks as much as the benefits of economic cooperation to citizens of the region, leading some to view it with less enthusiasm. Nevertheless, the overall importance placed on economic cooperation, and the positive attitudes towards it, remained high.

Educational Exchanges, Security and Military Cooperation, and Sports Competitions rated as mid-tier areas of importance for regional cooperation. There was also a great deal of variation from nation to nation in weighting the importance of these items. For example, Educational Exchanges ranked first in Laos and Myanmar and second in Brunei and Cambodia, but seventh in Malaysia and Singapore (both "importers" rather than "exporters" of exchange students). Conversely, Security and Military Cooperation ranked first in Singapore and second in Malaysia, but seventh in Laos and Thailand. Sports Competitions ranked second in Indonesia and third in Malaysia, but seventh in Brunei and eighth (last) in Singapore.

The least important aspects of integration and cooperation across the region were Cultural Exchanges and Political Cooperation. One of these two ranked last in all nations, except Singapore (where they ranked sixth and third respectively). In five countries they ranked seventh and eighth. In three countries they ranked sixth and eighth. In Thailand, Cultural Exchanges ranked fifth and Political Cooperation eighth. Overall, these results were extremely similar to those from the previous survey.

One difference from the prior survey was that "ASEAN scepticism" reported for Myanmar in 2007 was not seen in these or other questions in the 2014 survey. Conversely, less enthusiasm for integration and cooperation was registered in Thailand, at least among the primary university students (though not among students from the additional universities). Nevertheless, the responses from Thailand remained overall positive, just less strongly positive.

As was pointed out in the 2007 survey, students tend to focus on issues of people-to-people exchange (Tourism, Economic Cooperation, Educational Exchanges) more than state-to-state issues (Security and Military Cooperation and Political Cooperation). This was also true when students were asked about issues crucial to cooperation and awareness of ASEAN. The results in 2014 largely tracked with those in the 2007 survey.

In 2014, as in 2007, Poverty Reduction and Educational Exchanges ranked as the highest areas of priority. Poverty Reduction ranked first or second in every nation. Educational Exchanges ranked first through third everywhere except Singapore (fifth) and Malaysia (sixth).

Science and Technology Development remained third ranked overall, but slipped a bit to be very close in overall average ranking to Health and Disease Control, and Natural Resources and Environmental Management. All of these items tended to rank third to sixth in importance across all nations, with exceptions of a low rating for Science and Technology Development in Singapore (eighth) and divergent views on Health and Disease Control in Singapore (second) and Vietnam (seventh).

Disaster Prevention and Assistance ranked highly in Malaysia (second), the Philippines (third), and Singapore (third) but in the bottom half everywhere else. Regional Identity ranked last in five of the ten nations and in the bottom half in eight of the ten. However it ranked as the most important issue in Vietnam, and fourth overall in Thailand. As in 2007, Cultural Preservation was again the least important issue, ranking seventh or eighth in all but two nations — Indonesia (fifth) and Myanmar (sixth).

DESCRIBING ASEAN

In the 2014 survey, we included two additional sections to the survey. In the first, we asked respondents to write one word that they would use to describe a list of twenty countries and regions — ASEAN, the ten ASEAN member countries, and nine additional regions and/or countries for comparative purposes. These provide some insight into how students from across the region think about ASEAN and its members in their own words. Our analysis of these responses centred on those from the primary universities, due to the intensive labour involved in analysing this complex, qualitative set of data.

Across the region, words to describe ASEAN primarily related to regionalism (e.g. Southeast Asia, Asia, ten countries) and cooperation (organization, unity, etc.). Economic cooperation and the AEC specifically featured in the answers from about half of the universities. Similarly, five nations associated ASEAN with development. Singaporean and Thai students associate ASEAN with poverty, though Vietnamese and Bruneian students associated it with wealth.

Many students associated ASEAN with their own nation, for example 14 per cent of Indonesian students wrote "Indonesia" in reference to ASEAN. This sort of response was observed in all our sets of responses, except for those from Brunei and the Philippines. Diversity, culture, cultural diversity, and related terms were mentioned by all ten nations except for the Philippines and Thailand. The most negative descriptions of ASEAN were found in Singapore where about 11 per cent of students described ASEAN as "useless" (or a synonym) and Thailand where about 7 per cent described ASEAN as "stupid" (or similar). Conversely, about 15 per cent of Vietnamese students and 5 per cent of Singaporean students described ASEAN in positive terms.

The descriptions of individual ASEAN member nations were often complex and varied across the region, though there were also some dominant, primary association with each country.

Brunei was primarily described in terms of oil, wealth, its status as a sultanate, and its small size. Islam was an important descriptor for Brunei in Malaysia, Indonesia, Brunei, and Singapore, but not elsewhere.

Descriptions of Cambodia overwhelmingly centred on Angkor Wat and secondarily on poverty; though in several places, Cambodia was associated with development rather than poverty. Among other frequent descriptors were "culture" (or similar terms) and references to the Pol Pot and Khmer Rouge era. To a lesser extent, and in a minority of university samples, Cambodia was described in terms of agriculture, tourism, and Buddhism.

Indonesia's many islands and large size featured in all responses from across the region. Islam was an important descriptor for Indonesia from six nations, but not in Brunei, Malaysia, or Indonesia itself. Everywhere, except in Vietnam, Indonesia was associated with well-known places within the country, particularly Bali and Jakarta. There was a diversity of descriptions in economic terms. With Indonesia and a number of other countries, there was a tendency to associate the country with poverty or under-development by students from more affluent nations (such as Singapore, Malaysia, and Thailand) but described in terms of development, a good economy, or economic growth by students from less affluent nations (such as Cambodia and Laos).

Laos appeared to be the least known country in the region. Among other indicators, Laos rated the largest number of non-responses when students were asked to provide descriptions, particularly at universities other than Laos' immediate neighbours (i.e. other than Cambodia, Thailand, and Vietnam). Poverty, underdevelopment, and — to a lesser extent —

development were leading descriptors for Laos everywhere, except Thailand. A secondary set of responses across many countries related to traditional culture, ethnic dress, food, and natural resources.

Malaysia was described widely in ethno-religious (Malay, multiracial) and religious terms (associated with Islam). Reference was made in all university samples to tourism in reference to Malaysia, frequently citing the Malaysia tourism slogan "Truly Asia". Locations (especially Kuala Lumpur) and landmarks (particularly the KLCC or Twin Towers) featured prominently in descriptions of Malaysia across the region. Malaysia's economy was noted by students from over half of the nations, mostly in positive terms but in a few as "poor" or "developing". Also, given the timing of the survey, mention of air disasters was made in many university samples.

Myanmar was associated primarily with the country's politics. Aung San Suu Kyi, as an iconic figure, featured in response from all nations except Vietnam. Common reference was also made to the military government as well as to war and conflict. Students from all nations also associated Myanmar with poverty and development, except in Laos where respondents referred to investment and trade. Reference to Myanmar's Buddhist heritage was particularly strong in Thailand, Laos, and Cambodia, and elsewhere students made frequent reference to pagodas or specifically the Shwedagon Pagoda.

The two most common descriptors for the Philippines, found in all sets of responses, referred to natural disasters and islands. Other common associations made by at least four nations were in reference to language, pop culture, Manila, sports, and food items. Many descriptive terms prominent in some nations' descriptions — such as labour migration, the economy, tourism, religion or education — appeared only in a few nations' responses but not in others.

Singapore, by contrast, has a much more singular, common image across the region. The primary set of associations for Singapore, found across all university samples, centred on modernity, wealth, and the country's small size. A second order set of associations, also found in all the sets of responses, referred to tourism, cleanliness, and education.

Thailand also had a strong, similar image across the region, centring on tourism, food, and the country's political situation and conflict over the past decade. Other significant associations made were in reference to agriculture and exports, the transgender culture, and to elephants. Less universally, but in several countries, Thailand was described in terms of culture, popular culture, the monarchy, and religion.

The two main associations for Vietnam, to which all ten nations made reference, were war and/or politics and to the economy. The concepts of war and politics are grouped together due to both being closely linked and they are often primary or secondary terms except in the case of Vietnamese students' responses themselves. Reference was made everywhere as well to Vietnam's rapid economic growth. Other significant associations made reference to agricultural production, Vietnamese culture, food, and tourism.

COGNITIVE MAPS OF ASEAN

A final and additional question of the 2014 survey asked students to judge the similarities and differences among ASEAN member nations. The results allowed us to produce "cognitive maps" of the ASEAN members, in which the similarities and differences in the judgements of each sample of students are represented visually. The data are also contained in aggregate similarity matrices. Using another method, we are able to compare each sample's matrix to those from other universities to assess similarities and differences among the students' judgements, or put another way, between their perceptions of the relationship among Southeast Asian nations. These results are expressed as correlations, with 1 being perfect correlation (two sets of responses that are exactly the same) and 0 indicating no similarity between the responses.

Almost everywhere, the results (as with other parts of the survey) support a strong national framing of perceptions of the region. Within-nation correlations among the results were in almost all cases 0.9 or higher, which is extremely high. The greatest exception was in Malaysia, where results from Chinese-Malaysian UTAR students correlated only at 0.76 and 0.68 with Malay-Malaysian students from UM and East Malaysian students from Unimas; UM and Unimas students correlated with each other at 0.97. In fact, the UTAR students correlated much more highly (around 0.90) with students from Singapore.

Two other cases that exhibited some degree of ethno-religious or regional variance among the students' perceptions, falling substantially outside of the >0.90 range, were in the Philippines, where MSU students, mostly Muslim from the southern Philippines, correlated at 0.84 with students from both University of the Philippines Diliman and University of the Philippines Visayas; and in Indonesia, where the correlation of Unsyiah students from Aceh was 0.87 with Undana students in Kupang (West Timor). However, in both the Indonesian and Philippine cases, these within-nation correlations were higher than any across-nation correlations for these groups of students.

Where we drew samples from multiple within-nation universities, each national group of students, other than those mentioned above, produced fairly consistent cognitive maps of the region across the primary and additional universities. At the same time, the results demonstrate several transnational patterns of perceptions about the region.

A "Malay-Muslim" pattern was observed across Brunei, Indonesia (though not Undana), and Malaysia (at UM and Unimas, where the students were not themselves Malay-Muslim; though not at UTAR). In this pattern, the majority Muslim countries of Brunei, Indonesia, and Malaysia along with Singapore are clustered together and contrast primarily with the "CLMV" countries (Cambodia, Laos, Myanmar, and Vietnam) and secondarily with the Philippines and Thailand, which form a residual grouping. Some echoes of this are seen in the clustering of Malay-Muslim countries in the cognitive maps of both MSU in the Philippines and WU in Thailand, where our samples were at least 80 per cent Muslim.

The other major transnational pattern was a "Mainland-Maritime" pattern, shared by all student samples from Thailand (including WU), as well as those from Cambodia and Laos. In the Mainland-Maritime pattern, the strongest contrast among countries are between the five Mainland countries of Cambodia, Laos, Myanmar, Thailand, and Vietnam and the five Maritime countries of Brunei, Indonesia, Malaysia, Singapore, and the Philippines. Second-order contrasts then differentiated in varied ways among these two larger clusters of Mainland and Maritime countries.

A third pattern with some transnational reach is the "Singapore exceptionalism" pattern. In this pattern, Singapore is sharply contrasted with all other countries in the region. The "Singapore exceptionalism" pattern was produced by all students in Singapore (including Malay students from the National University of Singapore, when examined as a separate sample) and by the Chinese-Malaysian students from UTAR as well as Chinese-Malaysian students from UM when examined separately.

Aside from these transnational patterns, those produced by Myanmar, Filipino, and Vietnamese students were more unique to those countries. The Myanmar pattern shows some visual similarities to all three of the transnational patterns mentioned above — "Malay-Muslim", "Mainland-Maritime", and "Singapore exceptionalism"; but it is not highly correlated with any one of them. The Philippines pattern clusters the Philippines with Singapore, Indonesia, and Malaysia in contrast to the CLMV countries, with Brunei and Thailand as intermediaries between the two. And finally, the Vietnam pattern clusters Vietnam with its neighbours Cambodia and Laos, primarily in contrast to the Maritime countries but secondarily in contrast to Thailand and Myanmar.

A final, and perhaps the most intriguing of our findings, is evidence of what we might consider a transnational, centralized and elite perspective in thinking about the relationship among ASEAN members. In examining within and across-nation correlations, we found that the primary, "flagship" universities in our survey almost all correlated more highly with each other in their responses than did any of the additional universities to the additional universities in other nations. This suggests that along with strong national and subregional (e.g. Malay-

Muslim) framings of perceptions of Southeast Asia, there is also a general, shared, transnational frame-of-reference that is being absorbed by our primary university students (i.e. ones at top, centrally-located universities) but not, or less so, by our additional university samples (which are variously regional or vocational-technical schools). We suspect that this reflects a transnational elite discourse about the region to which students at elite universities are most attuned.

3
SUBJECTS AND METHODS

The survey targeted students at universities across Southeast Asia. We built on the methods and survey instrument employed in the 2007 ASEAN Awareness Survey. In 2007, we sampled students at one leading, "flagship" university in each ASEAN nation. For the 2014 survey, we returned to the same primary universities and also selected additional universities in six out of the ten countries, to further test the validity of our results and to probe for within-nation variation in those nations. At each university, the questionnaire was administered in the main language of instruction for that university. For simplicity, we refer to the universities involved in both the previous survey and the current survey as the "primary universities" and the additional universities in the current survey as "additional universities".

The primary universities were originally selected because they represented the top, public universities in each nation. Therefore the current students at those universities could be expected to represent a sample of future leaders and members of the nations' professional classes and to be important thought-leaders of the coming generation. While their views may not necessarily be nationally representative in a statistical sense — for instance, they may vary from older generations or from less educated members of the general population — nevertheless, we can expect that their views will matter to the future of how their individual nations and the region as a whole respond to and build on the ASEAN framework in coming decades.

In 2014, we were able to successfully replicate the 2007 survey at primary universities in nine of the ten ASEAN member states, at Universiti Brunei Darussalam (Brunei), Royal University of Phnom Penh (Cambodia), Universitas Indonesia, Depok Campus (Indonesia), National University of Laos (Lao PDR), University of Malaya (Malaysia), University of the Philippines Diliman (the Philippines), National University of Singapore (Singapore), Chulalongkorn University (Thailand), and Vietnam National University, Hanoi (Vietnam). In all cases, where we refer, for purposes of brevity, to data from a nation in cross-national comparisons, we are referring to the data from the primary universities amongst our samples.

In both 2007 and 2014, we sought to collect data at the University of Yangon (YU, Myanmar), but in both instances encountered difficulties due to the situation on the ground. In 2007, the University was closed to outsiders and was not conducting undergraduate courses. As an alternative, we sampled undergraduate "distance university students" who were taking university courses off campus at various sites around Yangon during the University's closure. For the 2014 survey, we again encountered difficulties, as the university was again closed to outsiders (due to student protests over the education law passed in September 2014), although it was conducting some undergraduate (but mostly postgraduate and diploma) courses. We were, however, able to complete the survey among undergraduate students at the University of Mandalay in central Myanmar. Difficulties in Yangon led our local research team to collect responses primarily from graduate students and some faculty members, rather than undergraduates, at YU. The number of responses were also significantly fewer than collected elsewhere and the sample from YU is significantly older than those at other universities. Our original intention was to use the Mandalay data as secondary, comparative data to that collected at Yangon. However, given the poor quality of the Yangon University data, particularly with respect to comparability with other samples, we have used the Mandalay data as our "primary university" data for Myanmar. We do report the results from Yangon University here, which provide some insights into the perspectives on ASEAN from Myanmar. YU is thus treated as an additional university in this report.

Primary Universities	*Abbreviation*	*Nation*	*Code*
Universiti Brunei Darussalam	UBD	Brunei	B1
Royal University of Phnom Penh	RUPP	Cambodia	C1
Universitas Indonesia, Depok	UI	Indonesia	I1
National University of Laos	NUOL	Lao PDR	L1
University of Malaya	UM	Malaysia	M1
University of Mandalay	MU	Myanmar	N2*
University of the Philippines Diliman	UP Diliman	Philippines	P1
National University of Singapore	NUS	Singapore	S1
Chulalongkorn University	CU	Thailand	T1
Vietnam National University, Hanoi	VNU-Hanoi	Vietnam	V1

Additional Universities	*Abbreviation*	*Nation*	*Code*
Universitas Syiah Kuala (Aceh)	Unsyiah	Indonesia	I2
Universitas Nusa Cendana (Kupang)	Undana	Indonesia	I3
Universiti Tunku Abdul Rahman	UTAR	Malaysia	M2
Universiti Malaysia Sarawak	Unimas	Malaysia	M3
University of Yangon	YU	Myanmar	N1*
University of the Philippines Visayas	UP Visayas	Philippines	P2
Mindanao State University	MSU	Philippines	P3
Singapore Polytechnic	SP	Singapore	S2
Khon Kaen University	KKU	Thailand	T2
Walailak University	WU	Thailand	T3
Saint John's University	SJU	Thailand	T4
Vietnam National University, Ho Chi Minh City	VNU-HCMC	Vietnam	V2

* see above

We also expanded our data collection to additional universities in Indonesia, Malaysia, the Philippines, Singapore, Thailand and Vietnam. These additional universities were selected through purposeful sampling — which is to say that we selected universities specifically to give us particular insights into variations that we might expect to find due to regional, socio-economic or ethno-racial diversity amongst particular national populations. We do not combine data across universities within nations to give a stronger (but false) sense of representativeness. Rather, we examine the extent to which responses across university samples tend to conform or to vary, which provides evidence of whether the responses we see from our primary universities can be taken to be relatively representative of a national view (at least of the current university generation). Or alternatively, the extent we see diverse or divergent views within nations along particular line of social difference (i.e. region, class, or ethnicity).

In Indonesia, we conducted the survey at two regionally disparate ends of the nation's vast archipelago. In addition to the primary university, Universitas Indonesia, Depok (UI, located in the greater Jakarta metropolitan region), we collected responses from students at the Universitas Syiah Kuala (Unsyiah) in Banda Aceh, and Universitas Nusa Cendana (Undana) in Kupang, West Timor. Not only are these universities and their students regionally diverse — Banda Aceh at the far northwest tip of Sumatra and Kupang in West Timor amongst the eastern islands of the archipelago — the students are also ethnically and religiously diverse. Students at Unsyiah are primarily Acehnese-Muslim, and while Indonesia as a whole is a predominantly Muslim nation, Aceh has a particularly strong Muslim identity within Indonesia. Students from Undana, on the other hand, are ethnically and regionally from Nusa Tenggara Timor (the East Nusa Tenggara region of Indonesia) and are predominantly Christian, as are many Indonesians in the eastern archipelago.

In Malaysia, our primary university sample was drawn from the University of Malaya, the nation's oldest public university, located in Kuala Lumpur. The student body is predominantly Malay-Muslim and this was reflected in our sample, which was over 80 per cent Malay. As a secondary university, we collected data from the Universiti Tunku Abdul Rahman (UTAR) at the main campus in Kupang (Perak State). UTAR is a relatively new university established in 2002 by the Malaysian Chinese Association, one of the component parties of the country's long-ruling National Front (Barisan Nasional) at the invitation of the Ministry of Education. UTAR's objective, at least in part, was to provide additional university opportunities to Chinese-Malaysians who were not able to find places in the nation's public universities due to ethnic quotas in place at those universities. The student body and our sample at UTAR is overwhelmingly (more than 90 per cent) Chinese-Malaysian.

In the Philippines, like Indonesia, we sought to sample students from regionally diverse universities. The additional university data reported here are from University of the Philippines Visayas (UP Visayas), located in Miagao, outside of Ilo-Ilo City in the central Philippines and from Mindanao State University (MSU) in Marawi City, Lanao del Sur on the island of Mindanao in the southern Philippines. Students from UP Visayas are mostly from the central Philippines. Students from MSU are largely from the southern Philippines and also largely from the Muslim minority within the majority-Catholic nation. We compare the results here from both universities to their counterparts at the University of the Philippines Diliman, located in greater Metro-Manila.

For Singapore, rather than regional diversity, we selected students from Singapore Polytechnic (SP) to compare to students from the National University of Singapore (NUS). Singapore now hosts several highly selective public universities, among which NUS is the oldest and most selective. SP is a member of Singapore's polytechnic school system, which is part of the Singapore academic streaming system. In general, Singaporean students who do not excel academically are usually streamed into either the Polytechnics or Institutes of Technical Education (ITE), both of which focus on training students for technical, professional careers. In general, it is most likely that students from NUS and other universities will move into professional or upper-middle class careers later in their lives, while Polytechnic graduates are more likely to fall socio-economically in the middle or working class. Thus the diversity amongst our Singapore samples is specifically educational attainment and, more generally, their likely future socio-economic status.

In Thailand, we were able to complete data collection at four universities. Two of our secondary universities in Thailand were selected to represent regional and ethnic diversity in the nation. Khon Kaen University (KKU) is located in the centre of the northeast or Isan region of Thailand, so students are predominantly from the northeast and over 80 per cent of our sample at KKU are from Isan. Walailak University (WU) is located in Nakhon Si Thammarat in the south. Although only 20 per cent of WU students are Muslim, we purposefully oversampled Muslim students in our survey. Thus, over 80 per cent of the WU sample are Muslim. Both KKU and WU are top-ranking public universities in Thailand, albeit with strong regional identities. The fourth university where we conducted the survey in Thailand was Saint John's University (SJU) in Bangkok. SJU is a technical-vocational university, which aims at practical, career-oriented education. The difference between SJU students and those from the others (particularly CU) mirrors the educational and socio-economic difference we tested between SP and NUS in Singapore.

Finally, in Vietnam, we were able to complete data collection at both Vietnam National University, Hanoi (VNU-Hanoi) and Vietnam National University, Ho Chi Minh City (VNU-HCMC). Again, as in Indonesia, the Philippines, and Thailand, comparative data from the two universities provides us with insights to regional variations within Vietnam; or conversely, provides evidence of strong national consensus within the nation insofar as students in both the north and south tend to respond to the survey in uniform ways.

At each university, a Research Coordinator (RC) supervised a number of Research Assistants (RAs), who collected responses to the questionnaire. For the most part, RCs were faculty members at the universities in question and RAs were undergraduate students. At each university, we collected simple convenience samples using a sample quota frame. For the convenience sample, student respondents were approached in public areas of the university campus and asked to complete the survey on a one-to-one basis or in small groups of three or four. We did not collect data from large classes, in order to get a more diverse and random sample of students. Students took about 10 to 15 minutes to complete the questionnaire on average and received a ballpoint pen as a token of appreciation.

The quota sample frame was used to approximate a random, or at least distributed, sample of respondents at each university. RAs were instructed to collect responses from "typical" undergraduate students at each university. In general, we instructed RAs to collect a balanced sample of male and female students, about 50 per cent each. We also instructed RAs to collect responses from a diversity of students based on their subject of study, so that no single field (e.g. social sciences and humanities) comprised more than 50 per cent of the respondents at any given university. For the most part, RAs were able to adhere to these parameters.

We received a total of 4,623 responses across the twenty-two universities. Our aim was to collect between 200 and 220 responses from each university, which was achieved in all cases except two. At SJU in Thailand, which is a relatively small school, we were only able to collect a sample of 178 respondents. At YU, we collected 177 responses, due to conditions described above. RAs collected beyond the target of 220 at both RUPP in Cambodia and SP in Singapore.

Overall the gender balance of the survey was 47 per cent male and 53 per cent female. The respondents were also spread across disciplines, with 40 per cent from the social sciences and humanities, 22 per cent from sciences, 14 per cent from engineering, and 22 per cent from other disciplines. There were a few cases where the gender balance of the samples was somewhat skewed — most notably at KKU and WU in Thailand and YU in Myanmar where the samples were less than 40 per cent male. But we have found no evidence that these gender-biased samples seriously affect the survey results in any way.

We did not set specific quotas for the students' year in university, but here, too, the respondents were fairly spread over first to fourth year undergraduates, with a few students included who were beyond fourth year (graduate students). The average age of the students in the sample was about 20 years old. And while a few younger and older students were included in the samples, the vast majority, more than 95 per cent, were in the range of 17 to 25 years old. Again, the YU sample is the only one that does not conform to this pattern.

At regional universities, we instructed RAs to collect samples that included at least 80 per cent of respondents from that region. Similarly, because we wanted to test the comparison between the mostly Malay-Malaysian student body at UM and mostly Chinese-Malaysian student body at UTAR, we instructed RAs to collect samples that included at least 80 per cent responses from each group respectively. Likewise, at WU in Thailand, although the university has only about 20 per cent Muslim students, we instructed RAs there to collect a sample that was at least 80 per cent Muslim from the south of Thailand.

Data was collected on a rolling basis between June 2014 and May 2015, based on the local university calendars (when schools were in session and students available) and the availability of RCs and RAs at each of the universities.

4

FINDINGS ON ATTITUDES, KNOWLEDGE, AND ORIENTATIONS TOWARD ASEAN

In both the 2007 and 2014 surveys, we have found that students around the region are overwhelmingly positive in their attitudes and orientations toward ASEAN. Across the region, we have found a degree of "ASEAN enthusiasm" amongst students, measured by the percentage of students who "strongly agree" with a range of questions on their perception of the importance of ASEAN and affinity for ASEAN (e.g. the degree to which they see themselves as citizens of ASEAN and see the future of ASEAN as important). In 2007, we reported that ASEAN enthusiasm was strongest in several of the newest and least affluent ASEAN nations (specifically Cambodia, Laos, and Vietnam). The least degree of ASEAN enthusiasm appeared in the most affluent ASEAN members, particularly Singapore but also Brunei. Singaporean students as a group displayed an attitude of ambivalence — neither strongly negative nor sceptical, but also not overwhelmingly positive. Amongst students from most of the other ASEAN nations (Indonesia, Malaysia, the Philippines, and Thailand), the aggregate orientation was overwhelmingly positive, but not to the same "enthusiastic" degree of the members mentioned above. In 2007, we also found a particularly interesting, bimodal distribution of responses amongst students surveyed in Myanmar. The majority displayed positive attitudes similar to that of most ASEAN member states, but a significant minority responded in ways that we termed "ASEAN scepticism". These students disagreed, or in many cases even strongly disagreed, across the same series of questions — e.g. that they did not feel ASEAN was of benefit to their nation, that they did not feel themselves citizens of ASEAN, and so on.

At the most general level, the results of the 2014 survey largely tracked with those of the 2007 survey. The overall attitudes of students across the region were positive. The greatest degree of ASEAN enthusiasm remained amongst students in Cambodia, Laos, and Vietnam. Students in Singapore continued to display a degree of ambivalence toward ASEAN. And elsewhere, the general attitude of students toward ASEAN is strongly positive, though not enthusiastic to the degree found in Cambodia, Laos, and Vietnam. At the same time, within this general overall similarity between the 2007 and 2014 results, there are important and instructive differences with respect to findings from particular nations. We highlight several of these differences here, and discuss them in greater detail in the remainder of this section of the report and the next.

The greatest change, or difference, in the results from any nation was found in Myanmar. The sample we draw on for this report did not display anywhere near the degree of "ASEAN scepticism" that we found in our 2007 sample. As elsewhere, the numbers of respondents answering that they "strongly disagree" with such statements as "ASEAN membership benefits my country" and "I feel that I am a citizen of ASEAN" were diminishingly small in Myanmar, as they tend to be everywhere else in Southeast Asia. The overall profile of responses from Myanmar in 2014 looks much more like the average and, in general, overwhelmingly positive pattern of responses found across the region. We are inclined to interpret this result as reflecting, to some degree, the normalization of Myanmar's status within ASEAN as well as the international community more generally. However, due to the difficulties of data collection in Myanmar, both in the 2007 and 2014 surveys, there may be other factors at play in the difference between the two results (discussed in the methodology section in Chapter 3 as well as below).

Another interesting shift was seen in responses from Thailand, specifically among students from Chulalongkorn University (CU), the primary university for Thailand in both surveys. In the 2014 survey, CU students display better objective knowledge about ASEAN, such as a much better ability to identify the ASEAN flag with ASEAN's bundled rice-stalks logo. While this increase in objective knowledge was most evident in Thailand, it is another notable trend across the region — that at least marginally, and sometimes significantly, students' objective knowledge about ASEAN appeared to increase across most nations in the region in the period between our two surveys. But in Thailand, we also see a marginal but noticeable drop in CU students' positive attitudes and affinity toward ASEAN. A long lasting and high-profile public campaign to raise awareness in preparation for the ASEAN Economic Community (AEC) took place in Thailand over several years prior to our second survey. We suggest below that we may be seeing here the effect of Thailand's involvement in ASEAN becoming at once more salient and more substantively debated; rather than simply taken for granted. At the same time, in comparing CU students to those of the additional Thai universities in our study, we see that these less positive orientations seem particular to students at the primary university. Possible reasons for this will be discussed in Chapter 5 of the report, which details responses from individual nations.

A final important point of comparison and departure between the 2007 and 2014 surveys is that in the earlier survey, we collected data from only one primary, flagship public university in each member nation. In the more recent survey, we were able to expand our scope to include data from a number of additional universities in several ASEAN member nations. In what follows, we primarily report on the results from the 2014 survey at the primary universities, and compare them to the results from the 2007 survey which was conducted at the same university in each case (with the exception of Myanmar, as explained in the methodology section in Chapter 3). In some instances we will also discuss results from additional universities in this section. In the following chapter, these will be discussed at greater length when reporting on results from each nation individually.

a. ATTITUDES TOWARD ASEAN AS A WHOLE

Our first set of findings refer to students' attitudes toward ASEAN as a whole — their affinity toward ASEAN measured in terms of them feeling they are a citizen of ASEAN, the benefits they see in the ASEAN membership, and the importance of ASEAN's future. In addition, we asked students to rate the similarities amongst ASEAN countries on three dimensions — cultural, economic, and political similarities. For these questions, as with most of the survey, we used an "agree/disagree" format which presents respondents with a forced choice; in other words, they are not allowed to give a neutral response. But we are able to measure the strength of their agreement, by differentiating those who "strongly agree" from those who simply "agree" (and likewise those who "disagree" from those who "strongly disagree"). Given the level of an overall agreement of 90 per cent or more, the differentiation between strong agreement and simple agreement becomes more analytically interesting. The current survey also allows us to compare not only between nations (based on the primary universities), but between the earlier and more recent survey as well as amongst different universities within nations. For the sake of consistency and presentation in non-technical language, we refer to difference between universities or between the 2007 and 2014 surveys of 5 to 15 per cent to be a "moderate" difference or change and more than 15 per cent to be a "substantial" difference or change. We consider a less than 5 per cent difference between universities or between the two surveys to be no difference or no change.

"I Feel that I am a Citizen of ASEAN"

Responses to this question were overwhelmingly in the affirmative, largely matching the positive responses in the previous 2007 survey (see Table 4.1). More than 90 per cent of respondents agreed with this statement at the primary universities in Cambodia, Laos, Malaysia, and Myanmar. More than 80 per cent agreed in Brunei, Indonesia, and Vietnam. The sentiment was less overwhelming, but still largely positive amongst students from the primary universities in the Philippines, Singapore, and Thailand.

The largest percentage who strongly agreed was in Cambodia, where two-thirds of students strongly agreed, matching the 2007 findings. This was followed by just under two-thirds of our sample in Myanmar, a tremendous shift from 2007 when less than 30 per cent strongly agreed that they felt themselves citizens of ASEAN and an even larger number strongly disagreed. Apart from

TABLE 4.1
"I Feel that I am a Citizen of ASEAN"
(Percentage of Students' Responses by Nation)

Primary Universities	Strongly Agree	Somewhat Agree	Somewhat Disagree	Strongly Disagree	Total Agree	Total Disagree
Brunei (B1)	35.5%	50.5%	11.0%	3.0%	86.0%	14.0%
Cambodia (C1)	67.5%	28.3%	4.2%	0.0%	95.8%	4.2%
Indonesia (I1)	34.6%	47.8%	13.7%	3.9%	82.4%	17.6%
Laos (L1)	39.6%	57.7%	2.7%	0.0%	97.3%	2.7%
Malaysia (M1)	36.0%	56.7%	7.4%	0.0%	92.7%	7.4%
Myanmar (N2)	63.9%	26.4%	7.2%	2.4%	90.4%	9.6%
Philippines (P1)	12.3%	53.9%	25.6%	8.2%	66.2%	33.8%
Singapore (S1)	19.3%	44.8%	24.1%	11.8%	64.1%	35.9%
Thailand (T1)	4.3%	51.0%	32.2%	12.5%	55.3%	44.7%
Vietnam (V1)	47.0%	36.9%	12.4%	3.7%	83.9%	16.1%
Average Primary	**36.0%**	**45.4%**	**14.1%**	**4.5%**	**81.4%**	**18.6%**
Additional Universities						
Unsyiah (I2)	67.0%	27.5%	3.0%	2.5%	94.5%	5.5%
Undana (I3)	82.1%	12.9%	1.0%	4.0%	95.0%	5.0%
UTAR (M2)	27.1%	50.0%	17.6%	5.2%	77.1%	22.9%
Unimas (M3)	35.3%	55.1%	7.8%	1.8%	90.4%	9.6%
YU (N1)	41.6%	44.5%	7.5%	6.4%	86.1%	13.9%
UP Visayas (P2)	23.6%	52.9%	19.7%	3.9%	76.4%	23.6%
MSU (P3)	45.4%	43.1%	9.6%	1.8%	88.5%	11.5%
SP (S2)	10.4%	62.5%	19.6%	7.5%	72.9%	27.1%
KKU (T2)	19.8%	51.9%	21.7%	6.6%	71.7%	28.3%
WU (T3)	34.2%	51.0%	14.4%	0.5%	85.2%	14.9%
SJU (T4)	22.5%	59.6%	14.6%	3.4%	82.0%	18.0%
VNU-HCMC (V2)	49.1%	36.9%	10.3%	3.7%	86.0%	14.0%
Average Additional	**38.2%**	**45.7%**	**12.2%**	**3.9%**	**83.8%**	**16.2%**
Average Total	**37.2%**	**45.5%**	**13.1%**	**4.2%**	**82.7%**	**17.3%**

Myanmar, the greatest increase in agreement was in Singapore and the greatest decrease was in Thailand. Singapore primary university students showed a substantial increase of nearly 15 per cent in overall agreement. Overall agreement in Thailand dropped by almost 12 per cent and strong agreement dropped from almost 20 to less than 5 per cent.

Overall agreement remained largely unchanged and at very high levels across Brunei, Cambodia, and Laos and at a high level in the Philippines. Malaysia showed a modest increase of agreement of just over 5 per cent. Agreement among Indonesian students from the primary university also increased moderately from 73 to 82 per cent, with those strongly agreeing increasing by more than 10 per cent. Vietnam showed a moderate decrease in agreement from 92 per cent in 2007 to 84 per cent in 2014, although the level of those strongly agreeing remained constant at slightly over 45 per cent. Agreement among Indonesian students from the primary university increased moderately from 73 to 82 per cent, with those strongly agreeing increasing by more than 10 per cent.

The general trend across the primary universities suggests a consistently strong or increasing sense of ASEAN citizenship, with Thai students being a striking exception, relating to the arguments detailed in Chapter 5 about the influence of the high-profile discourse about the AEC in Thailand over several years in the lead up to the 2015 launch.

Interestingly, with one exception, everywhere that we conducted the 2014 survey among additional universities, we found that the feeling of ASEAN citizenship was stronger among students from the additional universities that we sampled than from among the primary universities. The one exception was in Malaysia. The general sense of ASEAN citizenship was substantially greater between additional and primary university students in Thailand and moderately greater in Indonesia and Singapore. It was substantially greater at Mindanao State University (MSU) and moderately greater at the University of the Philippines Visayas (UP Visayas) than at UP Diliman. In Vietnam, while the difference was less than 5 per cent, it was still higher at the additional university. In Malaysia, the sense of ASEAN citizenship was substantially higher among the mostly Malay-Malaysian students at the University of Malaya (UM) as compared to the mostly Chinese-Malaysian students from Universiti Tunku Abdul Rahman (UTAR), though three-quarters of the latter still felt themselves ASEAN citizens and one-quarter strongly so. There was no substantial difference between students at UM and Universiti Malaysia Sarawak (Unimas, in Sarawak).

"Membership in ASEAN is Beneficial to My Country"

The generally positive views toward ASEAN citizenship were also reflected in respondents' answers to two questions on the benefits of ASEAN citizenship. These questions asked if they felt that membership in ASEAN was beneficial to their country and if their country's membership in ASEAN was beneficial to themselves.

With respect to whether their country benefited from membership in ASEAN, student agreement to the question was 85 per cent or higher for all primary and additional universities in all countries except in Thailand (see Table 4.2). Students from the primary universities in Brunei, Laos, and Vietnam all agreed at rates of over 95 per cent, while agreement in Cambodia, Indonesia, Malaysia, Myanmar, the Philippines, and Singapore all ranged between 85 and 95 per cent. While students from

TABLE 4.2
"Membership in ASEAN is Beneficial to My Country"
(Percentage of Students' Responses by Nation)

Primary Universities	Strongly Agree	Somewhat Agree	Somewhat Disagree	Strongly Disagree	Total Agree	Total Disagree
Brunei (B1)	33.5%	64.0%	2.5%	0.0%	97.5%	2.5%
Cambodia (C1)	50.4%	41.3%	7.5%	0.8%	91.7%	8.3%
Indonesia (I1)	33.7%	54.6%	9.8%	2.0%	88.3%	11.8%
Laos (L1)	49.6%	46.4%	3.2%	0.9%	96.0%	4.1%
Malaysia (M1)	14.3%	78.3%	6.9%	0.5%	92.6%	7.4%
Myanmar (N2)	56.0%	38.2%	3.9%	1.9%	94.2%	5.8%
Philippines (P1)	30.1%	56.9%	9.7%	3.2%	87.0%	12.9%
Singapore (S1)	31.3%	54.5%	9.0%	5.2%	85.8%	14.2%
Thailand (T1)	10.6%	60.6%	22.6%	6.3%	71.2%	28.9%
Vietnam (V1)	58.7%	36.7%	4.1%	0.5%	95.4%	4.6%
Average Primary	**36.8%**	**53.1%**	**7.9%**	**2.1%**	**90.0%**	**10.0%**
Additional Universities						
Unsyiah (I2)	54.5%	34.5%	6.5%	4.5%	89.0%	11.0%
Undana (I3)	64.7%	29.9%	3.5%	2.0%	94.5%	5.5%
UTAR (M2)	24.9%	60.8%	11.0%	3.4%	85.7%	14.4%
Unimas (M3)	13.8%	73.7%	11.1%	1.4%	87.6%	12.4%
YU (N1)	30.3%	61.7%	3.4%	4.6%	92.0%	8.0%
UP Visayas (P2)	44.9%	49.8%	4.8%	0.5%	94.7%	5.3%
MSU (P3)	48.2%	44.5%	6.0%	1.4%	92.7%	7.3%
SP (S2)	28.5%	63.2%	5.9%	2.5%	91.6%	8.4%
KKU (T2)	15.5%	55.9%	25.4%	3.3%	71.4%	28.6%
WU (T3)	23.4%	54.2%	20.0%	2.4%	77.6%	22.4%
SJU (T4)	30.3%	58.4%	6.7%	4.5%	88.8%	11.2%
VNU-HCMC (V2)	62.2%	35.5%	2.3%	0.0%	97.7%	2.3%
Average Additional	**36.8%**	**51.8%**	**8.9%**	**2.5%**	**88.6%**	**11.4%**
Average Total	**36.8%**	**52.4%**	**8.4%**	**2.4%**	**89.2%**	**10.8%**

Thailand generally agreed that membership in ASEAN benefited Thailand, their level of agreement at 71 per cent was much lower than the average across the region. These lower levels were found in the responses from Thai students at prestigious regional universities as well, but not at the vocational technical university located in Bangkok.

In comparison to the 2007 survey, agreement among primary university students in Thailand dropped substantially, from 89 to 71 per cent. In contrast, agreement among students surveyed in Myanmar rose substantially from 58 to 94 per cent among our Mandalay sample and 92 per cent among our Yangon sample. Brunei also saw a moderate increase from 85 to over 95 per cent. Rates of agreement were largely similar between the 2007 and 2014 surveys elsewhere, with essentially no change (less than 5 per cent) in Cambodia, Indonesia, Laos, Malaysia, and Vietnam. Both Singapore and the Philippines recorded modest declines in agreement from 92 and 94 per cent to 86 and 87 per cent, respectively.

"My Country's Membership in ASEAN is Beneficial to Me Personally"

As in the 2007 survey, attitudes toward the personal benefits of one's country's membership in ASEAN were generally lower than agreement on the general benefit of the country's membership, but at the same time, they were also uniformly positive across the region (see Table 4.3).

Rates of agreement were over 90 per cent in Laos, followed by agreement between 84 to 89 per cent in Brunei, Cambodia, and Vietnam. The highest rate of strong agreement (46 per cent) was in Vietnam followed by Laos (34 per cent), Cambodia (32 per cent), and Myanmar (29 per cent). Primary

TABLE 4.3
"My Country's Membership in ASEAN is Beneficial to Me Personally"
(Percentage of Students' Responses by Nation)

	Strongly Agree	Somewhat Agree	Somewhat Disagree	Strongly Disagree	Total Agree	Total Disagree
Primary Universities						
Brunei (B1)	18.0%	66.0%	13.5%	2.5%	84.0%	16.0%
Cambodia (C1)	31.7%	53.8%	12.1%	2.5%	85.5%	14.6%
Indonesia (I1)	19.0%	52.2%	22.4%	6.3%	71.2%	28.7%
Laos (L1)	33.6%	59.1%	6.4%	0.9%	92.7%	7.3%
Malaysia (M1)	5.4%	68.5%	23.7%	2.5%	73.9%	26.2%
Myanmar (Y2)	28.8%	38.5%	14.6%	18.1%	67.3%	32.7%
Philippines (P1)	15.7%	49.8%	24.0%	10.6%	65.5%	34.6%
Singapore (S1)	20.5%	51.4%	20.5%	7.6%	71.9%	28.1%
Thailand (T1)	9.1%	53.4%	31.3%	6.3%	62.5%	37.5%
Vietnam (V1)	45.9%	43.1%	7.8%	3.2%	89.0%	11.0%
Average Primary	**22.8%**	**53.6%**	**17.6%**	**6.2%**	**75.5%**	**24.5%**
Additional Universities						
Unsyiah (I2)	29.5%	45.0%	15.0%	10.5%	74.5%	25.5%
Undana (I3)	37.3%	41.3%	13.9%	7.5%	78.6%	21.4%
UTAR (M2)	7.7%	46.9%	34.5%	11.0%	54.6%	45.5%
Unimas (M3)	7.4%	65.9%	23.0%	3.7%	73.3%	26.7%
YU (N1)	9.09%	49.43%	22.16%	19.32%	58.52%	41.48%
UP Visayas (P2)	16.9%	58.5%	20.8%	3.9%	75.4%	24.6%
MSU (P3)	26.6%	53.7%	13.8%	6.0%	80.3%	19.7%
SP (S2)	10.8%	54.6%	25.0%	9.6%	65.4%	34.6%
KKU (T2)	12.3%	47.4%	32.9%	7.0%	59.7%	39.9%
WU (T3)	19.0%	54.2%	25.4%	1.5%	73.2%	26.8%
SJU (T4)	24.7%	57.3%	12.9%	5.1%	82.0%	18.0%
VNU-HCMC (V2)	55.6%	39.7%	4.2%	0.5%	95.3%	4.7%
Average Additional	**21.4%**	**51.2%**	**20.3%**	**7.1%**	**72.6%**	**27.4%**
Average Total	**22.0%**	**52.3%**	**19.1%**	**6.6%**	**74.3%**	**25.7%**

university students from Indonesia, Malaysia, Myanmar, and the Philippines all recorded rates of agreement between 65 and 75 per cent. Thailand again recorded the lowest rate of agreement at just over 62 per cent.

Comparing the 2007 and 2014 surveys, there was again a notable drop in agreement to this question at Thailand's primary university, from over 74 to under 63 per cent. Yet Thailand was the only nation where agreement with the personal benefit of ASEAN membership dropped. Very substantial increases were seen in Indonesia from less than 50 to over 70 per cent and in Myanmar from 26 to over 67 per cent (Mandalay) and 59 per cent (Yangon). Moderate increases were recorded in Brunei, Cambodia, Malaysia, Singapore, and Vietnam with no substantial change in Laos and the Philippines.

As with the question on ASEAN citizenship, the questions on the benefits of ASEAN membership both to the country and personally, generally saw similar or higher agreement among additional university students as compared to primary university students within each nation. An exception was again seen in Malaysia where UTAR students saw moderately less benefit to their country and substantially less benefit to themselves as compared to UM students. Again, results between UM and Unimas were nearly identical. Singapore Polytechnic (SP) students also saw less benefit to themselves personally as compared to National University of Singapore (NUS) students, though, interestingly, SP students rated the benefit to their country more highly.

Similarities among ASEAN Countries

The survey asked students about their perception of similarities amongst ASEAN countries based on three dimensions of cultural, economic, and political similarities. These dimensions were chosen because they appeared as important dimensions of similarity and difference in previous research on ASEAN. They also appear as inferentially discovered criteria among current students and survey respondents in the tests of similarity and difference amongst ASEAN countries conducted in the current survey (see triad analysis and one-word analysis elsewhere in this report).

On the whole, the perceptions of primary university students across the region have remained similar between the 2007 and 2014 surveys. In general, there is a tendency to see members of ASEAN as culturally similar but economically and politically dissimilar (see Tables 4.4, 4.5, and 4.6). On the whole, about two-thirds of primary university respondents see ASEAN members as culturally similar, two-fifths see them as economically similar and one-third see them as politically similar. None of these general averages changed substantially between the 2007 and 2014 surveys, though some moderate and a few substantial changes were seen in the responses from particular universities (see Table 4.7).

With regard to ASEAN members being culturally similar, the modal answer everywhere in the region was to somewhat agree with this statement. Overall agreement ranged between 61 per cent in Thailand to 82 per cent in Indonesia, with the exception of Singapore, where overall agreement was only 40 per cent. In Brunei, Laos, Malaysia, and Myanmar, general agreement rose substantially and in Laos and Vietnam, it rose moderately between the 2007 and 2014 surveys. Overall agreement dropped moderately in Cambodia, Singapore, and Thailand, with the largest of these drops of 13 per cent, being

TABLE 4.4
"ASEAN Countries are Similar Culturally"
(Percentage of Students' Responses by Nation)

Primary Universities	Strongly Agree	Somewhat Agree	Somewhat Disagree	Strongly Disagree	Total Agree	Total Disagree
Brunei (B1)	4.0%	63.5%	28.0%	4.5%	67.5%	32.5%
Cambodia (C1)	12.9%	64.2%	16.3%	6.7%	77.1%	23.0%
Indonesia (I1)	19.5%	62.0%	13.7%	4.9%	81.5%	18.6%
Laos (L1)	10.0%	65.0%	23.2%	1.8%	75.0%	25.0%
Malaysia (M1)	6.4%	54.7%	30.5%	8.4%	61.1%	38.9%
Myanmar (N2)	8.6%	61.2%	17.2%	12.9%	69.9%	30.1%
Philippines (P1)	5.1%	68.2%	17.5%	9.2%	73.3%	26.7%
Singapore (S1)	2.4%	37.7%	28.3%	31.6%	40.1%	59.9%
Thailand (T1)	1.4%	59.1%	37.5%	1.9%	60.6%	39.4%
Vietnam (V1)	18.4%	55.5%	16.1%	10.1%	73.9%	26.2%
Average Primary	**8.9%**	**59.1%**	**22.8%**	**9.2%**	**68.0%**	**32.0%**
Additional Universities						
Unsyiah (I2)	19.5%	56.0%	16.5%	8.0%	75.5%	24.5%
Undana (I3)	27.4%	34.8%	18.9%	18.9%	62.2%	37.8%
UTAR (M2)	6.7%	66.5%	20.6%	6.2%	73.2%	26.8%
Unimas (M3)	3.7%	55.6%	34.3%	6.5%	59.3%	40.7%
YU (N1)	1.1%	69.1%	10.9%	18.9%	70.3%	29.7%
UP Visayas (P2)	5.8%	63.1%	20.4%	10.7%	68.9%	31.1%
MSU (P3)	20.6%	55.5%	16.5%	7.3%	76.1%	23.8%
SP (S2)	5.4%	63.2%	24.2%	7.1%	68.6%	31.3%
KKU (T2)	10.8%	61.5%	24.4%	3.3%	72.3%	27.7%
WU (T3)	14.6%	55.6%	26.8%	2.9%	70.2%	29.8%
SJU (T4)	11.8%	69.7%	16.9%	1.7%	81.5%	18.5%
VNU-HCMC (V2)	15.5%	67.1%	14.1%	3.3%	82.6%	17.4%
Average Additional	**11.9%**	**59.8%**	**20.4%**	**7.9%**	**71.7%**	**28.3%**
Average Total	**10.5%**	**59.5%**	**21.5%**	**8.5%**	**70.0%**	**30.0%**

TABLE 4.5
"ASEAN Countries are Similar Economically"
(Percentage of Students' Responses by Nation)

	Strongly Agree	Somewhat Agree	Somewhat Disagree	Strongly Disagree	Total Agree	Total Disagree
Primary Universities						
Brunei (B1)	1.5%	30.0%	50.0%	18.5%	31.5%	68.5%
Cambodia (C1)	3.8%	29.6%	46.3%	20.4%	33.4%	66.7%
Indonesia (I1)	10.2%	46.8%	38.5%	4.4%	57.0%	42.9%
Laos (L1)	7.7%	47.3%	40.0%	5.0%	55.0%	45.0%
Malaysia (M1)	1.5%	48.3%	40.9%	9.4%	49.8%	50.3%
Myanmar (N2)	9.6%	52.6%	25.4%	12.4%	62.2%	37.8%
Philippines (P1)	0.5%	27.7%	43.3%	28.6%	28.2%	71.9%
Singapore (S1)	1.9%	16.0%	32.6%	49.5%	17.9%	82.1%
Thailand (T1)	1.4%	38.0%	54.8%	5.8%	39.4%	60.6%
Vietnam (V1)	12.5%	43.1%	26.4%	18.1%	55.6%	44.5%
Average Primary	**5.1%**	**37.9%**	**39.8%**	**17.2%**	**43.0%**	**57.0%**
Additional Universities						
Unsyiah (I2)	17.5%	55.0%	19.0%	8.5%	72.5%	27.5%
Undana (I3)	16.9%	34.3%	28.9%	19.9%	51.3%	48.8%
UTAR (M2)	4.3%	45.2%	36.2%	14.3%	49.5%	50.5%
Unimas (M3)	3.2%	41.0%	47.0%	8.8%	44.2%	55.8%
YU (N1)	4.6%	36.8%	30.5%	28.2%	41.4%	58.6%
UP Visayas (P2)	3.9%	32.9%	40.6%	22.7%	36.7%	63.3%
MSU (P3)	13.3%	43.6%	26.2%	17.0%	56.9%	43.1%
SP (S2)	2.1%	29.6%	35.0%	33.3%	31.7%	68.3%
KKU (T2)	8.9%	44.6%	42.3%	4.2%	53.5%	46.5%
WU (T3)	10.7%	52.2%	34.6%	2.4%	62.9%	37.1%
SJU (T4)	13.5%	55.1%	27.5%	3.9%	68.5%	31.5%
VNU-HCMC (V2)	8.4%	50.9%	23.8%	16.8%	59.3%	40.7%
Average Additional	**8.9%**	**43.4%**	**32.6%**	**15.0%**	**52.4%**	**47.6%**
Average Total	**7.2%**	**40.9%**	**35.9%**	**16.0%**	**48.1%**	**51.9%**

TABLE 4.6
"ASEAN Countries are Similar Politically"
(Percentage of Students' Responses by Nation)

Primary Universities	Strongly Agree	Somewhat Agree	Somewhat Disagree	Strongly Disagree	Total Agree	Total Disagree
Brunei (B1)	3.0%	18.0%	47.0%	32.0%	21.0%	79.0%
Cambodia (C1)	4.6%	45.8%	35.4%	14.2%	50.4%	49.6%
Indonesia (I1)	7.8%	41.0%	45.4%	5.9%	48.8%	51.3%
Laos (L1)	5.5%	27.3%	59.1%	8.2%	32.8%	67.3%
Malaysia (M1)	1.0%	24.6%	60.1%	14.3%	25.6%	74.4%
Myanmar (N2)	16.8%	38.3%	23.0%	22.0%	55.0%	45.0%
Philippines (P1)	1.8%	24.9%	49.8%	23.5%	26.7%	73.3%
Singapore (S1)	2.8%	13.7%	35.9%	47.6%	16.5%	83.5%
Thailand (T1)	0.5%	23.6%	59.1%	16.8%	24.0%	76.0%
Vietnam (V1)	13.8%	34.4%	24.8%	27.1%	48.2%	51.8%
Average Primary	**5.8%**	**29.2%**	**44.0%**	**21.2%**	**34.9%**	**65.1%**
Additional Universities						
Unsyiah (I2)	12.5%	42.0%	31.0%	14.5%	54.5%	45.5%
Undana (I3)	15.4%	36.3%	33.3%	14.9%	51.7%	48.3%
UTAR (M2)	2.9%	38.1%	39.5%	19.5%	41.0%	59.0%
Unimas (M3)	4.1%	28.9%	52.3%	14.7%	33.0%	67.0%
YU (N1)	2.3%	43.9%	33.9%	19.9%	46.2%	53.8%
UP Visayas (P2)	4.4%	28.5%	50.2%	16.9%	32.9%	67.2%
MSU (P3)	19.4%	34.6%	33.2%	12.9%	53.9%	46.1%
SP (S2)	5.4%	33.8%	33.3%	27.5%	39.2%	60.8%
KKU (T2)	6.6%	28.6%	54.8%	10.3%	35.2%	64.8%
WU (T3)	9.8%	30.2%	47.8%	12.2%	40.0%	60.0%
SJU (T4)	7.3%	37.6%	44.9%	10.1%	44.9%	55.1%
VNU-HCMC (V2)	11.7%	39.3%	22.0%	27.1%	50.9%	49.1%
Average Additional	**8.5%**	**35.1%**	**39.7%**	**16.7%**	**43.6%**	**56.4%**
Average Total	**7.2%**	**32.4%**	**41.6%**	**18.7%**	**39.7%**	**60.3%**

TABLE 4.7
General Overall Agreement/Disagreement on Similarity of ASEAN Countries
(Percentage of Students' Responses by Nation)

Primary Universities	Agree	Disagree	Agree +/-vs. 2007
Brunei (B1)	40.0%	60.0%	+7.3%
Cambodia (C1)	53.6%	46.4%	-4.6%
Indonesia (I1)	62.4%	37.6%	+2.3%
Laos (L1)	54.3%	45.8%	-3.9%
Malaysia (M1)	45.5%	54.5%	+3.6%
Myanmar (N2)	62.4%	37.6%	+22.8%
Philippines (P1)	42.7%	57.3%	-5.1%
Singapore (S1)	24.8%	75.2%	+0.0%
Thailand (T1)	41.3%	58.7%	-6.5%
Vietnam (V1)	59.2%	40.8%	-3.0%
Average Primary	**48.6%**	**51.4%**	**+1.3%**
Additional Universities			
Unsyiah (I2)	67.5%	32.5%	N.A.
Undana (I3)	55.1%	44.9%	N.A.
UTAR (M2)	54.6%	45.4%	N.A.
Unimas (M3)	45.5%	54.5%	N.A.
YU (N1)	52.6%	47.4%	N.A.
UP Visayas (P2)	46.2%	53.8%	N.A.
MSU (P3)	62.3%	37.7%	N.A.
SP (S2)	46.5%	53.5%	N.A.
KKU (T2)	53.7%	46.3%	N.A.
WU (T3)	57.7%	42.3%	N.A.
SJU (T4)	65.0%	35.0%	N.A.
VNU-HCMC (V2)	64.3%	35.7%	N.A.
Average Additional	**55.9%**	**44.1%**	**N.A.**
Average Total	**52.6%**	**47.4%**	**N.A.**

among Thailand's primary university students. Rates among Indonesian and Filipino students were essentially unchanged.

Overall assessments of economic similarity dropped moderately in Cambodia, the Philippines, and Thailand, but rose moderately in Indonesia, Laos, and Singapore. The rates were essentially unchanged in Brunei, Malaysia, and Vietnam. Among the Myanmar students surveyed, perceptions of economic similarity amongst ASEAN member nations rose substantially from 40 to over 60 per cent (for Mandalay; it remained at 40 per cent among our Yangon sample).

Perceptions of political similarity amongst ASEAN members also showed a sharp increase among Myanmar students surveyed, from overall perceptions of similarly at 28 per cent in 2007 to 55 per cent (Mandalay) and 46 per cent (Yangon) in the 2014 survey. Elsewhere there were moderate drops in perceptions of political similarity among primary university students in Laos and Vietnam, but in all other cases, the rates of agreement and disagreement remained essentially unchanged.

Comparing primary and additional universities within countries shows that in most instances, while there are some differences in degrees of judgement, the general pattern by which students tend to judge ASEAN members as similar or dissimilar, is consistent between universities. In other words, the results generally suggest that in each nation, there is a relatively consistent national frame-of-reference to how students view the relationship among ASEAN members. This corresponds to a strong tendency toward similar "cognitive maps" of Southeast Asia, discussed later in this report. Variations within nations are a matter of degree rather than actual differing views in almost all cases. The three exceptions are in Myanmar, Singapore, and Thailand. In the latter two cases, the differing views are on a single dimension — the cultural dimension among Singaporean students and the economic dimension among Thai students. In Myanmar, we found differing views on both the economic and political dimensions.

A solid two-thirds majority of SP students judged ASEAN countries to be culturally similar, whereas only a minority of NUS students (40 per cent) agreed. For the other two dimensions, both SP and NUS students overwhelmingly judged ASEAN countries to be economically and politically dissimilar. In both cases, the judgements (disagreement) of the NUS students were moderately to substantially stronger.

Thailand also showed somewhat divergent views between the primary and additional university students. At all universities, the students judged ASEAN members to be culturally similar. But while this was between 70 to over 80 per cent at additional universities, it was only 60 per cent at CU. Even more striking, while a solid majority of CU students (over 60 per cent) judged ASEAN countries to be economically dissimilar, Khon Kaen University (KKU) students were evenly split and students from Walailak University (WU) and Saint John's University (SJU) saw ASEAN countries as economically similar by solid majorities (63 and 68 per cent respectively). On the political dimension, while all Thai university student samples judged ASEAN countries as dissimilar, CU students again did so to a moderate to substantial degree more than their counterparts at the other three universities.

In Myanmar, 70 per cent of both Mandalay and Yangon respondents judged ASEAN countries to be culturally similar. But whereas the Mandalay sample judged ASEAN countries economically similar (62 per cent) and politically similar (55 per cent), the Yangon sample judged ASEAN countries dissimilar on these two dimensions by roughly similar percentages (59 and 54 per cent).

In Indonesia, Universitas Indonesia (UI) students judged ASEAN countries to be similar to a moderately greater degree than Universitas Syiah Kuala (Unsyiah) students in Aceh and to a substantially greater degree than Universitas Nusa Cendana (Undana) students in Kupang. Unsyiah students, however, judged ASEAN members substantially more similar economically than either UI or Undana students, with the UI students judging only moderately higher than Undana students in this dimension. All Indonesian students were about evenly split on the political similarity or dissimilarity amongst ASEAN members.

In Malaysia, UTAR students judged ASEAN countries to be culturally similar to a moderate degree more than both UM and Unimas students. All three universities were about evenly split with regard to economic similarity, though Unimas students recorded a slight tendency toward dissimilarity. And all three samples judged ASEAN countries to be politically dissimilar, though UM students to a substantially greater degree than UTAR students, with Unimas students falling in between.

Filipino students at all three universities judged ASEAN members to be culturally similar (more than two-thirds). University of the Philippines Diliman (UP Diliman) and UP Visayas students both judged ASEAN countries to be economically and politically dissimilar (by nearly or more than two-thirds). However MSU (Mindanao) students judged ASEAN members to be both economically and politically similar, albeit by slight majorities. Only on the economic dimension was there any notable difference between UP Diliman and UP Visayas students, with UP Diliman students asserting moderately stronger dissimilarity of ASEAN countries than UP Visayas students.

Students in Vietnam, at both universities surveyed, saw ASEAN members as culturally similar (to a strong degree), economically similar (to a modest degree) and were split on the political similarity or dissimilarity of ASEAN members. On every dimension, students from the Vietnam National University, Ho Chi Minh City (VNU-HCMC) judged ASEAN members to be more similar than did students from the Vietnam National University, Hanoi (VNU-Hanoi), though the difference was only moderately significant on the cultural dimension and negligible on the other dimensions.

b. KNOWLEDGE ABOUT THE REGION AND ASEAN

The survey employed a number of questions to assess students' knowledge about ASEAN. These included questions to test their objective knowledge about ASEAN and its individual member states as well as the cognitive salience of those countries. We did not include a long battery of questions to intensively probe students' knowledge about the organization and its structures. Rather, the questions posed were aimed at assessing general familiarity with the organization. These provide us with an insight into the general awareness respondents have about ASEAN as well as a comparative view of how this knowledge is distributed across the region.

As in 2007, students displayed a fairly high degree of general knowledge about ASEAN and its member states. In terms of our measures of objective knowledge, these generally remained the same or increased — particularly with regard to recognizing the ASEAN flag — between the 2007 and 2014 surveys. Interestingly, there was also a slight decrease in students' self-reported familiarity with ASEAN. Although, given that the decrease was at most a modest one, we would not make too much of this particular finding. It may be the case that as students have learned more about ASEAN in recent years — as measured by objective knowledge — they are more aware of how much they do not know about ASEAN and its member states, and thus self-report slightly less general familiarity.

"In General, How Familiar are you with ASEAN?"

The first substantive question in the survey asked students to subjectively assess their familiarity with ASEAN. The four scale answer set ranged from "Very Familiar" to "Somewhat Familiar", "A Little Familiar" or "Not Familiar at All". Across the region, the modal (most common) answer was "Somewhat Familiar", although in Indonesia, Myanmar, the Philippines, and Singapore the modal answer was "A Little Familiar". Combining "Very" and "Somewhat" to suggest overall familiarity, the majority of students across the region felt generally familiar with ASEAN (see Table 4.8). However, self-reported familiarity had dropped modestly overall from just over 60 to just over 55 per cent between the 2007 and 2014 surveys.

There were several large shifts in this self-reported familiarity within nations among students from primary universities. Cambodian students' self-reported general familiarity increased by almost 18 per cent and those from Myanmar increased by over 5 per cent. But the broader trend toward less self-reported familiarity was seen in substantial drops in the Philippines and Thailand and moderate drops in Indonesia, Laos, Singapore, and Vietnam. Brunei and Malaysia remained essentially the same.

Results from the additional universities reinforce the pattern of nationally-framed contexts. In most cases (Indonesia,

TABLE 4.8
"In General, How Familiar are you with ASEAN?"
(Percentage of Students' Responses by Nation)

Primary Universities	Very Familiar	Somewhat Familiar	A Little Familiar	Not at All Familiar	Total Familiar	Total Not Familiar
Brunei (B1)	8.5%	48.0%	4.0%	3.5%	56.5%	7.5%
Cambodia (C1)	5.0%	71.7%	22.9%	0.4%	76.7%	23.3%
Indonesia (I1)	4.4%	47.6%	48.0%	0.0%	52.0%	48.0%
Laos (L1)	15.9%	63.2%	20.5%	0.5%	79.1%	21.0%
Malaysia (M1)	3.5%	58.5%	37.0%	1.0%	62.0%	38.0%
Myanmar (N2)	1.5%	13.5%	45.5%	39.5%	15.0%	85.0%
Philippines (P1)	4.8%	37.8%	51.2%	6.2%	42.6%	57.4%
Singapore (S1)	3.3%	35.9%	40.0%	20.8%	39.2%	60.8%
Thailand (T1)	1.9%	51.0%	44.2%	2.9%	52.9%	47.1%
Vietnam (V1)	37.2%	44.7%	15.4%	2.8%	81.9%	18.1%
Average Primary	8.6%	47.2%	32.9%	7.8%	55.8%	40.6%
Additional Universities						
Unsyiah (I2)	11.0%	41.0%	46.0%	2.0%	52.0%	48.0%
Undana (I3)	8.5%	38.3%	50.3%	3.0%	46.8%	53.2%
UTAR (M2)	2.9%	17.9%	50.2%	29.0%	20.8%	79.2%
Unimas (M3)	3.8%	44.6%	45.5%	4.6%	48.4%	50.0%
YU (N1)	1.8%	18.9%	58.0%	21.3%	20.7%	79.3%
UP Visayas (P2)	4.8%	41.1%	46.9%	7.3%	45.9%	54.1%
MSU (P3)	7.1%	31.6%	45.8%	15.6%	38.7%	61.3%
SP (S2)	4.7%	27.7%	47.2%	20.4%	32.3%	67.7%
KKU (T2)	1.9%	57.2%	39.9%	1.0%	59.1%	40.9%
WU (T3)	7.6%	68.2%	23.2%	1.0%	75.8%	24.2%
SJU (T4)	5.1%	60.1%	34.3%	0.6%	65.2%	34.8%
VNU-HCMC (V2)	32.1%	52.8%	12.3%	2.8%	84.9%	15.1%
Average Additional	**7.6%**	**41.6%**	**41.6%**	**9.0%**	**49.2%**	**50.7%**
Average Total	**8.1%**	**44.1%**	**37.7%**	**8.5%**	**52.2%**	**46.1%**

Myanmar, the Philippines, and Vietnam), there is a negligible (within 5 per cent) difference between primary and additional universities, with respect to familiarity. While self-reported familiarity is moderately lower among SP students as opposed to NUS students, they share the same profile of about two-thirds claiming little or no familiarity. Differences in Thailand are also matters of degree, with a majority at all universities seeing themselves as generally familiar with ASEAN. CU students are about evenly split, with only slightly over half claiming to be very or somewhat familiar. This percentage rises to 59 per cent at KKU, 65 per cent at SJU, and 75 per cent at WU. The most dramatic within-nation divergence was found in Malaysia. Over 60 per cent of UM students rate themselves as generally familiar with ASEAN, but amongst UTAR students, nearly 80 per cent claim little or no familiarity. Unimas students fall in between at close to 50 per cent.

Two notable points arise from comparing the 2007 and 2014 surveys. First, the general pattern of subjective familiarity across the region remained largely the same. Students from Vietnam and Laos rated themselves as overall most familiar with ASEAN, and in 2014, Cambodian students also rated their familiarity comparatively highly. In both 2007 and 2014, Myanmar students rated their familiarity with ASEAN remarkably low compared to their counterparts elsewhere. But equally notable is that the moderate and, in some cases, substantial declines in subjective familiarity with ASEAN did not equate with notable drops in students' more objective knowledge of ASEAN as measured by other questions in the 2014 survey. These objective measures tend to suggest that, on the whole, students in the 2014 survey know as much or more about ASEAN than students did in the 2007 survey.

Indicators of Knowledge about ASEAN

The objective set of indicators of knowledge about ASEAN in the 2007 and 2014 surveys included identifying the ASEAN flag, the year of ASEAN's founding, listing ASEAN member states and identifying them on a nationally bordered but otherwise blank map of Southeast Asia (see Table 4.9). In general, recognition of the ASEAN flag rose notably between the 2007 and 2014 surveys, while other indicators of objective knowledge remained largely the same between the two surveys.

Averaged over all ten primary universities, recognition of the ASEAN flag rose from 75 to 85 per cent between the two surveys. Thailand's primary university students recorded a remarkable increase in their identification of the ASEAN flag, from 38 per cent in 2007 to 94 per cent in 2014. Cambodian students also recorded a substantial rise in recognition from 63 to 85 per cent between the two surveys. The only drop in recognition was among students from Myanmar, from 85 to 78 per cent between the surveys, comparing the 2007 Yangon sample and the 2014 Mandalay sample; however, the 2014 Yangon sample rated much higher — 97 per cent — recognition. Whereas in the 2007 survey, seven of the ten samples from primary universities had recognition rates of 75 per cent or more, in 2014 nine of the ten samples recorded three-quarters recognition or better. Only the Philippines was lower, at 48 per cent, though this was still an increase from the 39 per cent recognition recorded in 2007 among UP Diliman students.

Ability to select the correct date of ASEAN's founding from a choice of six years presented (1947, 1957, 1967, 1977, 1987, or 1997) remained largely consistent between the 2007

TABLE 4.9

Indicators of Knowledge about ASEAN

(Percentage of Students' Responses by Nation)

Primary Universities	% Flag Correct	% Year Correct	Countries Listed without Map (Avg.)	Countries Listed with Map (Avg.)	Countries Identified on Map (Avg.)
Brunei (B1)	98.5%	37.4%	9.3	9.6	8.3
Cambodia (C1)	85.4%	50.9%	9.5	9.3	5.6
Indonesia (I1)	94.1%	42.9%	9.8	9.7	7
Laos (L1)	86.4%	55.5%	9.7	9.6	NA
Malaysia (M1)	82.5%	56.3%	8.4	8.7	7.2
Myanmar (N2)	78.0%	29.2%	9.6	8.5	6.5
Philippines (P1)	47.9%	36.9%	8.7	7.4	4.9
Singapore (S1)	89.6%	43.4%	8.8	8	6.8
Thailand (T1)	94.2%	24.5%	9.7	10	8.4
Vietnam (V1)	91.2%	74.1%	9.6	8.7	7.1
Average Primary	**84.8%**	**45.1%**	**9.3**	**9.0**	**6.4**
Additional Universities					
Unsyiah (I2)	93.5%	50.0%	9.6	9.3	5.7
Undana (I3)	82.1%	50.3%	9.1	9.1	4.8
UTAR (M2)	50.5%	41.0%	9.9	9.5	6.5
Unimas (M3)	86.4%	44.6%	8.9	8.1	6.3
YU (N1)	97.2%	50.3%	9.7	8.8	7.8
UP Visayas (P2)	39.4%	36.5%	8.2	8.2	4.9
MSU (P3)	30.6%	29.7%	3.1	7.7	6.7
SP (S2)	89.6%	44.2%	8.6	8.4	6.2
KKU (T2)	98.1%	33.0%	9.6	9.8	8.4
WU (T3)	99.5%	38.4%	9.9	9.9	9
SJU (T4)	98.9%	20.2%	9.8	9.9	6.7
VNU-HCMC (V2)	78.9%	56.4%	9.8	9.6	9.3
Average Additional	**78.7%**	**41.2%**	**8.9**	**9.0**	**6.9**
Average Total	**81.5%**	**43.0%**	**9.1**	**9.0**	**6.7**

and 2014 surveys. Five of the ten primary university samples showed essentially no change. The overall average rates of correct identification across the ten primary university samples were 48 per cent in 2007 and 45 per cent in 2014. Cambodia and Vietnam scored moderate increases and Brunei and Laos moderate declines on this measure. The most substantial drop was among Indonesian primary university students, from 66 to 43 per cent. A closer inspection of the data show that the students' answers had shifted from 1967 (correct) to 1957 (incorrect), which suggests that they still have a general idea of the age of the Association.

As in 2007, we were not surprised that students, on the whole, were not particularly well versed in the specifics of ASEAN's history, though their responses across all countries suggest a rate of response better than mere guessing. While various nations have taken on board more education about ASEAN, it does not appear to be reflected in this detailed dimension of knowledge — the year of founding — but is reflected in the symbolic dimension, i.e. recognition of the ASEAN flag.

Listing and Mapping ASEAN Member States

In 2007, we were somewhat surprised at how well students did in being able to correctly list the ten ASEAN member states and to identify them on a blank map of Southeast Asia. In 2014, the primary university students across the region generally improved, if only marginally, on their already high scores on these measures. For both surveys, we asked half of the students sampled to simply list the names of the ten ASEAN member states. For the other half at each university sampled, we provided them with a blank map of

Southeast Asia and asked them to match the country with its location on the map.

When asked to simply list the ten countries of ASEAN, students from seven of the ten primary universities — those in Brunei, Cambodia, Indonesia, Laos, Myanmar, Thailand, and Vietnam — were able to list at least nine out of ten countries on average. Students from primary universities in Malaysia, the Philippines, and Singapore were able to list at least eight out of ten on average. The raw averages improved everywhere, except for minor drops in Brunei and Malaysia. Primary university student samples showed the most notable increases in Myanmar (from 8.5 to 9.6) and the Philippines (from 7.8 to 8.7).

When presented with a map and asked to list the ASEAN countries by location, the students did nearly as well. For this measure — listing the countries, though not necessarily identifying them correctly on the map — overall, their average across the region on this measure was essentially the same between 2007 (8.8) and 2014 (8.7). For half of the primary university samples, this measure was essentially unchanged. Malaysia, Philippine and Vietnam primary university students did moderately worse on this measure in the 2014 survey but the Myanmar students sampled did remarkably better, improving from 5.6 ASEAN countries listed in the 2007 survey to 8.5 in the 2014 survey. Thai students also did remarkably well — almost perfectly — with 103 out of 104 students correctly listing all ten ASEAN countries on the map test.

Although the Thai primary university sample identified only 8.4 of the countries in the correct location, this was the best among primary university students across the region (but a marginal drop from the 8.9 countries that Thai students from the same university got correct in the 2007 survey). As with other listing and mapping measures, there was little difference overall between the 2007 and 2014 surveys. In the former, students across the ten universities identified 6.8 countries correctly on the map and 6.9 correctly in the latter survey (note: data from the Lao university sample had to be excluded from this metric due to a translation error on the questionnaire). Again, the most noticeable difference within a particular country was in the Myanmar sample, which had correctly identified an average of 4.0 countries in 2007 and 6.5 countries in 2014. Moderate increases among Cambodian, Filipino, and Vietnamese students were offset elsewhere by moderate drops among Malaysian, Singaporean and Thai students.

Most, if not all, general trends observed in the 2007 survey were replicated in the 2014 survey. As in 2007, the cartographic knowledge of students' ability to identify countries on the map closely followed the conventional division between Mainland (Cambodia, Laos, Myanmar, Thailand, and Vietnam) and Maritime (Brunei, Indonesia, Malaysia, the Philippines, and Singapore) countries in Southeast Asia (see Table 4.10). With only four singular exceptions, students from Mainland nations identified Mainland countries more readily than Maritime countries; and the same held for students from Maritime nations more readily identifying those countries. Two exceptions were in the Malaysian and Singaporean students being able to more accurately identify Thailand rather than the Philippines. Myanmar students could more readily identify Singapore than they could either Cambodia or Vietnam. And Thai students identified Malaysia more readily on the map than any of the Mainland countries.

TABLE 4.10
Identification of Countries on Map

Primary Universities	Brunei	Cambodia	Indonesia	Laos	Malaysia	Myanmar	Philippines	Singapore	Thailand	Vietnam
Brunei (B1)	100.0%	70.0%	90.0%	65.0%	98.0%	65.0%	93.0%	96.0%	87.0%	66.0%
Cambodia (C1)	42.0%	86.6%	33.6%	71.4%	30.3%	48.7%	42.9%	47.1%	78.2%	74.8%
Indonesia (I1)	89.2%	43.6%	91.2%	51.0%	95.1%	39.6%	81.4%	94.1%	60.8%	45.1%
Laos (L1)	18.2%	25.5%	19.1%	24.6%	30.0%	30.0%	19.1%	22.7%	30.0%	39.1%
Malaysia (M1)	96.0%	37.4%	85.9%	41.4%	97.0%	47.5%	74.8%	96.0%	88.9%	46.5%
Myanmar (N2)	50.0%	64.7%	48.0%	71.6%	55.9%	100.0%	49.0%	65.7%	88.2%	55.9%
Philippines (P1)	49.1%	35.8%	60.0%	32.1%	60.0%	31.2%	96.4%	46.4%	36.7%	40.0%
Singapore (S1)	67.9%	45.3%	80.2%	45.3%	96.2%	45.3%	66.0%	99.1%	73.6%	61.3%
Thailand (T1)	72.1%	87.5%	75.0%	86.5%	92.3%	88.5%	76.9%	79.8%	98.1%	86.5%
Vietnam (V1)	61.3%	76.4%	69.8%	77.4%	65.1%	72.6%	67.9%	60.4%	76.4%	83.0%
Average Primary	**64.6%**	**57.3%**	**65.3%**	**56.6%**	**72.0%**	**56.8%**	**66.7%**	**70.7%**	**71.8%**	**59.8%**
Additional Universities										
Unsyiah (I2)	70.0%	37.0%	78.0%	31.0%	80.0%	46.0%	64.0%	73.0%	47.0%	40.0%
Undana (I3)	59.4%	31.7%	79.2%	40.6%	65.4%	36.6%	57.4%	58.4%	23.8%	31.7%
UTAR (M2)	86.7%	30.5%	71.4%	36.2%	97.1%	40.0%	74.3%	97.1%	86.7%	30.5%
Unimas (M3)	95.4%	28.4%	78.9%	36.7%	96.3%	33.0%	71.6%	91.7%	74.3%	32.1%
YU (N1)	70.9%	68.4%	64.6%	86.1%	74.7%	100.0%	76.0%	79.8%	92.4%	69.6%
UP Visayas (P2)	42.3%	25.0%	65.4%	36.5%	56.7%	26.9%	100.0%	47.1%	40.4%	50.0%
MSU (P3)	30.5%	21.4%	35.0%	13.2%	41.4%	14.4%	86.4%	31.7%	26.0%	21.0%
SP (S2)	55.8%	50.4%	67.0%	50.4%	88.5%	44.3%	53.1%	95.5%	68.1%	46.0%
KKU (T2)	68.6%	95.1%	82.4%	94.1%	92.2%	94.1%	64.2%	88.2%	99.0%	96.1%
WU (T3)	85.4%	88.4%	89.3%	87.4%	93.2%	93.2%	84.5%	90.3%	97.1%	90.3%
SJU (T4)	47.0%	67.0%	51.0%	73.0%	79.0%	76.0%	53.0%	54.0%	96.0%	71.0%
VNU-HCMC (V2)	52.4%	88.4%	64.1%	84.5%	66.0%	61.2%	68.9%	57.3%	76.7%	91.3%
Average Additional	**63.7%**	**52.6%**	**68.9%**	**55.8%**	**77.5%**	**55.5%**	**71.1%**	**72.0%**	**69.0%**	**55.8%**
Average Total	**64.1%**	**54.7%**	**67.2%**	**56.2%**	**75.0%**	**56.1%**	**69.1%**	**71.4%**	**70.2%**	**57.6%**

Summary Regarding General Knowledge

When comparing within-nation results among primary and additional universities, the measures of objective knowledge again match up fairly closely with regard to national frames-of-reference. In Indonesia, more than 90 per cent of students at both UI and Unsyiah identified the ASEAN flag, while over 80 per cent did at Undana. Just over half of the student sample at Unsyiah and Undana correctly identified the year of ASEAN's founding, moderately outscoring their peers at UI in the 2014 survey, but not matching the 2007 results from UI. All groups of Indonesian students could list more than nine ASEAN countries on average, though Undana students' performance was modestly lower than those at the other schools. Undana and Unsyiah students also performed substantially lower than UI students in correctly identifying ASEAN members on the map of Southeast Asia.

In the Philippines, UP Visayas students scored moderately lower in identifying the ASEAN flag, but on other measures, their scores were close to those of their UP Diliman peers. MSU students scored generally lower than their peers at other Philippine universities. These results reinforce the picture, found earlier in 2007, that students in the Philippines generally exhibit the lowest objective knowledge about ASEAN amongst students across the region. Scores of SP and NUS students were also remarkably similar across all measures and, while not as low as those in the Philippines, were consistently lower than regional averages (when the very low scores from the Philippines are excluded).

Scores from the four Thai universities tended to all follow a similar pattern, with very high recognition of the ASEAN flag and ability to list and identify ASEAN countries on a map, but modest to poor ability to identify the founding year (however, this may be due to the fact that Thai students were given the possible answers in Gregorian Christian years, rather than the Buddhist years which are more commonly used in Thailand). In Vietnam, students on the whole did well on the objective measures of knowledge about ASEAN, though with some variations between the two universities. VNU-Hanoi students scored well over 90 per cent on recognition of the ASEAN flag while only 79 per cent of VNU-HCMC students got this correct. VNU-Hanoi students also did much better — and remarkably well overall — in identifying the year of founding. While VNU-HCMC students scored substantially lower, their mark was still higher than any other primary or additional university in the survey. VNU-HCMC students also did better than Hanoi students in listing ASEAN members and identifying them on the map.

The greatest divergence in objective knowledge was again seen in Malaysia. UM students were far better than UTAR students at identifying the ASEAN flag and year of founding and moderately better at identifying ASEAN countries on the map. On the other hand, UTAR students scored substantially better in simply listing the ASEAN member states. Unimas students' responses were somewhat more similar to UM students, marginally better at identifying the flag, closer to UTAR students in identifying year of founding, intermediate in listing ASEAN members, but lowest in identifying them on a map.

The patterns of the relationship between primary and additional universities outlined above suggest that, in general, not only is there evidence of national framings in most countries, there was also a tendency for students from the primary universities to score marginally better than those at additional universities on their objective knowledge about

ASEAN. Given that the primary universities are, on the whole, the most academically selective schools in each nation, it is not surprising that students would tend to score somewhat higher on such objective knowledge tests. On the recognition of the ASEAN flag, it may also be the case that students at universities located in national political centres or capitals may have more exposure to such symbols.

c. ORIENTATION TOWARD THE REGION AND INDIVIDUAL COUNTRIES OF ASEAN

The survey provided further insights into students' orientation toward the region through questions on travel, work, and interest in ASEAN. We asked the students to complete the sentences "If I could travel to another country in ASEAN, I would most like to travel to …" and "If I could work in another country in ASEAN, I would most like to work in …". Using the agree/ disagree format, we also asked students to respond to the sentence "I would like to know more about other ASEAN countries". In addition to these direct questions on students' orientation toward the region, we were also able to use an analysis of the students' answers in listing the countries of ASEAN to assess the relative salience of the ten countries both within particular nations and across the region as a whole.

Salience of and Familiarity with Other Countries within ASEAN

We analysed the data collected from students listing the countries of ASEAN using free-list analysis techniques to determine which ASEAN countries are most salient to students from each primary university (see Tables D1–D11 in Appendix D). The countries are ranked by Smith's Salience Index (Smith's S), which combines the frequency and priority across individual respondents' lists to give a salience score; in other words, it measures how often and how quickly particular countries come to mind when students are asked to list the countries of ASEAN. As in the map test, neighbouring countries within the Mainland and Maritime regions tended to be more salient for students within those regions.

It is not surprising, given their centrality, that the two most salient countries overall across the region were Thailand and Malaysia (see Appendix D). It is notable that Thailand, with an overall average rank of 2.7 on the salience tables, is substantially more salient than Malaysia, with a combined 4.0 average rank. Thailand was amongst the top five most salient countries everywhere in the region. Salience of Malaysia was very high (first or second) amongst all Maritime nations but lower amongst students from Mainland nations.

Singapore, Indonesia, and Vietnam were closely grouped in average salience rank across the region (4.8, 4.9, and 4.9 respectively). Singapore tended to be the fourth to sixth most salient country in all nations. Vietnam also tended to range in the middle of the salience tables across the region and did not follow a notable Mainland-Maritime pattern; it had relatively high salience in Laos, Cambodia, and Singapore, but low salience in Brunei and Myanmar. Indonesia tended to rank high among respondents from the Maritime nations and low amongst those from Mainland nations.

The salience of Laos and Cambodia both followed a distinctive Mainland-Maritime pattern as well, with high salience in the former, and low salience in the latter. Interestingly, while students readily identified Cambodia's famous Angkor Wat on our "one-word" descriptive question and were often at a loss to come up with words to describe Laos, when it came to listing ASEAN members, Laos came up somewhat more readily than Cambodia. Myanmar, the Philippines, and Brunei were of relatively low salience across the region, with the minor exceptions of the salience of Myanmar (third) in Thailand and Brunei (fifth) in Indonesia.

The pattern of salience can further suggest to us a more refined understanding of the Mainland-Maritime configuration of ASEAN countries, with reference to their salience amongst students. The Mainland configuration centres on Thailand, Cambodia, Laos, and Vietnam, with Myanmar as something of an outlier. The first four nations all have a high cognizance of each other, ranking first through fourth in lists of all these nations — with the exception of Thailand where Vietnam is less salient (sixth after Malaysia) and Myanmar is more salient (third). The Maritime cluster likewise centres on Malaysia, Singapore, and Indonesia (all first through third on each of these nation's lists) with both the Philippines and Brunei as outliers, ranking fifth to tenth even amongst students from other Maritime nations.

Travel Destinations

In discussing travel and work destinations, we refer to destinations selected by more than 20 per cent of students within a sample or overall as primary destinations. Those chosen by 10 to 20 per cent, we call secondary destinations and those between 5 to 10 per cent, we label as tertiary destinations. If a destination is selected by less than 5 per cent of a sample, we consider that the destination "does not rate" amongst students at that university, nation, or the survey overall.

The most desirable travel destinations across the ten primary university samples were Singapore, Thailand, and Malaysia, which is consistent with the 2007 survey (see Table 4.11). In the 2007 survey, students from Brunei, Cambodia, Indonesia, Myanmar, the Philippines, and Vietnam had all rated Singapore, Thailand, and Malaysia as their first, second, and third travel destinations. In the 2014 survey, the picture is more mixed. In 2007, Singapore was the top primary travel destination for students from every country outside of Singapore, with the exception of Laos, where Malaysia was slightly preferred to Singapore (41 to 36 per cent). In 2014, Singapore replaced Malaysia by a wide margin (55 to 19 per cent) for students from Laos, though Malaysia remained their second most desirable travel destination (ahead of Vietnam at 7 per cent). As in 2007, desire to travel to Thailand barely registered among Lao university students. In 2014, Singapore remained the number one travel destination for Cambodian, Myanmar, Filipino, Thai, and Vietnamese students. But for primary university students in Brunei, Indonesia, and Malaysia, the 2014 survey found Thailand replacing Singapore in the number one spot by 6 to 8 percentage points.

While strong general interest in Singapore and Thailand remained at levels comparable to the 2007 survey, interest in travelling to Malaysia slipped in a number of places. And the average interest in travelling to Malaysia across the ten primary universities was only marginally higher than interest in travelling to Vietnam (both just over 7 per cent). While Vietnam had also appeared as the fourth most popular destination on average in the 2007 survey, it had rated less than half the interest shown to Malaysia (14 versus 6 per cent). In addition to the dramatic decline among Lao students noted above, interest in

TABLE 4.11
"If I Could Travel to Another Country in ASEAN, I Would Most Like to Travel to …"
(Percentage of Students' Responses by Nation)

Primary Universities	Bru	Cam	Indo	Laos	Mal	Mya	Phil	Sing	Thai	Viet	Other
Brunei (B1)	0.0%	1.5%	9.5%	0.5%	9.5%	1.5%	9.0%	27.0%	33.0%	5.0%	3.5%
Cambodia (C1)	1.3%	0.0%	2.5%	0.4%	3.8%	2.1%	3.8%	49.2%	25.8%	1.7%	9.6%
Indonesia (I1)	5.4%	1.0%	1.0%	1.5%	3.4%	1.0%	8.0%	27.8%	36.6%	11.7%	2.0%
Laos (L1)	2.3%	0.9%	3.2%	0.5%	18.6%	0.5%	3.2%	55.5%	2.7%	6.4%	6.4%
Malaysia (M1)	10.0%	4.5%	16.4%	1.5%	0.0%	2.0%	6.5%	15.4%	22.8%	8.5%	12.4%
Myanmar (N2)	1.5%	3.4%	4.4%	0.5%	3.9%	0.5%	2.4%	57.6%	18.5%	2.4%	4.9%
Philippines (P1)	0.5%	5.9%	5.5%	1.4%	12.3%	0.0%	0.0%	41.6%	17.4%	5.9%	9.6%
Singapore (S1)	5.3%	6.3%	6.3%	2.4%	17.4%	3.9%	3.4%	0.0%	38.7%	12.6%	3.9%
Thailand (T1)	7.8%	2.5%	2.5%	10.8%	5.4%	4.9%	2.5%	45.6%	0.0%	16.7%	1.5%
Vietnam (V1)	0.5%	0.5%	1.4%	5.6%	0.5%	0.9%	1.9%	74.7%	12.7%	1.4%	0.0%
Average Primary	**3.5%**	**2.6%**	**5.3%**	**2.5%**	**7.5%**	**1.7%**	**4.1%**	**39.4%**	**20.8%**	**7.2%**	**5.4%**
Additional Universities											
Unsyiah (I2)	16.0%	2.5%	0.5%	1.0%	4.5%	2.5%	3.0%	34.5%	26.5%	5.5%	3.5%
Undana (I3)	1.5%	2.5%	0.0%	1.5%	9.5%	0.5%	7.5%	48.8%	18.4%	2.5%	7.5%
UTAR (M2)	5.2%	4.8%	1.9%	0.0%	0.5%	1.0%	2.9%	34.8%	20.5%	4.8%	23.8%
Unimas (M3)	5.0%	7.7%	12.7%	1.4%	0.9%	1.8%	10.9%	13.6%	21.8%	8.6%	13.6%
YU (N1)	0.6%	5.5%	4.2%	1.8%	1.2%	0.0%	4.2%	55.8%	15.8%	10.9%	0.0%
UP Visayas (P2)	1.0%	3.4%	7.7%	0.0%	12.1%	0.5%	1.0%	36.2%	22.2%	2.4%	13.5%
MSU (P3)	1.8%	0.9%	4.1%	0.5%	25.4%	0.0%	0.0%	38.3%	4.6%	0.0%	24.4%
SP (S2)	11.7%	6.8%	7.7%	3.6%	11.3%	2.3%	2.3%	0.9%	35.6%	8.1%	9.9%
KKU (T2)	4.7%	2.4%	3.3%	12.7%	5.7%	5.2%	0.9%	51.9%	0.0%	11.3%	4.0%
WU (T3)	24.9%	0.5%	10.5%	2.5%	11.4%	2.0%	3.0%	40.8%	0.0%	4.0%	0.5%
SJU (T4)	9.6%	3.9%	6.7%	4.5%	2.3%	2.3%	3.9%	59.0%	0.0%	7.3%	2.8%
VNU-HCMC (V2)	0.5%	1.4%	4.2%	1.4%	2.3%	0.0%	1.9%	60.3%	24.8%	0.5%	1.9%
Average Additional	**6.9%**	**3.5%**	**5.3%**	**2.6%**	**7.2%**	**1.5%**	**3.5%**	**39.6%**	**15.8%**	**5.5%**	**8.8%**
Average Total	**5.3%**	**3.1%**	**5.3%**	**2.5%**	**7.3%**	**1.6%**	**3.7%**	**39.5%**	**18.1%**	**6.3%**	**7.2%**

travelling to Malaysia declined among students at every primary university with the exception of Singapore. Apart from Laos, the largest declines were among students from Brunei (from 19 to 9 per cent) and Indonesia (from 14 to 3 per cent). Indonesian students in particular showed much greater interest in travelling to Vietnam (12 per cent) or the Philippines (8 per cent) over Malaysia. The decline among Indonesian students may be attributable to increased tensions between the two nations over recent years, related to disputes over cultural heritage and labour migration. But reasons for the general decline elsewhere in the region is less clear — whether due to a decline in Malaysia's profile as a travel destination or alternatively due to the relative rise in desirability of other destinations in the region.

We noted in the 2007 survey that desirable travel destinations among ASEAN university students suggest an interest in travel to the most developed and modern places in the region, in contrast to the sort of "exotic" and "cultural" travel that may entice Western or other tourists from outside the region. In general, the 2014 findings continue to support such a conclusion. However, there is also some indication that ASEAN university students' imaginations are broadening with regard to travel in the region — with Thailand overtaking Singapore as the top ranked travel destination in some nations, Vietnam nearly matching Malaysia in general interest, and greater interest shown toward Indonesia and the Philippines in a number of nations. Nevertheless, the least affluent ASEAN members — Cambodia, Laos, and Myanmar — remain the countries where students show the least interest in terms of travel.

The 2014 survey, covering additional universities within six of the ASEAN member states, found the same overall pattern of desirability amongst students at those additional universities. The data demonstrate broad consensus within nations in most cases. But they also reveal some patterns in which there is a particular draw of certain countries within particular student bodies, generally based on region and co-ethnic factors. Of the six nations data reported here, the greatest internal consistency was found in Singapore and Vietnam, while data from Indonesia, Malaysia, the Philippines, and Thailand show evidence of regional and ethnic influences.

For both SP and NUS students, Thailand was a strong primary travel destination. Apart from Thailand, and given that they were selecting countries other than their own, Singaporean students displayed one of the most evenly spread selections of countries. Brunei, Cambodia, Indonesia, Malaysia, and Vietnam all rated as secondary or tertiary travel destinations for students from the two schools. Laos, Myanmar, and the Philippines did not rate.

Vietnamese students displayed the most overwhelmingly singular desire to travel to Singapore, at both VNU-Hanoi (75 per cent) and VNU-HCMC (60 per cent). Thailand rated a distant second choice at both universities, still a primary destination for VNU-HCMC students but only a weak secondary destination for VNU-Hanoi students. Hanoi students also rated Laos as a very weak tertiary destination. Otherwise, no other ASEAN countries rated as travel destinations of interest by our 5 per cent standard for students at either university.

Singapore and Thailand were primary travel destinations for Indonesian students from all three universities surveyed, except for Undana students who rated Thailand as a strong secondary destination. Secondary and tertiary destinations, however, show evidence of differentiated interest based on ethnic and regional differences in Indonesia. Brunei is a secondary destination for Unsyiah students from Aceh, but a weak tertiary destination for those at UI in Jakarta (Depok) and does not rate among Undana students in Kupang. Vietnam is of secondary interest for UI students and tertiary interest to Unsyiah students. The Philippines is a tertiary destination for both UI and Undana students, but not Unsyiah students. Only Undana students rated Malaysia as a tertiary destination and it did not rate among either UI or Unsyiah students. Cambodia, Laos, and Myanmar did not rate (5 per cent or higher) at any of the Indonesian universities.

The results from Malaysia, like those of Indonesia, demonstrate some ethnically- and regionally-based difference within a broader overall consensus around desirable travel destinations. Singapore and Thailand were both top travel destinations at all three Malaysian universities, but Thailand was the top and primary at UM and Unimas while Singapore was top and primary at UTAR. Thailand, though rated below Singapore, was also a primary destination for UTAR students. Singapore rated as a strong secondary destination for UM students and weaker secondary at Unimas. UM students rated both Indonesia and Brunei as secondary travel destinations (with Indonesia scoring slightly higher than Singapore). Indonesia was a secondary destination for Unimas students, but Brunei just barely rated as a tertiary destination. UM students also rated Vietnam and the Philippines as tertiary destinations. The Philippines was a secondary destination for Unimas students, while Vietnam along with Cambodia were tertiary. For UTAR students, apart from Singapore and Thailand, only Brunei rated as a weak tertiary travel destination amongst ASEAN countries. A large percentage of UTAR students (23 per cent;

compared to 12 per cent at UM and 14 per cent at Unimas) listed non-ASEAN countries in response to this question. Again Cambodia, Laos, and Myanmar did not rate among any group of Malaysian students, with the exception of Cambodia at Unimas.

Amongst Filipino students, Singapore was a strong primary travel destination for students at all three universities. Thailand was a weaker primary at UP Visayas and a strong secondary destination at UP Diliman, but did not rate among MSU students. Malaysia was another primary destination for MSU students, and a weaker secondary destination at both the Diliman and Visayas campuses. Indonesia rated as a tertiary destination (over 5 per cent) at both UP Diliman and UP Visayas, but did not rate (less than 5 per cent) at MSU. Cambodia and Vietnam rated as tertiary at UP Diliman. Laos and Myanmar did not rate at any of the three universities. Overall, the profile for UP Diliman and UP Visayas is largely similar. MSU was not too different, but did show evidence of a particular affinity toward Malaysia, though notably not toward the Muslim-majority countries of Brunei or Indonesia.

Results from Thailand demonstrate the allure of Singapore along with certain regional and ethnically based pulls — of KKU students to mainland neighbours and WU students to Malay-Muslim countries. Thai students from all four universities displayed an overwhelming interest (40 per cent or more) in travelling to Singapore. Brunei was the second rated country among WU students, where it was a strong secondary destination, and among SJU students, though only as a tertiary destination (59 per cent of SJU students selected Singapore; all other destinations were tertiary or did not rate). Brunei was also a tertiary destination for CU students, but did not rate among

KKU students. Indonesia and Malaysia were secondary, though weaker secondary destinations of interest among WU students. Indonesia rated as a tertiary destination for SJU students. And Malaysia rated as a weak tertiary destination for both CU and KKU students. But otherwise, Indonesia and Malaysia did not rate outside of WU.

The second choice destination for CU students was Vietnam, which was also a secondary destination for KKU students and tertiary destination among SJU students but did not rate at WU. The overall second destination (rated above Vietnam) for KKU students was Laos, which was also a weak secondary choice for CU students but did not rate at either SJU or WU. Myanmar was a weak tertiary destination for KKU students (and almost rated as tertiary for CU students). But otherwise, neither neighbouring Myanmar nor Cambodia rated among students from any of the Thai universities. The Philippines also did not rate at any of the Thai universities.

Work Destinations

As with travel destinations, work destinations also revealed some ethnic and regional specificity within broader overall national and ASEAN-wide consensus. The story here is less complex than with travel. As in the 2007 survey, in the current survey, Singapore again remained the overwhelming top destination for the primary university students from all ASEAN nations. About half to three-quarters of respondents listed Singapore at each primary university. As with travel, Thailand and Malaysia were second and third overall destinations for work. In 2007, Malaysia had been rated slightly higher than Thailand. In the current survey, Thailand came out slightly higher than Malaysia (see Table 4.12).

TABLE 4.12

"If I Could Work in Another Country in ASEAN, I Would Most Like to Work in …"
(Percentage of Students' Responses by Nation)

Primary Universities	Bru	Cam	Indo	Laos	Mal	Mya	Phil	Sing	Thai	Viet	Other
Brunei (B1)	1.5%	1.5%	5.0%	0.0%	24.0%	0.0%	2.5%	59.0%	4.0%	0.5%	2.0%
Cambodia (C1)	1.3%	2.5%	2.1%	0.4%	2.1%	1.3%	4.6%	48.3%	27.1%	1.3%	9.2%
Indonesia (I1)	4.4%	1.0%	2.9%	0.0%	3.4%	0.0%	1.5%	78.1%	6.8%	0.5%	1.5%
Laos (L1)	2.7%	1.4%	4.1%	2.7%	11.8%	0.0%	2.3%	56.4%	5.5%	5.9%	7.3%
Malaysia (M1)	20.0%	1.5%	5.5%	0.0%	1.5%	0.0%	2.5%	47.0%	7.0%	2.5%	13.5%
Myanmar (N2)	1.5%	1.0%	0.0%	0.0%	2.5%	3.9%	1.0%	78.3%	7.4%	1.0%	3.5%
Philippines (P1)	0.0%	1.4%	1.8%	0.0%	6.9%	0.0%	0.5%	68.8%	4.6%	3.2%	12.8%
Singapore (S1)	11.7%	1.1%	9.6%	1.1%	31.9%	2.1%	5.3%	3.7%	21.8%	4.8%	6.9%
Thailand (T1)	3.9%	0.0%	0.5%	4.9%	2.5%	1.0%	0.5%	72.1%	7.8%	3.4%	0.0%
Vietnam (V1)	0.5%	0.5%	0.5%	6.6%	1.9%	0.0%	1.4%	72.3%	9.9%	6.1%	0.5%
Average Primary	**4.7%**	**1.2%**	**3.2%**	**1.6%**	**8.8%**	**0.8%**	**2.2%**	**58.4%**	**10.2%**	**2.9%**	**5.7%**
Additional Universities											
Unsyiah (I2)	18.0%	1.0%	4.0%	1.5%	10.0%	1.0%	1.0%	48.5%	9.0%	2.0%	4.0%
Undana (I3)	3.5%	2.5%	2.5%	1.0%	9.0%	0.5%	5.0%	54.7%	12.9%	1.0%	7.5%
UTAR (M2)	5.3%	1.0%	0.0%	0.0%	3.8%	1.0%	0.0%	71.8%	1.0%	1.4%	14.8%
Unimas (M3)	16.7%	1.4%	3.7%	0.5%	3.2%	0.0%	0.9%	52.8%	4.2%	1.9%	14.8%
YU (N1)	1.9%	1.3%	0.6%	0.6%	1.3%	10.1%	0.0%	74.8%	7.6%	1.3%	0.6%
UP Visayas (P2)	0.0%	0.0%	2.0%	0.0%	10.7%	0.5%	1.0%	63.9%	5.9%	2.0%	14.2%
MSU (P3)	3.2%	0.0%	3.2%	0.0%	20.7%	0.5%	1.8%	43.8%	3.2%	0.9%	22.6%
SP (S2)	14.4%	2.9%	5.8%	5.8%	33.2%	0.5%	2.4%	6.7%	13.9%	3.9%	10.6%
KKU (T2)	3.8%	0.5%	1.9%	10.0%	5.2%	0.5%	1.4%	65.9%	4.7%	3.8%	2.4%
WU (T3)	22.4%	0.5%	3.0%	1.5%	23.9%	1.5%	2.5%	42.3%	2.0%	0.5%	0.0%
SJU (T4)	6.7%	0.0%	2.8%	1.1%	6.2%	1.1%	5.6%	60.1%	10.7%	2.3%	3.4%
VNU-HCMC (V2)	1.4%	0.5%	3.3%	0.5%	1.9%	0.5%	1.9%	72.4%	12.2%	3.7%	0.9%
Average Additional	**8.1%**	**1.0%**	**2.7%**	**1.9%**	**10.8%**	**1.5%**	**2.0%**	**54.8%**	**7.3%**	**2.0%**	**8.0%**
Average Total	**6.6%**	**1.1%**	**2.9%**	**1.7%**	**9.9%**	**1.2%**	**2.1%**	**56.4%**	**8.6%**	**2.4%**	**6.9%**

Only a few specific sets of students from particular nations saw significant opportunities for work in the region outside of Singapore (based on 10 per cent or more listing a particular country). Bruneian (24 per cent) and Lao (12 per cent) students listed Malaysia, Cambodian (27 per cent) students listed Thailand, and Malaysians (20 per cent) listed Brunei. For Singaporean students, their top three destinations for work outside their own country were Malaysia, Thailand, and Brunei. All of these findings are largely in keeping with patterns seen in the 2007 survey. Interest shown in the previous survey by Indonesian students for working in Brunei and Lao students working in Vietnam both declined substantially (from 22 to 4 per cent and from 15 to 6 per cent respectively).

Overall, there is little indication that the primary university students' imaginations with regard to seeking work outside their own nation but within ASEAN has expanded between the 2007 and 2014 surveys. For example, despite (or perhaps even because of) heavy promotion of the AEC in Thailand, which among other things is meant to ease restrictions on labour migration in the region, Thai primary university students in the 2014 survey showed more singular focus on Singapore and less interest in the possibility of work everywhere else in the region. Whether this will change, and the imagination of ASEAN students will widen into the future, as the AEC becomes a reality rather than a plan, will be a matter worth tracking.

The pattern of choices of work destinations within-nations as well as across ASEAN as a whole was much simpler, due to the overwhelming pull of Singapore. Between 40 to 80 per cent of students in every nation and from all universities rated Singapore as their top destination for work. On average across the region, Thailand was the second most popular destination for work. It rated as a primary destination for students from Cambodia's Royal Phnom Penh University (RUPP) and from Singapore's NUS; secondary for students from SP, Undana in Kupang (Indonesia), and VNU-HCMC; and tertiary for students from UI, National University of Laos (NUOL), UM, University of Mandalay (MU), and University of Yangon (YU) in Myanmar, VNU-Hanoi, Unsyiah in Aceh (Indonesia), and UP Visayas.

Brunei was a second choice for students at most predominantly Muslim universities — a primary destination for WU students in southern Thailand, UM students in Malaysia, and a strong secondary choice for Unsyiah students from Aceh (Indonesia); although Brunei did not rate among predominantly Muslim UI or MSU students. Brunei rated as a secondary destination for students from both Singapore schools as well as Unimas (Sarawak), and as a tertiary destination for SJU students in Thailand and UTAR students in Malaysia.

Malaysia also appeared to be a draw among Muslim students, as a primary work destination for WU students from Thailand, MSU students from the Philippines (Mindanao), and Universiti Brunei Darussalam (UBD) students from Brunei, and a secondary, albeit weak, destination for Unsyiah students. Again, it did not rate among UI students, who overwhelmingly (78 per cent) chose Singapore. But Malaysia's appeal was somewhat broader than Brunei's. It was a first choice and primary destination for NUS and SP students, secondary destination for students from Laos and UP Visayas, and tertiary destination for students from UP Diliman, Undana in Indonesia, and both KKU and SJU in Thailand.

Other than the overwhelming draw of Singapore and some selective interest in Thailand, Brunei, and Malaysia, there was little or no interest shown by students across the region for working in other ASEAN countries. Indonesia rated tertiary interest at both Singapore schools, at the UBD, and UM. Laos rated as a weak secondary choice at KKU and a tertiary choice among students from VNU-Hanoi and SP. The Philippines rated as a weak tertiary choice at NUS, Undana in Indonesia, and SJU in Thailand. Vietnam rated as a weak tertiary choice at NUOL. Cambodia and Myanmar did not rate as work destinations at any university across the region.

Interest in Learning about Other ASEAN Countries

The subsequent question "I would like to know more about other ASEAN countries" registered the same general and overwhelming interest in learning more about ASEAN neighbours that the 2007 survey revealed. There was also the same pattern of "ASEAN enthusiasm" registered among primary university students from the newer and generally less affluent ASEAN member nations as compared to those from the older and more affluent member nations. Overall agreement ranged between 84 per cent in Singapore and Thailand to 100 per cent in Laos. Apart from Singapore and Thailand, all other samples of primary university students agreed with this statement at rates of over 90 per cent. As we found in 2007, the highest rates of "strongly agree" were in Cambodia (90 per cent), Laos (76 per cent), and Vietnam (78 per cent). As with other parts of the survey, the "ASEAN scepticism" displayed by Myanmar students in 2007 had disappeared in the 2014 survey. Rather, both samples of Myanmar students from Mandalay and Yangon in 2014 displayed instead a pattern of ASEAN enthusiasm on this question, with 79 and 71 per cent strongly agreeing, 18 per cent and 27 per cent somewhat agreeing, and less than 3 per cent disagreeing with the statement (see Table 4.13).

TABLE 4.13
"I Would Like to Know More about Other ASEAN Countries"
(Percentage of Students' Responses by Nation)

Primary Universities	Strongly Agree	Somewhat Agree	Somewhat Disagree	Strongly Disagree	Total Agree	Total Disagree
Brunei (B1)	49.0%	47.5%	3.0%	0.5%	96.5%	3.5%
Cambodia (C1)	90.0%	8.8%	1.3%	0.0%	98.8%	1.3%
Indonesia (I1)	41.0%	52.7%	6.3%	0.0%	93.7%	6.3%
Laos (L1)	75.9%	24.1%	0.0%	0.0%	100.0%	0.0%
Malaysia (M1)	35.0%	59.1%	5.9%	0.0%	94.1%	5.9%
Myanmar (N2)	79.4%	17.7%	0.5%	2.5%	97.1%	2.9%
Philippines (P1)	52.8%	40.8%	5.5%	0.9%	93.6%	6.4%
Singapore (S1)	23.6%	60.4%	9.0%	7.1%	84.0%	16.1%
Thailand (T1)	25.0%	59.6%	12.5%	2.9%	84.6%	15.4%
Vietnam (V1)	77.8%	19.4%	1.4%	1.4%	97.2%	2.8%
Average Primary	**55.0%**	**39.0%**	**4.5%**	**1.5%**	**94.0%**	**6.1%**
Additional Universities						
Unsyiah (I2)	75.5%	22.5%	1.5%	0.5%	98.0%	2.0%
Undana (I3)	78.1%	21.4%	0.5%	0.0%	99.5%	0.5%
UTAR (M2)	33.3%	53.3%	11.0%	2.4%	86.7%	13.3%
Unimas (M3)	35.9%	59.5%	3.2%	1.4%	95.4%	4.6%
YU (N1)	71.0%	27.3%	1.7%	0.0%	98.3%	1.7%
UP Visayas (P2)	63.3%	34.8%	1.9%	0.0%	98.1%	1.9%
MSU (P3)	84.0%	16.0%	0.0%	0.0%	100.0%	0.0%
SP (S2)	13.8%	58.8%	22.1%	5.4%	72.5%	27.5%
KKU (T2)	60.1%	39.0%	0.5%	0.5%	99.1%	0.9%
WU (T3)	65.5%	33.0%	1.5%	0.0%	98.5%	1.5%
SJU (T4)	44.4%	47.8%	6.7%	1.1%	92.1%	7.9%
VNU-HCMC (V2)	78.0%	20.6%	0.5%	0.9%	98.6%	1.4%
Average Additional	**58.6%**	**36.1%**	**4.3%**	**1.0%**	**94.7%**	**5.3%**
Average Total	**56.9%**	**37.4%**	**4.4%**	**1.2%**	**94.4%**	**5.6%**

In nations where we sampled two or more universities, it was more common for there to be greater interest and enthusiasm for learning about other ASEAN countries from the additional rather than the primary universities. The only exceptions were in Malaysia and Singapore. Rates of enthusiasm, based on the "strongly agree" scores, between UM and UTAR were roughly similar, with moderately less overall interest among UTAR students. Singaporean students were overall the least interested and enthusiastic to learn more about ASEAN countries, with SP students reporting moderately less enthusiasm than their NUS peers.

While all students from Indonesian universities showed interest in learning about other ASEAN countries, students at Unsyiah and Undana both showed greater enthusiasm — strong agreement at more than 75 per cent as compared to 40 per cent at UI. MSU students showed substantially more enthusiasm and UP Visayas students showed moderately more enthusiasm than their peers at the primary university of UP Diliman. Thai students also fit the pattern of greater interest away from the primary university. Students at all three additional universities showed moderately more general interest and substantially more enthusiasm toward learning more about ASEAN countries. There was no significant difference in overall interest or enthusiasm between the two Vietnamese universities — where students at both VNU-Hanoi and VNU-HCMC exhibited some of the greatest enthusiasm observed across the region (only Cambodian students were substantially more enthusiastic).

d. SOURCES OF INFORMATION ABOUT THE REGION

We provided respondents with a list of fourteen possible sources of information about the region and asked them to circle all those from which they have learned about ASEAN. (We also gave them the option to circle "Other: _____" or "None of the above", but as responses to these selections were negligible we do not discuss them here.) The most and least frequently circled items were fairly consistent across the region and also largely consistent with the findings of the 2007 survey (see Table 4.14).

The frequency with which primary university students on the whole indicated the Internet as a source of information rose from 50 per cent in 2007 to 67 per cent in the 2014 survey. The Internet rose from being the fifth to the third most common source of information overall, surpassing newspapers and books, both of which declined moderately in the frequency with which respondents circled them; from 71 to 60 per cent for newspapers overall and from 65 to 57 per cent for books.

Radio also moderately declined in importance (from 40 to 35 per cent overall), with a substantial decline of 15 per cent in Cambodia and moderate declines of 10 per cent in both Laos and Vietnam. Movies showed a small rise overall from 12 per cent in 2007 to 16 per cent in 2014, but with a particularly dramatic rise from 9 to 78 per cent in the Philippines. All this suggests that while the general sources of information remain the same, some shifts are taking place in the mediascape of ASEAN, particularly with the Internet overtaking older media and sources of information. The rise in movies as a source of information may also signal some significance of pan-Asian or pan-ASEAN popular culture taking hold; though a deeper investigation would be necessary to confirm such a finding.

Consistent with the 2007 survey, television and schooling remained the first and second most important sources of

TABLE 4.14

Sources of Information about ASEAN:

Comparative Ranks (Primary Universities) Across Nations

Sources	Brunei	Cambodia	Indonesia	Laos	Malaysia	Myanmar	Philippines	Singapore	Thailand	Vietnam	Average	Percentage
Television	1	1	4	1	1	3	2	3	1	1	1.8	72.2%
School	4	2	1	2	4	5	1	1	2	2	2.4	71.1%
Internet	2	4	3	3	2	1	3	4	3	3	2.9	66.6%
Newspaper	2	6	5	4	5	2	3	2	5	4	3.9	60.0%
Books	6	3	2	6	3	4	5	5	6	5	4.6	56.5%
Friends	7	7	6	8	8	8	6	6	7	9	7.3	34.3%
Radio	5	5	11	7	9	7	9	9	8	6	7.7	34.5%
Advertising	10	8	9	5	10	10	8	12	4	8	8.2	31.5%
Sports	9	11	7	9	6	6	13	10	12	7	9	26.0%
Family	11	9	8	11	11	12	7	8	9	11	9.8	21.5%
Travel	8	14	10	10	13	13	10	7	9	12	10.7	19.3%
Movies	12	13	11	14	10	9	11	13	14	10	10.8	15.8%
Music	13	10	13	12	12	11	11	14	11	13	12.1	12.0%
Work Experience	14	11	14	13	14	13	14	11	12	14	13	8.7%

information about the region. School, as a source of information about ASEAN, remained noticeably low in Myanmar (38 per cent in 2007, 43 to 45 per cent in 2014) in contrast to the rest of the region. The Internet joined these as primary sources of information about ASEAN, along with newspapers and books (by which we expect that our respondents are referring to school textbooks). In the earlier survey, we identified the Internet and radio as secondary sources of information. While the Internet has become more important, radio has become less so.

In the 2014 survey, radio rated as a middling source of information along with friends, sports, and advertising. Amongst these, the frequency with which sports was indicated declined moderately (34 to 26 per cent) and the frequency of friends rose modestly (28 to 34 per cent). While the significance of sports declined somewhat in almost every nation, the decline was most noticeable in Vietnam (from 72 to 51 per cent), though Vietnam remained the country where sports was rated most highly. There is a strong possibility that the significance of sports may track closely with the immediacy of sporting events such as the Southeast Asian Games. The 2007 survey was conducted in the run-up to the 2007 SEA Games in Thailand, while the 2014 survey was conducted in an off-year for the biennial event (between hosting in Myanmar in 2013 and Singapore in 2015). With regard to friends, this source of information shifted from the ninth to sixth most common source of information, based on average rankings across all ten nations. While we would not necessarily read too much into this modest percentage increase, it may reflect the increasing importance of social media as a source of information in parallel with the increasing importance of the Internet.

Other possible sources of information provided as options — family, travel, movies, music, and work experience — all generally rated relatively low, as they had in the 2007 survey, though there was some increase in the significance of movies as noted above. The percentage of students reporting travel as a source of information generally rose across the region, with particularly dramatic increases in Brunei (11 to 42 per cent) and Laos (12 to 27 per cent). The percentage of Malaysian students in the primary university (UM) reporting travel as a source of information remained particularly low compared to their counterparts at other primary ASEAN universities (5 per cent in 2007 and 4 per cent in 2014, compared to a regional average of 19 per cent). Only the percentage of students in Cambodia, a much less affluent country, and at Undana in remote eastern Indonesia, rated travel at a similarly low level. Also of note, 17 per cent of UTAR students in Malaysia selected travel as a source of information, thus the low rating at UM cannot be generalized for all Malaysians. As with other aspects of the survey, this appears to reflect substantial differences between Malay and Chinese-Malaysian students. The response rate at Unimas was in between the two, at 8 per cent.

Several other within-nation variations were observed (see Table 4.14a). In addition to rating travel lower, Undana students specified radio substantially more frequently than their counterparts either at UI or Unsyiah in Aceh. UTAR students selected television (substantially) and radio (moderately) less frequently than their counterparts at UM, while the responses for UM and Unimas were essentially the same. In the Philippines, movies were a substantially less common source for UP Visayas and MSU students as compared to UP Diliman students. And in Singapore, advertising was moderately more common and travel moderately less common as sources of information for SP students compared to those from NUS.

TABLE 4.14a
Sources of Information about ASEAN:
Comparative Ranks within Nations

Sources	Indonesia			Malaysia		
	UI	Unsyiah	Undana	UM	UTAR	Unimas
Television	4	4	2	1	5	2
School	1	1	1	4	1	3
Internet	3	3	3	2	2	1
Newspaper	5	5	5	5	4	5
Books	2	2	4	3	3	4
Friends	6	6	8	8	6	7
Radio	11	11	7	9	12	9
Advertising	9	8	9	7	11	6
Sports	7	7	6	6	9	7
Family	8	9	12	11	10	11
Travel	10	10	14	13	7	13
Movies	11	12	10	10	8	9
Music	13	14	11	12	13	11
Work Experience	14	13	13	14	14	14

Sources	Philippines			Singapore	
	UP Dilliman	UP Visayas	MSU	NUS	SP
Television	2	3	3	3	3
School	1	1	1	1	1
Internet	3	2	2	4	2
Newspaper	3	5	5	2	4
Books	5	4	4	5	5
Friends	6	6	5	6	6
Radio	9	9	10	9	10
Advertising	8	8	7	12	7
Sports	13	10	9	10	9
Family	7	7	12	8	8
Travel	10	12	11	7	11
Movies	11	10	8	13	12
Music	11	14	13	14	14
Work Experience	14	13	14	11	13

TABLE 4.14a   (*continued*)

Sources	Thailand				Vietnam	
	CU	KKU	WU	SJU	VNU-Hanoi	VNU-HCMC
Television	1	1	1	2	1	4
School	2	3	3	1	2	1
Internet	3	2	2	2	3	2
Newspaper	5	5	5	4	4	3
Books	6	6	6	6	5	5
Friends	7	7	7	8	9	8
Radio	8	9	10	10	6	6
Advertising	4	4	4	5	8	8
Sports	12	11	12	11	7	7
Family	9	9	8	7	11	12
Travel	9	8	9	9	12	11
Movies	14	14	13	12	10	10
Music	11	10	11	13	13	13
Work Experience	12	13	14	14	14	14

On the whole, however, there is strong support in the data to suggest that not only are sources of information relatively uniform across the region, they are even more common within particular nations. In Thailand, for instance, sources of information across all four Thai universities were extremely similar, with only minor variations in rank importance and percentage responses across the fourteen items. Only one item varied across the universities by more than two ranks (music, ranked tenth for KKU students and thirteenth for SJU students). And only a few varied by as much as 10 per cent in the number of responses. The largest percentage variation was with regard to the Internet between CU students (63 per cent) and KKU students (84 per cent), but for both the rank of the Internet amongst items was similar (third and second respectively). Similar consistency was found between VNU-Hanoi and VNU-HCMC, with the only substantial gap between the two being television, which had 81 per cent of responses and was ranked first at VNU-Hanoi, and 65 per cent of responses and a ranking of fourth at VNU-HCMC.

While the increasing similarity of sources of information, for instance with the general decline of radio and rise of the Internet, is notable, this should not lead to the conclusion that there are no differences of importance. Amidst the similarity, both across and within nations, it is noteworthy that affluence or socio-economic status appears to have some influence on students' sources of information. Radio, for instance, still remains somewhat more important, not only in less affluent countries such as Cambodia, but also in somewhat less affluent and remote areas within countries, such as Kupang, West Timor Indonesia, where Undana is located. Similarly, travel as a source of information tends to be less significant for students from more remote areas or among less affluent groups within and across nations.

e. ASPIRATIONS FOR INTEGRATION AND ACTION

The final substantive findings on which we can compare the 2007 and 2014 surveys relate to students' aspirations for the region and for ASEAN. These aspirations were measured in two questions, one which used the agree/disagree format to elicit students' opinions of the importance of eight aspects of integration and cooperation, and a second which asked students to select from among eight choices, those that they felt were most crucial for ASEAN to address in order to enhance cooperation and awareness. Students were given the option to list other responses, but the scores for this option were negligible and thus not discussed here.

In comparing the responses across nations and universities and in comparing the 2007 and 2014 survey findings, we mainly compared the ranking of items. For the aspects of integration and cooperation, we used rankings based on the number of respondents who "strongly agreed" that the item was important. For the eight issues for cooperation and action, we ranked the items based on the number of respondents from a particular university who circled the item. In comparing differences or changes in the rankings, we refer to a difference of one rank as negligible, a difference of two or three ranks as slight and a difference of four or more as substantial. In all cases, those who are interested in a more detailed or specific comparison should refer to both the frequency of responses and relative ranking of items reported in the tables summarizing each aspect of integration in Appendix E.

Aspects of Integration and Cooperation

We asked respondents to indicate their agreement or disagreement on the following eight aspects of integration and cooperation: Cultural Exchanges, Economic Cooperation, Development Assistance, Educational Exchanges, Security and Military Cooperation, Political Cooperation, Sports Competitions, and Tourism. As in the 2007 survey, we again found that overall agreement on the importance of these items was strikingly and strongly positive across the region (see Table 4.15).

In eight out of ten cases, 90 per cent or more of primary university respondents strongly or somewhat agreed on the importance of each item (see Table 4.15*a*). Total agreement averaged over the eight items was over 90 per cent in all nations apart from Singapore (89 per cent) and Thailand (84 per cent). Like elsewhere in the survey, the "ASEAN scepticism" apparent in Myanmar in the 2007 survey disappeared in the 2014 survey.

TABLE 4.15
Overall Attitudes Toward Aspects of Integration and Cooperation (averaged over all eight): Aspects of Integration Ranked Importance (based on "Strongly Agree"; Primary Universities)

Aspects	Brunei (B1)	Cambodia (C1)	Indonesia (I1)	Laos (L1)	Malaysia (M1)	Myanmar (N2)	Philippines (P1)	Singapore (S1)	Thailand (T1)	Vietnam (V1)	Average Rank	Average (Strongly Agree)
Tourism	1	1	1	4	1	5	1	3	2	4	2.3	65.0%
Development Assistance	5	4	4	2	5	2	2	5	1	1	3.1	63.3%
Economic Cooperation	3	3	5	3	4	3	3	2	3	3	3.2	62.7%
Educational Exchanges	2	2	3	1	7	1	4	7	4	5	3.6	60.3%
Security Cooperation	4	5	6	7	2	6	5	1	7	2	4.5	51.7%
Sports Competitions	7	6	2	5	3	4	6	8	6	6	5.3	52.2%
Cultural Exchanges	6	8	7	6	8	7	7	6	5	8	6.8	46.9%
Political Cooperation	8	7	8	8	6	8	8	3	8	7	7.1	41.3%

TABLE 4.15a
Overall Attitudes Toward Aspects of Integration and Cooperation
(average over all eight)

Nation	Strongly Agree	Somewhat Agree	Somewhat Disagree	Strongly Disagree	Total Agree	Total Disagree
Brunei (B1)	60.6%	35.2%	3.6%	0.6%	95.8%	4.3%
Cambodia (C1)	59.2%	34.5%	5.4%	0.9%	93.7%	6.3%
Indonesia (I1)	61.1%	35.1%	3.4%	0.5%	96.2%	3.9%
Laos (L1)	54.0%	39.7%	5.5%	0.7%	93.8%	6.3%
Malaysia (M1)	43.5%	52.1%	3.9%	0.5%	95.6%	4.4%
Myanmar (Y1)	65.5%	29.9%	3.2%	1.4%	95.3%	4.7%
Philippines (P1)	57.0%	35.1%	6.7%	1.3%	92.1%	7.9%
Singapore (S1)	44.1%	44.6%	6.2%	5.2%	88.7%	11.4%
Thailand (T1)	35.2%	48.6%	13.3%	2.9%	83.8%	16.2%
Vietnam (V1)	74.3%	21.6%	3.1%	1.5%	95.9%	4.6%
Average	55.4%	37.6%	5.4%	1.6%	93.1%	7.0%

Nation	Items Not Seen as Important (>10% General Disagreement)
Brunei (B1)	Political Cooperation (15.5%)
Cambodia (C1)	Cultural Exchanges (12.0%), Political Cooperation (10.9%)
Indonesia (I1)	None
Laos (L1)	Security Cooperation (15.9%), Political Cooperation (27.8%)
Malaysia (M1)	Cultural Exchanges (11.8%)
Myanmar (Y1)	Political Cooperation (12.0%)
Philippines (P1)	Security Cooperation (13.7%), Political Cooperation (16.0%)
Singapore (S1)	Educational Exchanges (12.3%), Security Cooperation (10.9%), Sports Competitions (29.4%)
Thailand (T1)	Cultural Exchanges (12.5%), Security Cooperation (32.7%), Political Cooperation (38.5%), Sports Competitions (24.4%)
Vietnam (V1)	None

In 2007, our Myanmar sample registered general disagreement of 10 per cent or more on every one of the eight items. In 2014, only a few items registered general disagreement across our two samples. The importance of Political Cooperation was met with disagreement in both Yangon (16 per cent) and Mandalay (12 per cent), along with Cultural Exchanges (14 percent) and Security Cooperation (11 per cent) in Yangon. These track closely with regional trends — for instance, Political Cooperation was the least important aspect overall and found disagreement of 10 per cent or more in Brunei, Cambodia, Laos, the Philippines, and Thailand as well. As in the 2007 survey, the greatest ASEAN enthusiasm, as measured by strong agreement overall, was found in Vietnam. But in the 2014 survey, Myanmar students (based on the Mandalay sample) jumped to second place in this regard. Bruneian students also registered substantially more responses of strong agreement. Strong agreement rates fell moderately in the Philippines and Singapore.

The drop in enthusiasm for ASEAN among our sample of primary university students in Thailand noted elsewhere in the survey was reflected clearly in responses to this set of questions on the important aspects of integration. In 2007, the frequency of answering with "strongly agree" among CU students was similar to students elsewhere. In 2014, strong agreement by CU students dropped to last among the ten primary universities; from 50 per cent in 2007 to 35 per cent in 2014. This was nearly ten points lower than responses from primary university students from the next two lowest nations (Malaysia and Singapore). Thai primary university students also registered four out of the eight items on which 10 per cent or more disagreed overall that the item was of importance (Cultural Exchanges, 13 per cent; Security Cooperation, 33 per cent;

Political Cooperation, 39 per cent; and Sports Competitions, 24 per cent).

With respect to how the eight aspects of integration and cooperation ranked in importance across the region (based on the percentage of those who "strongly agreed" in each nation), this remained the same between the 2007 and 2014 surveys, with one exception — Economic Cooperation dropped from first- to third-ranked in importance (see Table 4.15b). Tourism moved from second- to first-ranked followed by Development Assistance. This shift is particularly interesting in light of 2014 representing a period of transition to the AEC which emphasizes economic integration and cooperation over other aspects of ASEAN community building. As noted elsewhere, and particularly with respect to Thailand, we see this as indicative of the fact that in Thailand and elsewhere, public discussion of ASEAN economic integration raises not only consciousness but also debate on the issue. Awareness of ASEAN and plans for the economic community inevitably raise concerns about possible negative consequences — challenges that come along with the opportunities the AEC will afford — and thus less easy acceptance or enthusiasm for the economic dimension of ASEAN cooperation.

That said, the relative drop in enthusiasm for economic cooperation should not mask the fact that in absolute terms, it remains one of the most important items for our respondents across all nations. In fact, it rated consistently as the third most important item in seven nations. It was fifth in Indonesia and fourth in Malaysia, but not by large margins behind other items. Economic Cooperation rated as the second most important item for Singapore primary university students.

TABLE 4.15b
Overall Attitudes Toward Aspects of Integration and Cooperation (averaged over all eight): Rank in 2014 vs. 2007, Primary Universities

Aspects	Brunei (BI)	2007	Cambodia (CI)	2007	Indonesia (II)	2007	Laos (LI)	2007 (Corrected)	Malaysia (MI)	2007	Myanmar (YZ)	2007	Philippines (PI)	2007	Singapore (SI)	2007	Thailand (TI)	2007	Vietnam (VI)	2007 (Corrected)
Tourism	1	2	1	1	1	2	4	5	1	2	5	5	1	1	3	4	2	5	4	2
Development Assistance	5	4	4	4	4	4	2	3	5	4	2	3	2	4	5	3	1	2	1	1
Economic Cooperation	3	3	3	2	5	3	3	1	4	3	3	4	3	3	2	1	3	1	3	3
Educational Exchanges	2	5	2	3	3	5	1	2	7	7	1	1	4	2	7	7	4	3	5	6
Security Cooperation	4	1	5	6	6	7	7	7	2	1	6	8	5	8	1	2	7	7	2	4
Sports Competitions	7	6	6	5	2	1	5	6	3	5	4	2	6	7	8	8	6	6	6	8
Cultural Exchanges	6	8	8	7	7	6	6	4	8	8	7	7	7	5	6	6	5	4	8	5
Political Cooperation	8	7	7	8	8	8	8	8	6	6	8	6	8	6	4	5	8	8	7	7

Note: Data corrected for Laos and Vietnam; 2007 Report errata.

Comparing our 2007 and 2014 survey results amongst the primary university students within each nation, there were no substantial differences in rank importance, based on the number of students selecting that item. While there were some slight shifts (i.e. by two or three ranked places), overall the results show a strong consistency between the two surveys (even these "slight shifts" were generally by two ranked places and rarely three). In most nations, students registered only slight shifts in rankings on two or three items. The Philippines had the most number of slight shifts in rankings — on five out of the eight items. In Cambodia, there were only negligible shifts (at most one ranked place) across all eight items (see Tables 4.16 and 4.16*a*).

We also found, when taking the additional universities into account in the 2014 survey, that the ranking of items within nations tended to be largely consistent, with a few slight variations (see Table 4.15*c*). We only found substantial differences amongst responses from Thailand and Malaysia. In Thailand, substantial variation was found with respect to only one item between two universities (CU and SJU) across the four university samples. The variations amongst UM, UTAR, and Unimas students in Malaysia were more significant.

No substantial differences were found in the results from Indonesia, the Philippines, Singapore, and Vietnam, though slight differences appeared in all four nations. In Indonesia, Unsyiah and Undana students ranked Tourism lower and Economic Cooperation higher than UI students. Unsyiah students ranked Economic Exchanges slightly higher than UI students. In the Philippines, UP Diliman, UP Visayas, and MSU rankings were nearly identical, with very slight differences in UP Visayas' higher ranking of Political Cooperation (sixth) compared to

TABLE 4.15c
Overall Attitudes Toward Aspects of Integration and
Cooperation (averaged over all eight):
Comparative Ranks within Nations

Aspects	Indonesia			Malaysia		
	UI	Unsyiah	Undana	UM	UTAR	Unimas
Tourism	1	4	3	1	1	5
Development Assistance	4	5	5	5	5	3
Economic Cooperation	5	3	2	4	2	4
Educational Exchanges	3	1	3	7	3	7
Security Cooperation	6	6	6	2	4	2
Sports Competitions	2	2	1	3	7	1
Cultural Exchanges	7	8	8	8	6	8
Political Cooperation	8	7	7	6	8	6

Aspects	Philippines			Singapore	
	UP Diliman	UP Visayas	MSU	NUS	SP
Tourism	1	1	1	3	5
Development Assistance	2	2	1	5	4
Economic Cooperation	3	3	3	2	3
Educational Exchanges	4	4	4	7	7
Security Cooperation	5	5	5	1	1
Sports Competitions	6	7	6	8	8
Cultural Exchanges	7	8	8	6	6
Political Cooperation	8	6	7	3	2

Aspects	Thailand				Vietnam	
	CU	KKU	WU	SJU	VNU-Hanoi	VNU-HCMC
Tourism	2	1	2	1	4	3
Development Assistance	1	2	3	4	1	1
Economic Cooperation	3	3	4	5	3	2
Educational Exchanges	4	4	1	3	5	5
Security Cooperation	7	7	7	6	2	4
Sports Competitions	6	5	5	2	6	7
Cultural Exchanges	5	6	6	7	8	6
Political Cooperation	8	8	8	8	7	8

TABLE 4.16
Slight Shifts in Relative Ranking of Items Between
2007 and 2014 Surveys[1]

Aspect of Cooperation	Shift in Ranking (from 2007 to 2014)
Cultural Exchanges	lower in Laos, the Philippines, and Vietnam
Economic Cooperation	lower in Indonesia and Laos
Security Cooperation	lower in Brunei; higher in Myanmar, the Philippines, and Vietnam
Educational Exchanges	lower in Brunei and the Philippines; higher in Indonesia
Sports Competitions	lower in Myanmar; higher in Malaysia and Vietnam.
Political Cooperation	lower in Myanmar and the Philippines; higher in Singapore
Development assistance	lower in Singapore; higher in the Philippines
Tourism	lower in Vietnam; higher in Thailand

Note: [1] Corrected data from ISEAS publication of 2008: Vietnam and Laos rankings were reported/printed incorrectly there.

TABLE 4.16a
Slight Shifts in Relative Ranking of Items Between
2007 and 2014 Surveys by Nation

Nation	Shift in Ranking
Brunei	Security Cooperation higher; Educational Exchanges lower
Cambodia	Negligible
Indonesia	Educational Exchanges higher; Economic Cooperation lower
Laos	Economic Cooperation and Cultural Exchanges lower
Malaysia	Sports Competitions higher
Myanmar	Security Cooperation higher; Sports Competitions and Political Cooperation lower
Philippines	Development Assistance and Security Cooperation higher; Educational Exchanges, Cultural Exchanges, and Political Cooperation lower
Singapore	Political Cooperation higher; Development Assistance lower
Thailand	Tourism higher
Vietnam	Security Cooperation and Sports Competitions higher; Tourism and Culture Exchanges lower

UP Diliman students (eighth). Ranking amongst Singaporean students showed negligible variation overall. The only slight variation was on the ranking of the importance of Tourism — third amongst NUS students and fifth amongst SP students. Difference between VNU-Hanoi and VNU-HCMC students were also largely negligible. The only slight differences were on Security Cooperation, which VNU-Hanoi students ranked slightly higher, and on Cultural Exchanges, which they ranked slightly lower.

Rankings amongst Thai students were largely similar with only one substantial difference: SJU students ranked Sports Competitions as the second most important aspect of integration, which was substantially higher than CU students (sixth) and slightly higher than KKU and WU students (both fifth). And there were a few slight differences amongst Thai universities on other aspects. WU students ranked Educational Exchanges first amongst all eight aspects of integration, which was slightly higher than students at all other Thai universities. WU and SJU students ranked Development Assistance slightly lower than CU and KKU students. SJU students also ranked Economic Cooperation slightly lower than CU and KKU students and ranked Cultural Exchanges slightly lower than CU students.

The greatest variations were found in Malaysia, with numerous slight and a couple of substantial differences amongst UM, UTAR, and Unimas students. At both UM and UTAR, Tourism was ranked first, and Development Assistance fifth. Tourism was fifth and Development Assistance third among Unimas students. UTAR students ranked Educational Exchanges as substantially more important and Sports Competitions as substantially less important as compared to both UM and Unimas students. They also ranked Economic Cooperation and Cultural Exchanges as slightly more important, and Security and Political Cooperation as slightly less important as compared to UM and Unimas students.

Issues Crucial to Cooperation and Awareness

For the final question about ASEAN, asked on both the 2007 and 2014 surveys, we presented students with eight issues and asked them to circle the issues that they felt were the most crucial to enhancing regional cooperation and awareness. In comparing the results from the 2007 and 2014 surveys, we found that the overall pattern of more and less important issues for students from the primary universities remained consistent. However, having completed the survey at ten universities in 2007 and twenty-two in 2014, we became aware of methodological issues that arose with the format of this question, which make direct, detailed comparisons between university samples somewhat difficult to interpret. The problem, which we explain next before turning to the substantive results, does not invalidate our results entirely, but limit their interpretive power.

The main methodological problem was that respondents varied in how they answered the question. The intent of the question was for students to circle all issues that apply, in other words as many or as few of the issues as they felt were crucial. In the 2007 survey, we noted that this led to a great deal of variation in how students answered the question — circling many or few issues. In the 2014 survey, it became even more apparent that students were interpreting the instructions in different ways. Some students were clearly circling only one answer rather than several. This was particularly apparent at CU and KKU in the 2014 survey, which may be the result of how research assistants were conveying the instructions or how Thai students tended to interpret the wording of the instructions. This makes comparison of percentage responses between universities unhelpful, because large variations are an artefact of how students interpreted the instructions.

A partial solution to this variation, which we used in interpreting results of the first survey and use again here, is to convert the percentages at each university into rankings. This standardizes the pattern of responses across each university, and it is on this basis that we will discuss the substantive results below. While this is a partial solution, it is not perfect. At some universities, there are large, substantive differences between the rankings (e.g. between first and second or fourth and fifth ranked items). But in some cases, the percentage differences in rankings are very small, and thus the difference between rankings is, at best, negligible. In some instances, for example, four or five items may be separated by only a few percentage points, particularly among items of middle rank. Thus it may be that an item ranked third and an item ranked sixth are much more similarly rated than the second and third or sixth and seventh items within one sample. Those interested in detailed comparisons from particular sets of respondents should refer to both the rankings and to the percentage responses at universities to assess within-university rankings.

With those caveats in mind, we can report that the findings not only suggest that the overall ranking of the importance of issues we asked about remained largely the same between the 2007 and 2014 surveys, there is also evidence for a strong influence of national frames-of-reference with regard to students' orientations toward ASEAN, with a few notable instances where students within nations vary across the universities in our sample.

The overall ordered ranking of issues in our questionnaire remained the same between 2007 and 2014 when averaged across the ten primary university samples. Reduction of Poverty and Economic Disparities remained the most important issue. In fact, it ranked as the first or second most important issue at every primary and additional university in the 2014 survey, with the single exception of VNU-HCMC, where it ranked sixth. Educational Improvements and Exchanges ranked second overall, and again was ranked as the first or second most important issue in the 2014 survey at seven out of ten primary universities and fifteen out of twenty-two universities overall. It ranked third at both Vietnamese universities and fifth at both Singapore universities. In Malaysia, it ranked sixth at UM, but first at UTAR and third at Unimas.

Science and Technology Development and Applications, Health Maintenance and Disease Control, and Natural Resources and Environmental Management, all ranked closely together in the middle of the list of eight items. Almost all university samples ranked these between third and sixth. Science and Technology Development ranked lower at the Singapore universities (seventh at SP; eighth at NUS) but higher at VNU-HCMC (second). Health and Disease Control ranked higher in Singapore (second at both schools), but lower in Vietnam (seventh and eighth). Natural Resources and Environmental Management ranked relatively low in both Indonesia and Vietnam (sixth at the primary university and seventh at additional universities in both cases).

Disaster Prevention, Relief and Recovery Assistance ranked slightly behind Science and Technology Development, Health and Disease Control, and Environment. While eight of twenty-two universities ranked Disaster Prevention and

Assistance fourth to sixth, this item exhibited some of the greatest variations in importance across the region. It ranked second at UM and third at both UP Diliman and UP Visayas in the Philippines and at both Singapore schools. But it ranked seventh at UTAR and Unimas in Malaysia and UI, and seventh or eighth in Cambodia, Laos, Myanmar, and all the Thai universities, except SJU where it ranked fourth.

Regional Identity and Solidarity Enhancement, and Cultural, Literary and Artistic Preservation and Promotion continued to be the issues of least importance to students, as they had been in the 2007 survey. Regional Identity ranked last at thirteen of the twenty-two universities in 2014 and among the bottom half at all universities with three notable exceptions. At CU in Thailand, it ranked fourth in 2014 (and third in 2007). At both Vietnamese universities, this issue ranked first among all eight. Cultural Preservation, on the other hand, ranked among the bottom four issues at twenty universities and as seventh or eighth at thirteen of the twenty-two universities. The only instances where it rated highly were at Unimas in Malaysia and with our 2014 Yangon sample. In both instances, it ranked second (though the difference amongst items in both these samples was very small in percentage terms).

Overall the ranking of items by students in 2007 and 2014 in our primary university samples remained largely stable. For fifty-eight items across the ten universities, there was no change or negligible change (by one rank) between surveys. Sixteen items showed slight changes and only six showed substantial change. The most substantial changes were in the data from Brunei. The importance of Educational Improvements and Exchanges rose from fifth to first while Cultural Preservation slipped from second to seventh. While we do not have an explanation for the latter — other than the fact that this brings Bruneian students more in line with regional norms — the increase in the former may be related to UBD's strong push over the past several years to position itself as an international and world-class university. In both the Philippines and Singapore, Disaster Prevention and Assistance rose from seventh to third in importance. We would speculate that this may be due to the attention given to Typhoon Haiyan in November 2013 in both countries. The other two substantial, within-nation changes between the 2007 and 2014 surveys were the decrease in the importance of Regional Identity in Myanmar (from fourth to eighth) and increase in the importance of Poverty Reduction in Vietnam (from fifth to first). Again, while we do not have any specific explanations for these shifts, in both cases they bring the response more in line with regional norms.

Within-nation comparisons of primary and additional universities on the question of crucial issues for cooperation and awareness generally lends support to the idea that, along with there being general overall consensus across the region, in most cases there is as strong or stronger consensus within nations on how students view the importance of these issues. Singaporean students at NUS and SP, for example, ranked the eight items almost identically, with only a few negligible differences. Differences in ranking of issues was identical or negligibly different in Indonesia, with only two minor exceptions. Unsyiah students ranked Disaster Prevention and Assistance slightly higher than UI students and Health and Disease Control slightly lower than both UI and Undana students.

Filipino students at the three universities sampled also displayed only slight differences. UP Diliman and MSU students ranked Natural Resources and Environmental Management slightly higher than their UP Visayas counterparts. UP Diliman and UP Visayas rated Disaster Prevention and Assistance slightly higher than MSU students. And UP Visayas and MSU students rated Health and Disease Control slightly higher than UP Diliman.

In Malaysia, differences amongst UM, UTAR, and Unimas students were negligible or slight, with three substantial exceptions. UTAR students ranked Educational Exchanges substantially higher than UM students, with Unimas falling in between. UM students rated Disaster Prevention and Assistance substantially higher than both UTAR and Unimas students. And Unimas students rated Cultural Preservation substantially higher than both UM and UTAR students.

Overall rankings by Thai university students across all four universities tended to be very similar — with Poverty Reduction and Educational Exchanges ranking as the top two issues across all four universities and Cultural Preservation ranking last or near last. Three of the four universities also ranked Disaster Prevention and Assistance at or near the bottom, the exception being SJU, where students ranked it fourth amongst the eight issues. While there were also some slight difference in ranking for Health and Disease Control, Natural Resources and Environmental Management, and Science and Technology Development, all of these issues ranked in the middle (between third and sixth) at all four universities. The final item, Regional Identity and Solidarity Enhancement ranked fourth at CU and seventh at SJU, with KKU and WU falling in between.

Ranking of issues at VNU-Hanoi and VNU-HCMC was identical or negligibly different on five of the eight issues. They differed substantially on ranking Poverty Reduction (first at VNU-Hanoi and sixth at VNU-HCMC; though it is perhaps

notable that the HCM ranking for 2014 is very similar to the
Hanoi ranking in 2007). VNU-HCMC students gave slightly
higher rankings to both Science and Technology Development
and Cultural Preservation. But despite these differences, one
particularly strong indication of how national frames-of-reference
influence students' perceptions appears in Vietnamese students'
ranking of the importance of Regional Identity and Solidarity
Enhancement. In both the 2007 and 2014 surveys, VNU-Hanoi
students ranked this issue first amongst the eight issues, as
did VNU-HCMC students in the 2014 survey. With a few minor
exceptions, this issue ranked last or near the bottom among
students from all other nations and universities.

5
NATIONAL SUMMARIES

BRUNEI

Students from the Universiti Brunei Darussalam (UBD) demonstrated generally good knowledge of ASEAN. They scored almost perfectly (98.5 per cent) on their ability to identify the ASEAN flag, replicating their performance on the 2007 survey. They also had the second highest score amongst primary university students (after Thailand) on identifying ASEAN member countries on a map of Southeast Asia. They were about average for the region in identifying the year of ASEAN's founding. Their perceptions of similarity amongst ASEAN countries was somewhat below average regionally for the economic and political domains. Bruneian students scored the highest of all primary universities in viewing ASEAN membership as beneficial to their own country and amongst the highest in seeing their country's membership as being beneficial to them personally, though when measured in terms of strong agreement (ASEAN enthusiasm), they score closer to average for the region. Overall, Bruneian students held positive views of ASEAN, common to students in the region generally. With respect to the view of Brunei held by students from other countries, as in the 2007 survey, it remains overall the least salient country generally to students from elsewhere. The tendency to report Brunei as a possible destination for work dropped somewhat in the 2014 survey, particular in Indonesia, though it remained at more than 10 per cent in both Singapore and Malaysia.

CAMBODIA

Cambodian students from the Royal University of Phnom Penh (RUPP) remained among the strongest "ASEAN enthusiasts" amongst primary university students. They remain among the most oriented toward seeing themselves as citizens of ASEAN (two-thirds "strongly agree") and in wanting to learn about other ASEAN countries (90 per cent "strongly agreeing"). They also displayed better objective knowledge of the region as compared to the 2007 survey, with substantially higher percentages of students who could identify the ASEAN flag and year of founding, though their cartographic knowledge remained somewhat below regional averages. In both the 2007 and 2014 surveys, Cambodian students tended to see ASEAN members as similar culturally, dissimilar economically, and were evenly divided on whether ASEAN countries are similar politically. Their view of both cultural and economic similarities was somewhat lower in the 2014 survey. Although Cambodian students' perception that ASEAN membership benefited their country dropped marginally, they remained among the most strongly in agreement with this benefit and their perception of personal benefit even increased slightly. The 2007 survey highlighted the varied mediascapes of ASEAN nations with respect to Cambodia, where the Internet and newspapers were of relatively low importance as sources of information about ASEAN, whereas radio was relatively high. In the 2014 survey, we see in Cambodia and elsewhere a levelling of the variation in mediascapes. In particular, in Cambodia, Laos, Myanmar, and Thailand, the Internet has become a much more important source of information. Radio has diminished as a source of information for Cambodian students. However, the importance of newspapers remains low in comparison to elsewhere — suggesting that variations in mediascapes have not disappeared altogether.

INDONESIA

In both the 2007 and 2014 surveys, Indonesian students were generally positive in their attitudes toward ASEAN. Overall, Indonesian students rate the highest regionally, along with Vietnamese students and Myanmar students (in the 2014 survey, Mandalay sample), as seeing similarities among ASEAN members. In 2014, the Universitas Indonesia (UI) students rated ASEAN members as very similar culturally, similar economically, and were evenly split on whether ASEAN members are similar politically. These findings on cultural and political similarities mirrored the 2007 survey. The number of students seeing ASEAN members as economically similar increased substantially. On objective knowledge, UI students remained among the best regionally in listing the names of ASEAN countries and identifying the ASEAN flag, but fared worse in selecting the year of ASEAN's founding. However, a close look at the pattern of answers shows that those who answered wrongly still tended overwhelmingly to choose an answer (1957 or 1977) close to the correct year. Among students at the additional Indonesian universities in the 2014 survey, students at Universitas Syiah Kuala (Unsyiah) in Banda Aceh did as well as UI students in identifying the ASEAN flag and almost as well in listing ASEAN countries. Students from the Universitas Nusa Cendana (Undana) did not do quite as well on the flag and listing tasks, though their objective knowledge was generally as good as the averages across primary universities regionally.

Students from Unsyiah and Undana exhibited greater ASEAN enthusiasm and interest in ASEAN compared to students from UI. With respect to wanting to know more about ASEAN, about three-quarters of both Unsyiah and Undana "strongly agreed", compared to about half of the students at UI. Similarly, Unsyiah and Undana students displayed greater ASEAN enthusiasm in answers on the benefits of ASEAN, feeling they are citizens of ASEAN, and on ASEAN's future being important.

One notable shift in attitudes among Indonesian students was a decline in affinity for their Malay-Muslim neighbours, Brunei and Malaysia (particularly the latter). UI students showed markedly less interest in travelling to Malaysia and Brunei, and somewhat less interest in Singapore; by contrast, their interest in travelling to the Philippines, Thailand and Vietnam increased. Thailand replaced Singapore as the top travel destination among UI students, though Singapore remained the top destination for students from the additional universities. Students from UI also showed less interest in working in Brunei or Malaysia, and an even more overwhelming orientation toward working in Singapore compared to the 2007 survey. While Unsyiah and Undana students also favoured Singapore, they were more open to other destinations. Unsyiah students' second most common choice was Brunei. For Undana students, it was Thailand. And for both, Malaysia remained a common third choice, selected by about 10 per cent at both universities, as compared to less than 4 per cent of UI students.

LAOS

Students from the National University of Laos (NUOL) remain among the most objectively knowledgeable about ASEAN among students in the region, although their scores on the objective knowledge questions dipped somewhat, while those of students elsewhere mostly increased between the 2007 and 2014 surveys. In comparison to the 2007 survey, in 2014, Lao students rated ASEAN members somewhat more similar economically and somewhat less similar politically. Overall, three-quarters continued to see ASEAN members as culturally similar.

Although Lao students remained very positive toward ASEAN, there is some evidence that the strong ASEAN enthusiasm found in 2007 had waned somewhat in the 2014 survey. Whereas in 2007, three-quarters "strongly agreed" that ASEAN membership benefited their country, in 2014, the number had dropped to half. But 96 per cent overall continued to agree that ASEAN membership was beneficial. Modest drops in enthusiasm were found in other questions, though the overall orientation of Lao students toward ASEAN remained very positive.

As in the 2007 survey, Lao students remained relatively unenthusiastic about travelling or working in their culturally and linguistically close neighbour, Thailand. With regard to the view of Laos amongst students from other ASEAN nations, along with Brunei, it was commonly the least salient and most unfamiliar.

MALAYSIA

Students from the University of Malaya (UM) reported a stronger sense of ASEAN members' cultural similarity in the 2014 survey as compared to the 2007 survey. They remained divided on ASEAN nations' economic similarity and continued to see ASEAN countries as politically dissimilar by a three-to-one margin. In both surveys, more than 90 per cent continued to see membership in ASEAN as beneficial to their country and more than two-thirds saw their country's membership as beneficial to them personally. While over 90 per cent felt they are citizens of ASEAN, that ASEAN's future is important, and that they want to know more about other ASEAN countries, the number that strongly agreed with these items tended to be at or below averages across the region.

The mostly Chinese-Malaysian students at the Universiti Tunku Abdul Rahman (UTAR) showed some modest, though not extreme, differences from their mostly Malay-Malaysian counterparts at the UM. Students from Universiti Malaysia Sarawak (Unimas) in Sarawak tended to have responses very similar to those from the UM students. UTAR students, like UM and Unimas students, see ASEAN countries as culturally similar (though somewhat more so than UM and Unimas students) and are divided on whether ASEAN members are economically similar. As with UM and Unimas students, they tend to see ASEAN members as politically dissimilar, but not to the same degree. They see somewhat less benefit of ASEAN membership to themselves personally in comparison to UM and Unimas students. And only three-quarters, as opposed to over 90 per cent at UM and Unimas, see themselves as citizens of ASEAN. With regard to objective knowledge, UTAR students did better in listing ASEAN countries, but did not perform as well in identifying the ASEAN flag, the date of ASEAN's founding, or locating ASEAN countries on a map of Southeast Asia. The general impression of these varied measures is that the UTAR students have somewhat less affinity for ASEAN in contrast to UM and Unimas students.

MYANMAR

In the 2007 survey, respondents from Myanmar displayed a disparate set of orientations toward ASEAN. While most respondents showed a generally positive attitude toward ASEAN, a substantial minority displayed a degree of negative attitudes, or scepticism toward ASEAN, rarely in evidence amongst responses from the rest of the region. In contrast, the responses gathered from the students of both the University of Mandalay (MU) and University of Yangon (YU) in the 2014 survey reflected a more generally positive orientation toward ASEAN, much more in line with norms elsewhere in Southeast Asia. In the following, we compare the 2007 results from Yangon with the 2014 results from Mandalay, given problems with the 2014 Yangon data (see our discussion of methods in Chapter 3).

In 2007, only 60 per cent of Myanmar respondents in Yangon agreed that membership in ASEAN benefited their country, with a quarter strongly agreeing but a quarter strongly disagreeing. Only a quarter agreed that Myanmar's ASEAN membership benefited them personally, with 60 per cent strongly disagreeing. In the 2014 survey in Mandalay, over 90 per cent agreed and over 55 per cent strongly agreed that ASEAN membership benefited their country, with more than two-thirds responding that their country's membership benefited them personally. Similarly the number of Myanmar respondents who felt themselves ASEAN citizens rose from under 60 to over 90 per cent between the 2007 and 2014 surveys. And in 2014, over 95 per cent said that ASEAN's future is important (not asked in the 2014 survey).

With regard to objective knowledge about ASEAN, in 2014, Myanmar respondents fared better at identifying ASEAN countries on a map of Southeast Asia but scored moderately lower (78 as compared to 85 per cent) at identifying the ASEAN flag, while other indicators were largely unchanged. A large difference between the 2007 and 2014 surveys was observed, however, in

Myanmar respondents' perceptions of similarity amongst ASEAN countries. Across all domains (cultural, economic, and political), a majority of 2014 Mandalay respondents viewed ASEAN countries as more similar than different. Averaged across all three domains, Myanmar respondents in 2014 rated ASEAN countries as more similar than any other set of primary university respondents in our survey (at 62 per cent, they equalled students at UI in Indonesia). The reverse had been the case in the 2007 survey, where Myanmar students averaged rating of similarity was only 40 per cent.

In a simple comparison of the 2007 and 2014 surveys, the overall impression is that the ASEAN scepticism evident in the earlier survey has been replaced by responses that look much more like the norm — of general positive attitudes — elsewhere in Southeast Asia. Our confidence in interpreting these data is complicated, however, by difficulties encountered in data collection in Myanmar. While a straight comparison of responses from YU students between 2007 and 2014 would be preferable, the results here can at the very least allow us to conclude that the ASEAN scepticism evident in the 2007 survey does not extend to our Myanmar respondents in the 2014 survey (in either our Mandalay or Yangon samples). We think that this is due largely to events in the intervening period, which have seen Myanmar normalize relations with much of the world generally and integrate more fully into the ASEAN region. Alternatively, it could be that, at least in some respect, this reflects differences between students at the nationally central university in the city of Yangon and those at a regional centre in Mandalay. Further research would be necessary to test this hypothesis.

THE PHILIPPINES

In 2014, as in 2007, students from the University of the Philippines Diliman (UP Diliman) displayed the weakest overall knowledge of ASEAN. Only just under half were able to identify the ASEAN flag and on average, they were able to list fewer than nine ASEAN countries and identify fewer than five on a map of Southeast Asia. While there were some marginal improvements in ASEAN knowledge among UP Diliman students between the 2007 and 2014 surveys, they remained at or near the bottom across all measures compared to their counterparts at primary universities elsewhere.

UP Diliman students were generally in line with regional norms in seeing ASEAN membership as beneficial to the Philippines (the rate of agreement was marginally lower in 2014 at 87 per cent, compared to 94 per cent in 2007). In both 2007 and 2014, about two-thirds of UP Diliman students saw their country's membership as beneficial to them personally and saw themselves as citizens of ASEAN. With regard to perceptions of similarity and difference across the region, strong majorities of UP Diliman students viewed the countries of ASEAN as culturally similar but economically and politically dissimilar. This was true as well of students from the University of the Philippines Visayas (UP Visayas) located in the central Philippines. Students from the Mindanao State University (MSU), however, saw ASEAN members as both economically and politically similar, along with being culturally similar.

In other respects as well, survey results from UP Visayas reflected those at UP Diliman. In objective knowledge, UP Visayas and MSU students scored similarly low or lower than their UP Diliman counterparts. On the other hand, they were somewhat more likely to view ASEAN membership as beneficial to the Philippines, to themselves personally, and to see themselves as citizens of ASEAN. At all three universities, well over 90 per cent of students stated that they wanted to learn more about other ASEAN countries, with the rates of overall agreement and strong agreement highest at MSU.

SINGAPORE

Students from the National University of Singapore (NUS) displayed the same degree of ambivalence toward ASEAN in the 2014 survey that we had seen in the 2007 survey (though, as we reported then, this was not the sort of negative scepticism toward ASEAN found among a sizeable minority in 2007 in Myanmar). While majorities of just under two-thirds felt they were citizens ASEAN and 85 per cent felt that ASEAN membership benefited their country, these were low compared to averages across the region. Over 60 per cent saw ASEAN members as culturally dissimilar and over 80 per cent saw ASEAN countries as economically and politically dissimilar. Overall, NUS students' perception of the dissimilarities amongst ASEAN countries was far above those of students from other nations. Objective knowledge across the items asked in the survey was also at or below regional averages among NUS students.

For the 2014 survey, we also sampled Singaporean students at Singapore Polytechnic (SP), which is a technical-vocational school. The result of the survey at SP mirrored those at NUS in most respects. With regard to measures of objective knowledge and the benefits of ASEAN, SP students scored very similarly to their NUS counterparts. They rated slightly higher in agreeing that they feel themselves citizens of ASEAN, though not with respect to strong agreement. They also did not have as strong a perception of dissimilarity amongst ASEAN countries. While they agreed with their counterparts at NUS, albeit not so strongly, that ASEAN countries are dissimilar economically and politically, unlike NUS students, a solid majority of SP students rated ASEAN countries as culturally similar.

As in the 2007 survey, Singapore continued to hold a central position for both travel and work amongst students from elsewhere in the region. In 2014, Singapore's overwhelming desirability as a destination for work remained unrivalled. However, the desirability of Thailand as the number one travel destination overtook Singapore among students from several countries in the 2014 survey.

THAILAND

Changes in the survey results in Thailand between 2007 and 2014 are among the most interesting in this study. There has been tremendous promotion of the ASEAN Economic Community (AEC) in Thailand during the intervening years between surveys and the responses from Chulalongkorn University (CU), the primary university selected in Thailand, appear to reflect the high level of ASEAN awareness promoted through schools (now equipped throughout the nation with ASEAN resource rooms), public advertising, news, and other avenues. In the 2007 survey, CU students rated last in identifying the ASEAN flag and year of founding. In the 2014 survey, CU students were among the best on the flag question (with 94 per cent correct; second only to Brunei), though their ability to select the year of founding was still poor. (Note: In both surveys, only about a quarter of Thai students were able to select the year correctly. However, this may be due to the fact that the years were given according to the

Gregorian, Christian calendar, while Thais more regularly figure years by the Buddhist calendar.) CU students also scored high in listing ASEAN countries and highest regionally in identifying them on the map of Southeast Asia.

In other respects, however, there was a notable though not overwhelming shift *away* from affinity with ASEAN amongst CU students. They rated themselves as less familiar with ASEAN generally (the objective measures above notwithstanding). Although a majority (71 per cent) still agreed that ASEAN membership was valuable to their country, this was far less than in the 2007 survey (89 per cent), and even more so among those who strongly agreed (10 compared to 30 per cent in 2007). Those that strongly agreed that membership of Thailand benefited them personally also fell from 20 to less than 10 per cent. Those that saw themselves as citizens of ASEAN also dropped by 10 per cent. And while 89 per cent felt that the future of ASEAN was important, this was the lowest of any primary university (with a regional average of over 95 per cent). Only 31 per cent strongly agreed that ASEAN's future was important, 10 points less than either Singapore or Malaysia; and much less than all other students from primary universities, whose "strong agreement" ranged from 55 to almost 85 per cent.

CU students' perception of overall similarities amongst ASEAN members also dropped more than anywhere else in the region. They still saw ASEAN members as culturally similar, though less so than in the 2007 survey. Their sense of economic dissimilarity grew between the two surveys, but their sense of the political dissimilarity among ASEAN countries remained the same (with one-quarter agreeing and three-quarters disagreeing with the statement "ASEAN countries are politically similar").

In the 2014 survey, we were able to collect data from three additional universities in Thailand: Khon Kaen University (KKU) and Walailak University (WU), both of which are leading public universities, but located in the northeast and south of Thailand respectively, and Saint John's University (SJU), which is a vocational-technical school located in Bangkok. At each regional university, we purposefully sampled students from the northeast (KKU) and Muslim students from the south (WU).

On the whole, the trend among these additional universities in Thailand was that they have somewhat more affinity for ASEAN as compared to CU students. The responses from KKU tended to be the closest to those from CU, with more deviation amongst WU and SJU students. Students from all three additional universities saw themselves as citizens of ASEAN to a greater degree than CU students (55 per cent at CU, 72 per cent at KKU, 82 per cent at SJU and 85 per cent at WU). Students at the three additional universities all agreed that ASEAN's future is important at rates of 92 to 96 per cent. In terms of the benefit of ASEAN membership to their country, KKU students matched the regional low of CU students (71 per cent). WU students were slightly higher (77 per cent agreement). SJU students (88 per cent) were closer to the average across Southeast Asia (90 per cent). SJU students also heavily regarded Thailand's membership as personally beneficial (82 per cent). CU and KKU students were again the lowest across the region (approximately 60 per cent), while WU students fell in between (73 per cent). Students from all three additional universities also showed greater interest in learning about other ASEAN countries and more self-reported familiarity with ASEAN than their counterparts at CU.

Both WU and SJU students differed significantly from CU students with regard to their view of similarities and differences amongst ASEAN member nations. They, along with KKU students, had a stronger view of cultural similarity of ASEAN countries in comparison to CU students. And while they, like CU students, saw ASEAN members as politically dissimilar, they did not register this to the same degree. The most remarkable difference was with regard to perceptions of economic similarity or difference. While overall 40 per cent of CU students saw ASEAN countries as economical similar and 60 per cent did not, the reverse was true for WU (63 and 37 per cent) and even more so for SJU students (68 and 32 per cent). KKU students fell in between CU and other students on both these measures — of similarity and difference in the political and economic domains.

Finally, students from the additional universities in Thailand generally did as well or better than CU students with regard to objective knowledge about ASEAN. They scored even higher in correctly identifying the ASEAN flag (over 98 per cent at all three universities) as well as on the tasks of listing ASEAN members and identifying them on a map of Southeast Asia. SJU students fared slightly worse on the map identification task, but this is not surprising as this is an academically-oriented question and prior academic performance is the primary metric on which they have been streamed to SJU as opposed to the other three top public universities; but even SJU students did about as well on this task as the regional average across primary, largely elite, universities.

These varied findings from amongst the Thai universities raise interesting questions as to the sources of this variation. The high scores on objective knowledge are not surprising, given the attention to AEC preparation that current university students would have been subject to in recent years, when they were attending secondary school. However, more detailed research would be needed to explain the other discrepancies between CU students and those from additional (regional and vocational) universities. Based on the attention to the AEC as well as the political situation in Thailand over the past several years, we would suggest, at least hypothetically, that the following may be at play. First, with regard to the CU students, the fact that they know more about ASEAN but feel less affinity for ASEAN may reflect some of the unintended effects of consciousness raising in AEC preparation. In the years before 2007, there was some general awareness of ASEAN, and of Thailand's role in the Association. Actual knowledge about ASEAN was somewhat less, but attitudes toward ASEAN were generally favourable. From 2007 to 2014, in the run-up to the AEC, the focus on the need to prepare for the AEC — or else to lose out — made ASEAN more visible, but also raised a more active debate over the benefits and drawbacks of ASEAN and AEC membership. In this scenario, ASEAN awareness at the same time raised, at least for some Thai and specifically CU students, a greater level of concern or scepticism over the value of membership and Thailand's role in the Association (though we would note again that the overall attitudes toward ASEAN remain positive, just somewhat less positive than in 2007).

The above hypothesis still leaves us with the puzzle of why there is a difference between CU students and their counterparts at regional and technical universities. Here we would suggest that the answer may lie with social, economic, and political stratification and difference amongst typical CU students in comparison to KKU, WU, or SJU students. CU's reputation is that of an elite and relatively conservative university within Thailand's educational system. In the politically-charged atmosphere that has engulfed Thailand for nearly a decade, CU students are more likely than not to be affiliated with the "yellow-shirt" movement, which among other things has promoted conservative Thai nationalism in recent years. CU has literally been at or near the centre of a great deal of the political protest and counter-protest that has gone on in central Bangkok over the years between 2007 and 2014. All of this may influence a more inward-looking, Thailand-centred perspective amongst CU students, in comparison to those at regional universities (KKU, WU) or the technical vocational students (SJU) who, on the whole, may be less politically oriented and/or less oriented toward the elite, nationalist "yellow-shirt" politics.

Before turning from this summary of the Thailand data, we would emphasize again that further research would be needed to confirm (or refute) the hypothesized explanations provided above. What the data from Thailand demonstrate most clearly is that while there are very often trends of similarity across universities within particular nations, suggesting strong national framings of attitudes and orientations toward ASEAN, there are also cases, as in Thailand here, where attitudes and orientations toward ASEAN within particular nations are not uniform and explanations for such diversity are worth further investigation.

VIETNAM

Students from the primary university in Vietnam, Vietnam National University, Hanoi (VNU-Hanoi), showed a strong degree of ASEAN enthusiasm in both the 2007 and 2014 surveys. They were at or near the top of measures regionally in seeing their country's membership in ASEAN as beneficial, of feeling that they personally benefit from Vietnam's ASEAN membership, and in seeing themselves as citizens of ASEAN. Additionally in the 2014 survey, 83 per cent strongly agreed that the future of ASEAN is important; the highest of any primary university in the region. VNU-Hanoi students are also amongst the most inclined, along with students from Indonesia and Myanmar (in the most recent survey), to see ASEAN members as being similar to each other. VNU-Hanoi students overwhelmingly (74 per cent) saw ASEAN countries as culturally similar. A majority (over 55 per cent) saw ASEAN members as economically similar. And they were about evenly split on whether ASEAN members are politically similar. VNU-Hanoi students also rated amongst the best regionally in their objective knowledge about ASEAN.

In the 2014 survey, Vietnam National University, Ho Chi Minh City (VNU-HCMC) was included as an additional university in Vietnam. In this case, unlike Thailand discussed above, the responses from VNU-Hanoi and VNU-HCMC closely matched each other. VNU-HCMC students scored slightly lower on their objective knowledge of the region, but still mostly near or above average for universities across the region. They matched or exceeded their peers at VNU-Hanoi in their positive orientations towards ASEAN regarding the benefits to their country, the benefits to themselves personally, seeing themselves as citizens of ASEAN, and seeing the future of ASEAN as important. They also matched or exceeded VNU-Hanoi students across all cultural, economic, and political domains in seeing ASEAN members as similar to each other.

We noted in the 2007 survey that Vietnam appeared to be an emerging, alternative destination for travel and work, after the most favoured destinations of Singapore, Thailand, and

Malaysia. In the 2014 survey, this remained the case in terms of travel, but fewer students listed Vietnam as a destination for work, particularly among Lao students (6 per cent in 2014 as opposed to 15 per cent in 2007) and Singaporean students (5 per cent as opposed to 10 per cent).

6
DESCRIPTIONS OF ASEAN AND MEMBER COUNTRIES

In the 2014 survey, we presented students with a list of twenty nations and regions, and asked them to write one word to describe each. The list included ASEAN, the ten member nations, and nine additional countries and regions, for comparative purposes (to compare how ASEAN and its members are described as compared to other regions and countries). As our main basis of comparison, we have translated and analysed the data from the ten primary national universities covered in the survey (see Chapter 3: Subjects and Methods for details; here as elsewhere, the primary university for Myanmar is the University of Mandalay [MU]). In this chapter, we present findings of how the students from those universities across the ten nations describe ASEAN and its members.

The data was organized by words, concepts (collections of largely synonymous words), and domains (collections of similar concepts). For example, dress, dance, or Islam would be words organized under the concepts of "culture" (dress, dance) and "religion" (Islam), all of which are collected under the "Cultural Domain" (in contrast to Political, Economic, or Geographic Domains). On the basis of the data collected, we identified eight distinct domains through which students think about countries and regions: Economics, Politics, Culture,

Ethno-racial Concepts, Human Mobility (including Tourism and Labour Migration), Geography and Places, Symbols and Characteristics, and Disasters and Crime. The analysis below refers mainly to the "concept" level of analysis (combinations of synonymous words). Concepts are referred to as primary if they constitute more than 10 per cent of items from a national sample, secondary if between 5 to 10 per cent of all items, and tertiary if between 2 to 5 per cent of all items. Items constituting less than 2 per cent of responses are not considered, except in special cases.

ASEAN

The words associated with ASEAN across all ten nations are primarily related to cooperation and regionalism. In all nations, from 9 to over 28 per cent of responses referred to regional concepts, such as Southeast Asia, Asia, or Ten Countries. Similarly words that referred to cooperation, such as Cooperation, Organization, Unity, ranged from 8 to 33 per cent.

The ASEAN Economic Community (AEC) was mentioned specifically by 20 per cent of respondents from Laos and by 4 per cent in Indonesia and Thailand. Only one respondent mentioned the AEC in Cambodia and Brunei, but other references were made to economic cooperation by about 4 per cent of Cambodian students. Economic cooperation did not figure prominently in the responses from Malaysia, Myanmar, the Philippines, Vietnam, and Singapore. Thai (5.1 per cent) and Singaporean (2.7 per cent) students associated ASEAN with poverty while students from Vietnam (14.1 per cent), Myanmar (13.3 per cent), Indonesia (5.9 per cent), the Philippines (2.9 per cent), Singapore (2.7 per cent) and Brunei (2.1 per cent) associated ASEAN with development or progress. Students from Vietnam (7.6 per cent) and Brunei (3.1 per cent) also associated ASEAN with wealth, but not the other eight nations.

References to ASEAN symbols, such as the ASEAN flag and logo, were common as were references to the Southeast Asian Games (SEA Games). In Cambodia, for example, over 13 per cent of students referenced the ASEAN flag or logo. In Indonesia, the Philippines, Myanmar, and Malaysia, 6 to 8 per cent of responses referred to the SEA Games or to sports generally. A large number (10.3 per cent) of Thai students wrote "rice" in reference to ASEAN, which may refer to the ASEAN logo (ten stalks of rice bound together), to the economic and cultural centrality of rice, or both.

Many students associated their own country with ASEAN. The frequency was highest in Indonesia, where 11.2 per cent wrote the name of their own country ("Indonesia") in reference to ASEAN. This was followed by Malaysia (6.5 per cent), Thailand (5.6 per cent), Cambodia (5.4 per cent), Singapore (5.4 per cent), Laos (4.4 per cent), Myanmar (4 per cent), and Vietnam (2.2 per cent).

Diversity, culture, cultural diversity, and related terms were mentioned by all ten nations except for the Philippines and Thailand. These terms relating to culture and diversity were seen in Brunei (9.3 per cent), Cambodia (8.6 per cent), Malaysia (5.9 per cent), Singapore (5.4 per cent), Indonesia (5.3 per cent), Laos (3.4 per cent), Myanmar (2.6 per cent), and only one respondent mentioned the term "diversity" in Vietnam.

Negative perceptions came across as primary, secondary and tertiary concepts in the responses of three nations respectively: Singapore, Thailand, and Vietnam. In Singapore, 10.8 per cent of response items referred to ASEAN as "useless" (or a synonym). Similarly, in Thailand, 6.7 per cent of the response items were synonyms for "stupid", while 3.8 per cent of the response items from Vietnam were synonyms for "weak". At the same time, four nations also included positive perceptions of ASEAN, and these were Brunei, Myanmar, Singapore, and Vietnam. These were reflected in tertiary concepts from Brunei (3.6 per cent) and Singapore (4.8 per cent), while they were primary concepts in Myanmar (14.7 per cent) and Vietnam (14.6 per cent).

Among other unique, though mainly tertiary concepts from particular nations: Cambodian students associated ASEAN with Singapore (4.9 per cent) and with yellow or white skin (2.2 per cent); Filipino students, on the other hand, associated ASEAN with the colour brown (2.4 per cent), which could be an indicator of race or ethnicity. Indonesians associated ASEAN with Malay (4.4 per cent); Lao students with tourism (8.3 per cent); Malaysian (5.3 percent) and Vietnamese (10.8 per cent) students with peace; Singaporeans (3.7 per cent) and Malaysians (2.9 per cent) associated ASEAN with politics. Bruneian students also associated ASEAN with food (2.1 per cent).

BRUNEI

Students from the ten nations perceived Brunei in terms of its oil, wealth, status as a sultanate, and small size. Oil was, on the whole, the most common association with Brunei in all the nations except three: Thailand (42.4 per cent), Cambodia (43.6 per cent), Laos (32.4 per cent), Myanmar (31.2 per cent), Singapore (22.3 per cent), Malaysia (15.7 per cent), and Indonesia (14.9 per cent). Oil was a secondary concept in Brunei (8.6 per cent) and a tertiary concept in the Philippines (4.3 per cent) and Vietnam (4.0 per cent).

Wealth (rich or a synonym) registered as a primary concept in six nations, with the exception of Brunei, Cambodia, and

Vietnam, where it was a secondary concept, and the Philippines, where it was a tertiary concept: Thailand (18.1 per cent), Indonesia (17.9 per cent), Laos (17.0 per cent), Malaysia (16.9 per cent), Singapore (13.4 per cent), Myanmar (10.4 per cent), Vietnam (9.7 per cent), Cambodia (7.4 per cent), and the Philippines (4.3 per cent). In several nations, specific reference was made to money (Singapore, 5.0 per cent) and to gold and diamonds (Thailand, 4.5 per cent; Singapore, 3.9 per cent; Laos, 3.8 per cent; the Philippines, 3.6 per cent; Vietnam, 3.2 per cent; and Malaysia, 2.2 per cent). However, the term "poor" also appeared in the Vietnam data as a primary concept (12.9 per cent).

The third most common and universal association with Brunei was its status as a sultanate (with words for "king", "kingdom", or a synonym), though the prominence of this concept varied from overwhelmingly primary in Indonesia to tertiary in Vietnam: Indonesia (25.4 per cent), the Philippines (12.8 per cent), Singapore (10.6 per cent), Myanmar (10.4 per cent), Brunei (9.6 per cent), Malaysia (8.4 per cent), Thailand (6.8 per cent), Laos (6.6 per cent), Cambodia (5.9 per cent), and Vietnam (3.2 per cent).

Brunei's small size appeared in all nations, except Myanmar, and varied in prominence, ranking from a primary concept in Vietnam to a tertiary concept in Brunei: Vietnam (40.3 per cent), Indonesia (8 per cent), Laos (6.6 per cent), Cambodia (5.9 per cent), Thailand (4.5 per cent), the Philippines (3.7 per cent), Malaysia (3.4 per cent), Singapore (2.2 per cent), and Brunei (2.0 per cent).

Islam was associated as an overwhelmingly primary concept among Malaysian students and also as primary concept among Bruneians and Indonesians: Malaysia (38.2 per cent), Brunei (10.7 per cent), and Indonesia (10 per cent). It was secondary among Singaporean and Myanmar students, and tertiary among Cambodian students: Singapore (8.9 per cent), Myanmar (7.8 per cent), and Cambodia (3.5 per cent). It did not appear to a significant degree (less than 2 per cent) in responses from Laos, Thailand, and Vietnam. Among the Malaysian students, it was not simply Islam, but specifically the implementation of Islamic law ("syariah" or "hudud") which registered sharply (in 52 out of the 68 overall references to Islam).

Numerous other descriptors were mentioned in only one or two nations. Cambodian and Lao students associated Brunei with dress (4 and 2.7 per cent respectively) and sports (2.5 and 2.7 per cent respectively). Lao students also associated Brunei with the natural environment (6.6 per cent; sea, forest, river, etc.) and with food (4.4 per cent). Singaporean students associated Brunei with jungle and forests (3.3 per cent). Indonesians (8.5 per cent) and Malaysians (2.2 per cent) associated Brunei with its moniker "Darussalam" which means "abode of peace" in Arabic. Singaporean students associated Brunei with synonyms for "boring" (4.4 per cent) but also "peaceful" (2.6 per cent). Myanmar (6.5 per cent) and Cambodian (3.5 per cent) students referred to Brunei in terms of tourism and desirability (3.5 per cent; "nice"; "want to visit").

CAMBODIA

Angkor Wat is a primary association for Cambodia across all ten nations, referenced by two-thirds of both Cambodian students themselves (67.8 per cent) and Lao students (66.3 per cent), and prominent in all other countries as either the first (Thailand, 36.8 per cent; Myanmar, 36.6 per cent, the Philippines, 35.2 per cent; Singapore, 22.5 per cent; Malaysia, 14.4 per cent; Brunei, 13.4 per cent) or second (Vietnam, 28.7 per cent;

Indonesia, 13.6 per cent) primary concept used in reference to Cambodia.

After Angkor Wat, the second most common image of Cambodia was that of "poor" and "developing". Vietnamese students responded with "poor", "poverty", or synonyms (33.8 per cent) more commonly than with Angkor Wat. Malaysian students (10.8 per cent) referred to Cambodia more commonly as "poor" rather than "developing"; as did Singaporean students (13.9 per cent) and Bruneian students (8.3 per cent) and, to lesser degree, Thai students (3.6 per cent) and Filipino students (2.8 per cent). Elsewhere, students tended to refer to the country as "developing" as much or more so than "poor". Indonesian students were evenly split in referring to either poverty or developing (total 5.8 per cent), whereas both Cambodian (4.2 per cent) and Lao students (3.4 per cent) mainly referred to Cambodia as "developing" but not "poor". Myanmar students were split on referring to the country as developing or poor (7 per cent) or developed and successful (5.6 per cent).

The leading response in Indonesia was "flower" (32.5 per cent), as the Indonesian word for Cambodia (*Kamboja*) is also the name of a popular flower (*frangipani*). Flower also appeared in the responses from Singapore (3.2 per cent).

"Culture", along with references to "dance" and similar terms, was a primary concept in Brunei (12.7 per cent) and a secondary or tertiary concept in responses from Laos (7.2 per cent), Malaysia (5.0 per cent), Cambodia (5.9 per cent), the Philippines (3.9 per cent), and Singapore (2.1 per cent). Phnom Penh was another common secondary and tertiary association in the Philippines (8.9 per cent), Myanmar (5.6 per cent), Laos (5.5 per cent), Cambodia (5.9 per cent), Brunei (3.2 per cent), and Indonesia (2.6 per cent)

References to the Khmer Rouge and Pol Pot era were prominent in Singapore (11.2 per cent), the Philippines (10.6 per cent), Brunei (7 per cent), Indonesia (6.8 per cent), Vietnam (5.1 per cent), Malaysia (4.3 per cent), and Myanmar (2.8 per cent) but not elsewhere among students from other nations. Indonesian students made reference to Cambodia's politics through terms such as "republic" and "democracy" (4.2 per cent). Thai students prominently associated Cambodia with the country's long-standing leader "Hun Sen" (13.0 per cent) and to the military (2.1 per cent). They also made reference to frictions between Thailand and Cambodia through terms such as "barbarian", "thief", and "enemy" (3.1 per cent) and reference to Phra Viharn (2.1 per cent), the disputed temple complex on the Thai–Cambodia border. On the other hand, other Thai students referred to Cambodia as "neighbour" (3.6 per cent) or in one case "friend" (note: the Thai phrase for "neighbour" contains the word "friend"). Thai students (3.1 per cent) also associated Cambodia with immigrant labour.

Agriculture, and specifically rice, registered as a tertiary concept with Cambodia in Malaysia (5.0 per cent), Singapore (4.3 per cent), Indonesia (3.1 per cent), and Thailand (2.1 per cent). Malaysian, Bruneian, and Singaporean students made reference to tourism (7.9 per cent, 7.0 per cent, and 2.1 per cent respectively) as well as Buddhism (3.6 per cent, 3.8 per cent, and 2.1 per cent respectively). Myanmar students made the most references to Buddhism (7 per cent) and also general positive terms (8.5 per cent; good, good to visit, beautiful, etc.).

Finally, Malaysian students also associated Cambodia with Cham Malays (3.6 per cent), an ethnic group in Cambodia that are predominantly Muslim. Singaporean students made reference to community involvement projects (8.0 per cent), along with ethnic clothes (2.1 per cent). Lao students used the term "black" (2.4 per cent), conforming to a common use of racial terms by Lao students generally (three Cambodian students themselves also referred to Cambodia with the term "yellow skin").

INDONESIA

Indonesia's large number of islands was reflected across all ten nations, with words like "island(s)": Vietnam (34.4 per cent), Thailand (33.1 per cent), the Philippines (20.5 per cent), Cambodia (15.3 per cent), Malaysia (14.4 per cent), Myanmar (13.2 per cent), Laos (12.1 per cent), and Singapore (7.9 per cent). Only Indonesians and Filipinos used the word "archipelago" more often than "island" (4.9 per cent and 20.5 per cent respectively). Its vast size was also significant among Malaysian (6.6 per cent), Brunein (5.1 per cent), Thai (5.1 per cent), Singaporean (4.2 per cent), Vietnamese (3.2 per cent), and Cambodian (1.9 per cent) students.

Islam was another common concept for Indonesia across the nations, except among Bruneian, Indonesian, and Malaysian students where responses were considered negligible: Cambodia (9.9 per cent), Thailand (7.3 per cent), the Philippines (5.7 per cent), Vietnam (5.6 per cent), Singapore (4.8 per cent), Laos (4.4 per cent), and Myanmar (2.9 per cent).

All nations except Vietnam also displayed their knowledge of certain places in Indonesia, such as Bali and Jakarta: Brunei (17.4 per cent), the Philippines (16.5 per cent), Cambodia (14.8 per cent), Malaysia (12.7 per cent), Myanmar (11.8 per cent), Thailand (10.7 per cent), Singapore (9.5 per cent), Laos (11.5 per cent), and Indonesia (10.8 per cent).

Indonesia's economic status and development was a point of contention. To Cambodian (8.4 per cent), Lao (8.8 per cent), and Myanmar (7.4 per cent) students, Indonesia was associated with the concept of "economy", which included words like "advanced", "good economy", "business hub", and "economic growth". On the other hand, Malaysian, Bruneian, and Vietnamese students perceived Indonesia as poor (9.9 per cent, 4.6 per cent, and 4.0 per cent respectively), and Indonesians themselves perceived their country as developing (8.3 per cent). Singaporeans as well as Bruneians described Indonesia as "cheap" (5.8 per cent and 10.8 per cent respectively). However, along with "poor", Vietnamese students also described Indonesia as "developed", which shows that it is a point of contention within the country. Thais and Filipinos did not refer to Indonesia in economic terms.

Some nations also associated Indonesia with its resources and exports: Laos (coffee + oil = 8.2 per cent) Singapore (6.3 per cent), and Cambodia (3.4 per cent). Food was another common concept: Brunei (11.8 per cent), Singapore (6.3 per cent), the Philippines (6.3 per cent), Malaysia (4.4 per cent), Laos (3.8 per cent, Cambodia (3.4 per cent), Thailand (2.2 per cent), and Indonesia (2 per cent). Indonesia was also associated with natural disasters such as tsunamis and earthquakes among students from Thailand (12.4 per cent), Malaysia (8.3 per cent), Vietnam (8 per cent), the Philippines (6.8 per cent), Laos (6.6 per cent), Brunei (3.6 per cent), and Cambodia (2 per cent). In Myanmar (8.8 per cent), students associated Indonesia with volcanos.

Cambodian (7.9 per cent) and Lao (4.4 per cent) students associated Indonesia with their dressing. Some Cambodian students (1.9 per cent) highlighted Indonesia as an ASEAN member — the only nation to do so. Malaysian students highlighted the concept of immigrants (4.4 per cent), reflecting

Malaysia's status as a labour importer. Both Bruneians and Singaporeans also reflected this, with 5.1 per cent and 3.2 per cent respectively writing "maids". Singapore was the only nation to highlight "haze" (5.3 per cent) as one of the descriptions. Only Singaporeans (5.8 per cent) and Indonesians (5.9 per cent) associated the country with corruption. Some Malaysian (5.5 per cent), and Thai (2.8 per cent) students also described the country as "friendly" and "friend" respectively. Thais used the word "Indian(s)" (2.8 per cent), a translation of the Thai word *khek*, a unique ethno-racial Thai word used to describe foreigners from South Asian and Muslim countries (Indians, Arabs, and Malay-Muslims). Myanmar (7.4 per cent) students mentioned Joko Widodo and Indonesia's presidential system.

LAOS

Laos is one of the consistently least known countries, across Brunei, Indonesia, Malaysia, Myanmar, the Philippines, and Singapore; though not amongst three of its immediate neighbours of Cambodia, Thailand, and Vietnam. For the former nations, Laos rated the largest or near largest number of non-responses. For example, among University of Malaya students, less than two-thirds (64.7 per cent) of the number of items written for Malaysia (191) were recorded as descriptors for Laos (124). Moreover, beyond simple non-responses or "I don't know", items from Singapore (17.0 per cent), Brunei (8.1 per cent), the Philippines (8.0 per cent), Malaysia (5.6 per cent), Myanmar (4.7 per cent), and Indonesia (3.7 per cent) were words such as "foreign", "not famous", or "unknown". Conversely, Thai students registered strong cultural affinity for Laos as a neighbour (11.7 per cent) and "same as Thai" (4.3 per cent). Respondents from Vietnam

(17.5 per cent) and Singapore (5.2 per cent) also expressed that Laos is "friendly" and "good".

Also in Vietnam (35.6 per cent), Malaysia (20.2 per cent), Singapore (18.5 per cent), Indonesia (18.2 per cent), Myanmar (14.3 per cent), the Philippines (10.9 per cent), and Brunei (5.1 per cent), poor and underdeveloped was the leading, primary concept associated with Laos. One exception was in Indonesia where 25.8 per cent wrote "spice" as the word "*laos*" is an Indonesian word for the commonly used spice *galangal*. Myanmar (7.9 per cent) students also rated Laos as developing. In Cambodia, poor or developing was a secondary concept (8.4 per cent) for Laos. For Lao students themselves, developing (but not poor) was a secondary concept (5.1 per cent) to describe their own country. Thai students did not associate Laos with poverty or underdevelopment, but rural (3.7 per cent) did register as a tertiary concept.

Lao students themselves associated their country with notions of culture (12.1 per cent), as did Cambodian (9.3 per cent), Bruneian (6.6 per cent) and Malaysian (6.5 per cent) students. Other nations, such as the Philippines (5.8 per cent) and Thailand (3.7 per cent) also associated Laos with its traditional dressing even though none of their respondents explicitly indicated the term "culture". Filipino, Cambodian, and especially Thai students exhibited close cultural familiarity with Laos, associating the country with specific ethnic dress (Cambodia 7.9 per cent, the Philippines 5.8 per cent, and Thai 3.7 per cent) and food (Thai 15.4 per cent, Cambodia 3.7 per cent, and the Philippines 3.6 per cent). Food, particularly papaya salad (*som tam*) and sticky rice, was also a secondary concept (5.6 per cent) for Laos among Lao students. Singaporean students associated Laos more generally with rice and fish (5.9 per cent). Vietnamese students did not respond with any culture or food-related terms.

Lao students highlighted the specific sites of Thatluang (25.1 per cent), the Victory Arch (14.9 per cent), and Luang Prabang (4.2 per cent). For Cambodian students, Vientiane (19.2 per cent) was their primary association for Laos and Vat Phou Temple (9.8 per cent) a secondary association. Myanmar (7.9 per cent) students identified Vientiane. Thai students noted Luang Prabang and at a lesser frequency, Vientiane (5.9 per cent combined).

For Thai students, the ethnonym or ethnolinguistic term "Lao" was a primary (19.1 per cent) association, which also appeared as a secondary concept in the Philippines (6.5 per cent) and a tertiary concept in Indonesia (4.8 per cent) and Singapore (4.4 per cent). Thai (4.8 per cent) and Cambodian (2.8 per cent) students also made reference to the language. Thai students mentioned Isan (2.7 per cent), the northeast region of Thailand which borders Laos and whose people are ethno-linguistically close to Lao.

Respondents alluded to nature-related terms in their primary concepts, with Lao (21.3 per cent), Bruneian (11.8 per cent), Thai (10.6 per cent), and Vietnam (10.6 per cent) students associating Laos with terms like "forest", "nature" and "natural resources". Various references to nature were a secondary concept in the Philippines (8.0 per cent) and Singapore (6.7 per cent) and a tertiary concept in Cambodia (3.7 per cent). Vietnam (5.6 per cent) and the Philippines (2.2 per cent) also mentioned wildlife-related terms, of which "elephant" featured prominently.

Laos' position as a landlocked country came across as a primary concept in Malaysia (12.9 per cent), a secondary in Indonesia (9.6 per cent) and Myanmar (9.5 per cent), and a tertiary in Cambodia (4.2 per cent), Vietnam (2.5 per cent), and Thailand (2.1 per cent). For Malaysians (6.5 per cent), Vietnamese (3.8 per cent), Indonesians (3.2 per cent), Filipinos (2.9 per cent), and Singaporeans (2.2 per cent), the small size of the country registered as secondary and tertiary concepts.

For Malaysian (6.5 per cent), Lao (6.0 per cent), and Bruneian (5.1 per cent) students, tourism in general was a secondary concept.

For the Philippines (19.6 per cent), Indonesia (18.2 per cent), Brunei (12.5 per cent), and Malaysia (10.5 per cent), ASEAN or Asia was a primary concept associated with Laos.

War is a tertiary concept for Singapore (3.0 per cent) and Brunei (2.2 per cent). Communism was a tertiary concept for the Filipinos (2.2 per cent). For Cambodians (4.7 per cent), both politics and the communist system combine to form a tertiary concept. Some Singaporeans (6.7 per cent), Filipinos (6.5 per cent), Vietnamese (2.5 per cent), and Indonesians (2.1 per cent) had particularly negative perceptions of Laos, as seen through their choice of the words "bad", "chaos", or a variety of synonyms. Thais, on the other hand, referred to Laos as peaceful (3.2 per cent). None of the Lao respondents indicated any political terms in their responses.

Cambodia (9.8 per cent), Myanmar (9.5 per cent), and Brunei (6.6 per cent) expressed Buddhism-related terms as a secondary concept. Only among Filipinos (4.3 per cent) and Singaporeans (3.7 per cent) did Buddhism register as a tertiary concept. Lao students themselves associated their country with "Champa" (5.6 per cent), most likely in reference to the Dok Champa national flower or Lao Champa TV station. Human mobility was a secondary concept for Brunei (5.1 per cent) and a primary one for Malaysia (4.8 per cent), whose respondents responded with labour-related terms. Finally, Malaysians uniquely associated Laos with sports (3.2 per cent) and Singaporeans uniquely with overseas community involvement projects (3.0 per cent).

MALAYSIA

Students from all ten nations perceived Malaysia in terms of ethnicity or religion, and, with the exception of Malaysian and Myanmar students, they associated Malaysia with tourism. Students from Malaysia described their own nation as "multiracial" (16.8 per cent). Ethno-racial terms, particularly "Malay", registered as a primary term in Indonesia (14.1 per cent) and a secondary or tertiary term in the Philippines (9.2 per cent), Brunei (8.2 per cent), Malaysia (4.0 per cent), Thailand (3.8 per cent), and Singapore (3.0 per cent). The term "Indian" or "*khek*" (see the section under Indonesia above) is uniquely featured as a tertiary concept for Malaysia (3.8 per cent) among Thai students.

"Religion" or "Islam" registered as a primary term in Thailand (19.9 per cent), Cambodia (15.9 per cent), and Myanmar (10.8 per cent). It is a tertiary concept for the Philippines (3.8 per cent), Laos (2.5 per cent), Singapore (2.5 per cent), and Indonesia (2.4 per cent). But religion and Islam did not feature among responses from Brunei and Vietnam nor amongst Malaysian students themselves.

Respondents from eight nations perceived Malaysia in terms of tourism and indicated terms such as "Truly Asia" or "tourism" in their responses. References to tourism as a primary term were made by Laos (23.2 per cent) and the Philippines

(21.6 per cent), a secondary term by Brunei (6.7 per cent), and as a tertiary term by Indonesia (4.4 per cent), Cambodia (4.2 per cent), Singapore (3.4 per cent), Vietnam (3.2 per cent), and Thailand (2.7 per cent). Other terms related to tourism were also noted. Students from Brunei (14.9 per cent), Singapore (5.4 per cent) and Thailand made reference to casinos (2.7 per cent).

As for landmarks, "Twin Towers" and "KLCC" were noted as a primary term in the responses from Laos (29.8 per cent), Cambodia (22.0 per cent), Vietnam (22.0 per cent), Brunei (19.0 per cent), the Philippines (13.0 per cent), and Thailand (10.2 per cent) and a secondary concept for Malaysia (9.9 per cent) and Myanmar (5.8 per cent). The capital "Kuala Lumpur" was mentioned extensively by respondents from the Philippines (7.6 per cent), Laos (6.6 per cent), Indonesia (5.4 per cent), Cambodia (4.2 per cent), and Malaysia (4.2 per cent) while Singaporeans referred to Johor Bahru (5.1 per cent). Indonesia (5.4 per cent) and Laos (5.1 per cent) referred to the capital Kuala Lumpur while Singapore referred to Johor Bahru (5.1 per cent).

References to air disasters were noted as secondary or tertiary terms in some nations. The Malaysian Airlines disasters appeared in the responses of the Philippines (9.7 per cent), Vietnam (7.1 per cent), Myanmar (5.4 per cent), Brunei (5.1 per cent), Singapore (4.4 per cent), and Indonesia (3.9 per cent).[1]

Students from Malaysia (11.0 per cent), Brunei (10.8 per cent), Myanmar (9.5 per cent), and Singapore (5.9 per cent) also referred to politics and political leaders. In addition, students from Singapore referred to corruption (5.4 per cent). Singaporean and Malaysian students also referred to "boleh" (from the catchphrase "Malaysia boleh" or "Malaysia can") as a tertiary term (3.4 per cent and 2.1 per cent respectively). The political slogan "1Malaysia" was also mentioned by Malaysian respondents (6.8 per cent).

Respondents from Singapore (6.9 per cent), Brunei (5.6 per cent), and Myanmar (4.5 per cent) made reference to criminal activities and disorder. Thailand (3.2 per cent) referred to terrorism and Cambodia (2.3 per cent) to human trafficking and human rights abuses.

Other terms that were common in the data include those relating to culture and food. Terms used to describe culture, including references to "dress", were seen in the responses from Cambodia (12.6 per cent), Malaysia (5.2 per cent), the Philippines (2.2 per cent), and Thailand (2.2 per cent). "Food" was noted in the responses from Singapore (14.8 per cent), Malaysia (7.9 per cent), Thailand (3.2 per cent), and the Philippines (2.2 per cent).

Words related to Malaysia's economic development appeared as primary to tertiary concepts across most nations. More positive terms, such as "strong economy" and "rich", were noted in the following cases: Vietnam (19.0 per cent), Myanmar (14.9 per cent), the Philippines (8.6 per cent), Cambodia (7.9 per cent), and Laos (6.1 per cent). Less positive terms like "poor" and "developing" were noted in Vietnam (10.3 per cent), Malaysia (5.8 per cent), Brunei (2.1 per cent), and featured once or twice in responses from Cambodia and Malaysia. Cambodia also listed "agriculture" (3.7 per cent) and Thailand listed "oil" (4.3 per cent) as one of Malaysia's economic resources.

For responses related to human mobility, Cambodia and Indonesia used the word "workers" (8.4 per cent) and "Indonesian migrant workers" (4.9 per cent) respectively. Myanmar (10.8 per cent) students similarly associated Malaysia with "jobs", "many go there to work", and similar terms.

In addition, responses from some nations described the relationship between the respondents' nations and the country described. Indonesia indicated a strong anti-Malaysia sentiment,[2] with Indonesia using words like "thief" (12.2 per cent), "plagiarism" (11.7 per cent), and "rival" (5.4 per cent). Myanmar (5.4 per cent) students associated Malaysia with religious discrimination. However, terms used to express positive bilateral relations, such as "neighbours", were found in responses from Singapore (14.8 per cent), Indonesia (10.2 per cent), and Brunei (2.6 per cent). Thailand referred to Malaysia as "south" (14.5 per cent) and "better than Thailand" (2.2 per cent).

References to the geographical attributes and landscape of Malaysia were made by Laos (4.5 per cent), Thailand (4.3 per cent), Vietnam (3.2 per cent), and Cambodia (2.3 per cent).

Some salient concepts were only used by one nation. Bruneian respondents used the term "entertainment" (6.7 per cent), students from Malaysia mentioned positive terms like "peaceful" and "unique" (12.6 per cent) and also referred to "my country" (5.2 per cent), while Singaporean students used the word "toll" (3.0 per cent).

MYANMAR

Perceptions of Myanmar among students from the ten nations, in most cases, are primarily in reference to the country's politics. Aung San Suu Kyi is an iconic figure featured in data yielded from all nations except Vietnam. It is a primary concept in Thailand (12.2 per cent) and Cambodia (10.4 per cent), secondary in Myanmar (8.4 per cent; including a couple of references to General Aung San, her father),

Laos (7.9 per cent), Singapore (7.8 per cent), and tertiary in Indonesia (4.9 per cent), Malaysia (4.9 per cent), Myanmar (4.9 per cent), Brunei (2.1 per cent), and the Philippines (2.0 per cent).

In terms of bilateral ties, many Thai (8.2 per cent) students associated Myanmar with historical enmity ("enemy", "Bayinnaung"). Granted, other Thai (3.1 per cent) students referred to Myanmar instead simply as "neighbour", Vietnamese (8.8 per cent) and Singaporean (2.4 per cent) students indicated that Myanmar is "friendly" or a "friend". The other nations like Brunei (6.4 per cent), Vietnam (3.9 per cent), and Malaysia (2.1 per cent) expressed positive sentiments for Myanmar, such as "interesting" and "beautiful". Conversely, students from some nations like Singapore (5.4 per cent), Indonesia (4.9 per cent), Brunei (2.9 per cent), and the Philippines (2.7 per cent) also expressed that Myanmar was "foreign" or "unknown". Bruneians (12.9 per cent) and Indonesians (11.5 per cent) also associated Myanmar generally with ASEAN or Asia.

The junta or military government was also widely associated with Myanmar; primary in Singapore (22.2 per cent), Indonesia (17.6 per cent), Cambodia (14.5 per cent), and Malaysia (10.6 per cent) and secondary in the Philippines (9.5 per cent) and Thailand (7.1 per cent). Malaysian (9.2 per cent), Singaporean (9.0 per cent), and Indonesian (4.9 per cent) students referred to war or conflict in association with Myanmar. Bruneian students combined both war and the military junta into a primary concept (12.9 per cent). For Lao students, both "open" (3.7 per cent) and "closed" (2.1 per cent) appeared as tertiary associations. Vietnamese students primarily referred to Myanmar as a "Kingdom" (6.9 per cent).

Vietnamese (24.5 per cent), Malaysian (10.6 per cent), and Singaporean (7.2 per cent) students associated Myanmar with poverty and development, as did Bruneian (4.3 per cent), Filipino (4.1 per cent), Cambodian (4.3 per cent), and Indonesian (3.3 per cent) students. The primary concept for Myanmar (15.7 per cent) students themselves was underdevelopment. At the same time, others in Myanmar (10.8 per cent) rated the country as developing. Conversely, students from Laos associated Myanmar's economy only with investment and trade (5.3 per cent) and with fisheries and agriculture (3.7 per cent). Singaporean students associated Myanmar with rice (3.6 per cent). Thai students associated Myanmar with the presence of resources (3.1 per cent). Cambodian students associated Myanmar with drugs (2.9 per cent) and agriculture (2.4 per cent).

For Thai students, the primary association for Myanmar was with labour (15.8 per cent) and also maids (4.6 per cent). For Malaysian (13.4 per cent) students too, their primary association for Myanmar was with labour in the form of migrant workers. Singaporean (5.4 per cent) students associated Myanmar specifically with maids. Malaysian (7.0 per cent), Bruneian (6.4 per cent), and Indonesian (3.8 per cent) students, on the other hand, associated Myanmar with "Rohingya".

Among Myanmar's Buddhist, mainland neighbours — the Thai, Cambodian and Lao students — associations with Myanmar's Buddhist heritage were particularly strong. Cambodian (7.2 per cent) students made the most substantial association between Myanmar and Buddhism generally while temple-related or pagoda-related terms were mentioned by respondents from Laos (20.1 per cent), Myanmar (13.3 per cent), Thailand (12.8 per cent), the Philippines (6.8 per cent), Brunei (5.0 per cent),

Cambodia (4.8 per cent), Singapore (4.8 per cent), Indonesia (3.3 per cent), and Vietnam (2.0 per cent).

Lao (12.7 per cent), Cambodian (6.3 per cent), Malaysian (2.1 per cent), and Thai (2.0 per cent) students associate Myanmar with traditional clothing, particularly the "*longyi*" or Burmese sarong. Similarly, Myanmar (10.8 per cent), Bruneian (8.6 per cent), Filipino (8.2 per cent), Lao (7.9 per cent), Cambodian (7.2 per cent), Singaporean (5.4 per cent), and Malaysian (2.8 per cent) students also associated Myanmar with its culture in general. Thai (3.6 per cent) and Cambodian (3.4 per cent) students made reference to "*thanaka*", the traditional cosmetic powder that many Burmese apply to their faces.

Brunei (9.3 per cent), the Philippines (4.8 per cent), Indonesia (2.7 per cent), and Cambodia (2.4 per cent) made reference to the food of Myanmar. In terms of sporting events, concepts that have been featured include HBT (Hassanal Bolkiah Trophy) for Brunei (5.0 per cent) and "soccer" for Vietnam (2.0 per cent).

In two countries — the Philippines (27.2 per cent) and Indonesia (14.8 per cent) — a significant association was the former international name of Myanmar, "Burma". The former name is also a secondary term in Singapore (6.7 per cent), Brunei (4.3 per cent), and Malaysia (4.2 per cent).[3] Thai (4.6 per cent), Vietnamese (3.9 per cent) and Lao (3.7 per cent) students associated Myanmar with Yangon. However, only Lao (2.6 per cent) students associated Myanmar with the new capital of Naypyitaw. Vietnamese (10.8 per cent), Filipino (8.2 per cent), Bruneian (5.0 per cent), Cambodian (3.9 per cent), Thai (2.6 per cent), and Lao (2.1 per cent) students made reference to

Myanmar's natural landscape, citing concepts like "beach" and "nature".

THE PHILIPPINES

The two universal associations that feature in the descriptions of the Philippines are natural disasters and islands. There was considerable variation in the extent to which these two concepts were used, but Thailand, Vietnam, and Cambodia used these concepts in the greatest proportion. Students from all ten nations, except from the Philippines, described the Philippines as an island nation. This registered as a primary or secondary term in Thailand (32.1 per cent), Cambodia (17.6 per cent), Laos (13.6 per cent), Indonesia (11.7 per cent), Brunei (11.1 per cent), Vietnam (10.6 per cent), Myanmar (9.1 per cent), and Singapore (8.9 per cent), and as a tertiary term in Malaysia (3.9 per cent). Students from all ten nations also referred to natural disasters: Vietnam (56.3 per cent), Thailand (11.1 per cent), Myanmar (10.4 per cent), Cambodia (9.0 per cent), Brunei (7.8 per cent), Laos (5.1 per cent), Malaysia (5.9 per cent), Indonesia (5.1 per cent), Singapore (3.4 per cent) and the Philippines (2.7 per cent).

Other common associations made by at least four nations were in reference to language, pop culture, Manila, sports, and food items. Language, especially Tagalog, was a primary or secondary term in responses from Indonesia (13.7 per cent), Brunei (10 per cent), Thailand (9.5 per cent), Malaysia (6.5 per cent), and Cambodia (6.7 per cent), and a tertiary term in Singapore (3.9 per cent) and Myanmar (3.9 per cent). Pop culture exports from the Philippines were referenced by students from Malaysia (20.9 per cent) and Cambodia (15.2 per cent) as a primary term, and by Brunei (8.9 per cent), Indonesia (6.1 per cent), Vietnam (3.5 per cent), Singapore (2.2 per cent) and

Thailand (2.1 per cent) as a secondary or tertiary term. Myanmar (6.5 per cent) associated the Philippines with dance and festivals. The capital Manila was mentioned by students from Cambodia (12.4 per cent), the Philippines (11.7 per cent), Myanmar (7.8 per cent), Laos (6.8 per cent), Indonesia (6.6 per cent), Malaysia (5.2 per cent), and Brunei (4.4 per cent).

Sports, especially boxing, was a primary term in the responses from Laos (11.9 per cent), and occurred less significantly in the responses from Thailand (4.7 per cent), the Philippines (4.4 per cent), Cambodia (2.4 per cent) and Indonesia (2.0 per cent). References to various food products was a primary term from Brunei (18.3 per cent), while it was seen as secondary or tertiary term from the Philippines (5.3 per cent), Indonesia (5.1 per cent), Laos (4.5 per cent), Singapore (3.4 per cent), and Thailand (2.1 per cent).

Concepts about tourism, the economy, and the labour flows were mentioned by three nations. Words relating to tourism, were mentioned by students from Brunei (7.8 per cent), Laos (4.5 per cent), and Malaysia (3.3 per cent). Words relating to culture registered as tertiary terms in Laos (4.0 per cent), Malaysia (3.3 per cent), and Cambodia (2.4 per cent). References to the economy occurred as a secondary or tertiary term in six countries, with students from the Philippines using the concept poverty (8.7 per cent), students using the word "poor" from Vietnam (8.5 per cent) and Malaysia (5.9 per cent), students from Myanmar (11.7 per cent) and Brunei (2.8 per cent) using the word "developing" (2.8 per cent), while students from Laos (4.0 per cent) and Cambodia (2.4 per cent) used positive or neutral terms. References to "maids" formed a strong primary concept in the responses from Singapore (37.4 per cent), a secondary concept in Brunei (6.7 per cent), while a small percentage of responses from Laos (4.5 per cent) referred to migrant workers from the Philippines.

Some descriptors, referring to religion, appearance, education, and identity, were used in only two nations. There were also generic terms used by the students. Education was associated with the Philippines by Thailand (11.1 per cent) as a primary term and Laos (6.8 per cent) as a secondary term. Myanmar (3.3 per cent) noted the Philippines as "good at English". Some Cambodian and Malaysian students made references to the appearance of people from the Philippines, generally in a positive or neutral way (5.2 per cent and 4.6 per cent respectively). Religion was mentioned in a small percentage of the responses from Cambodia (Christian: 4.3 per cent) and Singapore (Catholic: 2.2 per cent). Students from the Philippines also used the concept Pinoy (6.7 per cent), while a smaller percentage of responses from Singapore also used this concept (2.8 per cent). Myanmar (11.7 per cent) students referred to the Philippines using "good" or similar words though others (5.2 per cent) used negative terms "dislike it" or "don't want to go". Students from Brunei and Vietnam used "good" (both 2.8 per cent), while students from Singapore also referred to the Philippines using positive terms such as "friendly" (5.6 per cent), but a few used negative terms like "bad" (2.8 per cent).

Myanmar (10.4 per cent) made reference to the Philippine presidential system. Other concepts, generally low secondary and tertiary terms, were only found in the responses from single nations. For example, students from Indonesia gave responses different from the other nations, making references to ASEAN (7.1 per cent) and politics (4.6 per cent), as well as conflict (3.0 per cent). Some students from Malaysia referred to "Sulu"

(5.2 per cent). Some students from Thailand referred to the Philippines as the "same as Thai" (3.7 per cent).

SINGAPORE

The descriptions of Singapore, across the ten nations, are primarily centred on the themes of modernity, wealth, and the country's size. Associations made towards tourism, cleanliness, and education are also often seen across the ten nations. Words related to modernity and development were used in all ten nations: Myanmar (28.4 per cent), the Philippines (25.0 per cent), Malaysia (21.7 per cent), Indonesia (17.2 per cent), Thailand (16.8 per cent), Laos (16.2 per cent), Brunei (15.9 per cent), Vietnam (12.9 per cent), Singapore (12.2 per cent), and Cambodia (10.7 per cent). Wealth and a robust economy were also strongly associated with Singapore: Malaysia (17.9 per cent), Vietnam (14.0 per cent), Cambodia (13.8 per cent), Brunei (12.8 per cent), the Philippines (11.3 per cent), Indonesia (7.9 per cent), Thailand (7.7 per cent), Laos (6.1 per cent), and Singapore (4.9 per cent). Interestingly, only students from Singapore (5.4 per cent), Thailand (3.1 per cent), and the Philippines (2.5 per cent) specifically referred to Singapore's comparatively high cost of living. Another common association observed in all ten nations was with Singapore's small size: Thailand (11.7 per cent), Indonesia (10.8 per cent), Malaysia (8.2 per cent), Vietnam (5.6 per cent), Cambodia (5.3 per cent), Singapore (4.9 per cent), the Philippines (4.4 per cent), Laos (4.1 per cent), Brunei (3.6 per cent), and Myanmar (3.4 per cent).

References to the lion and Merlion statue were common and often primary across nations with the exception of Vietnam: Thailand (30.6 per cent), Laos (26.9 per cent), Cambodia (26.2 per cent), the Philippines (20.6 per cent), Myanmar (18.2 per cent), Indonesia (13.8 per cent), Brunei (9.2 per cent), Malaysia (6.5 per cent), and Singapore (4.4 per cent). References made towards tourism as a concept was observed in all nations with the exception of Singapore and Vietnam: Brunei (29.2 per cent), Malaysia (17.9 per cent), Indonesia (13.3 per cent), the Philippines (8.8 per cent), Thailand (7.7 per cent), Cambodia (7.1 per cent), Laos (6.1 per cent), and Myanmar (5.7 per cent).

Many students also perceived Singapore as having a clean and desirable environment, with the exception of those from Cambodia: Vietnam (53.4 per cent), the Philippines (11.8 per cent), Brunei (10.3 per cent), Singapore (10.2 per cent), Thailand (10.2 per cent), Myanmar (8.0 per cent), Indonesia (7.9 per cent), Laos (7.1 per cent) and Malaysia (6.5 per cent). Singapore is also associated with education across the nations, except among Bruneians, Singaporeans and Malaysians: Myanmar (9.1 per cent), Laos (5.6 per cent), the Philippines (3.9 per cent), Cambodia (3.6 per cent), Indonesia (3.9 per cent), Thailand (2.6 per cent), and Vietnam (2.2 per cent).

There were also some associations made by some nations which often appeared as tertiary concepts. Lao students were unique in highlighting "white" as one of the concepts (2.5 per cent), perhaps in reference to the majority Chinese population in Singapore. Some Indonesian students positively associated Singapore with the concepts "welfare" (3.0 per cent) and "cool" (3.0 per cent). They also associated Singapore with "neighbour" (2.5 per cent), while Malaysia did not even include that in any of their responses. Singaporean (2.9 per cent) and Thai (2.6 per cent) students also made references to the concept of food. Some Malaysian students mentioned "Pedra Branca" (2.2 per cent), alluding to the dispute that Singapore and Malaysia had over this territory for almost three decades, and also brought up the association between "Chinese" (2.7 per cent) and Singapore. Some Cambodian students referred to Singapore as "dragon" (2.2 per cent), which is linked to Singapore's rapid development as a nation. The political situation in Singapore was also highlighted in Brunei (2.6 per cent) and Singapore (2.9 per cent), with the reference to Lee Kuan Yew, a political figure, and also indirectly in the Philippines (4.9 per cent), where this concept describes both the policies implemented and the political situation in Singapore. Singaporeans also mentioned the concept of "Singlish" (2.0 per cent), which is part of their cultural identity. Both Philippines (2.9 per cent) and Singapore (2.4 per cent) also had responses which consist of negative perceptions of Singapore.

THAILAND

The three main associations made by students from all ten nations in reference to Thailand were related to tourism, food, and the political situation. Students from the ten nations referred to Thailand as a tourist destination, both directly and in reference to shopping and to specific places, especially Bangkok, but also popular tourist areas like Chiang Mai. These terms registered as strong primary concepts, except in Thailand and Vietnam, where they were secondary and tertiary: Cambodia (38.3 per cent), Brunei (35.7 per cent), Singapore (29.2 per cent), Laos (21.3 per cent), Malaysia (21.2 per cent), Indonesia (19.7 per cent), the Philippines (16.4 per cent), Myanmar (12.1 per cent), Thailand (5.5 per cent), and Vietnam (2.8 per cent). Another common association was food, where it registered as a primary term in Brunei (19.9 per cent), Thailand (17.9 per cent), and Singapore (15.1 per cent), as a secondary term in Laos (8.3 per cent), the Philippines (6.9 per cent), Malaysia (6.1 per cent), and Indonesia

(5.4 per cent), and as a tertiary term in Cambodia (4.3 per cent) but not in Myanmar.

Thailand was also perceived in terms of its political situation and unrest by respondents from all nations except for Brunei. This occurred as a strong primary term in Laos (33.3 per cent), Malaysia (25.7 per cent), and Vietnam (11.9 per cent), as a secondary term in Cambodia (11.3 per cent), Singapore (8.3 per cent), and Thailand (6.0 per cent), and as a tertiary term in Myanmar (3.6 per cent), Indonesia (3.4 per cent) and Vietnam (2.8 per cent). Although Thailand is a popular tourist destination, the widespread perception of its political situation being unstable suggests that tourists may think twice about visiting the country.

Other significant associations made were in reference to agriculture and exports, the transgender culture, and to elephants. Agriculture and exports, especially rice, were mentioned as secondary terms in responses from Vietnam (8.0 per cent), Singapore (6.3 per cent), Cambodia (5.7 per cent), and Laos (5.1 per cent). References to the transgender subculture in Thailand were noted as primary terms in the responses from Vietnam (33.5 per cent), the Philippines (20.8 per cent), Indonesia (13.3 per cent), and Singapore (12.0 per cent), as a secondary term from Myanmar (6.2 per cent) and Brunei (5.6 per cent), and as a tertiary term in Malaysia (3.9 per cent). "Elephant" occurred as a strong primary term among Indonesian (25.6 per cent) and Filipino (21.8 per cent) students, while a smaller proportion of students in Malaysia (8.9 per cent), Brunei (8.7 per cent), Thailand (5.5 per cent), and Singapore (3.1 per cent) did so.

Other secondary and tertiary concepts mentioned by at least three nations were in reference to culture, pop culture, the monarchy, and religion. Terms relating to culture were noted in the responses from Brunei (7.1 per cent), Cambodia (6.1 per cent), Malaysia (4.5 per cent), and Myanmar (3.6 per cent), while the concept "smile" was associated with Thailand by Thai (8.0 per cent) and Singaporean students (3.6 per cent). References to pop culture including films and stars were noted in the responses from the Philippines (8.9 per cent), Indonesia (5.9 per cent), Brunei (5.6 per cent), Vietnam (4.0 per cent), Cambodia (3.5 per cent), and Laos (2.3 per cent). The monarchy, particularly the king, was mentioned by students from Thailand (5.5 per cent), Indonesia (4.4 per cent), Singapore (3.6 per cent), Myanmar (3.6 per cent), and Brunei (2.0 per cent). References to religion, especially Buddhism, were noted in responses from Vietnam (9.7 per cent), the Philippines (6.9 per cent), Myanmar (4.8 per cent), Indonesia (3.9 per cent), Brunei (3.1 per cent), Cambodia (3.0 per cent), Malaysia (2.8 per cent), and Singapore (2.1 per cent).

Positive references to the economy as a secondary concept were made by students from Vietnam (9.1 per cent), Myanmar (7.2 per cent), Malaysia (6.1 per cent), and Cambodia (5.7 per cent). Malaysian students also made references to language (2.8 per cent) and used the terms "neighbour" (2.8 per cent). Singaporean (12.0 per cent) and Myanmar (6.0 per cent) students wrote "good for shopping".

Lao students used tertiary terms that were not found in the responses from other nations, including the Chao Phraya River (2.3 per cent), news and advertising (2.3 per cent), and Krungsri (2.3 per cent).

Overall, besides references to political unrest, students from all ten nations generally used neutral or positive terms to describe Thailand. In Myanmar, for example, students used a variety of terms related to "good" (9.6 per cent) and "polite"

(8.4 per cent); though some Myanmar students did use terms such as "arrogant" (2.4 per cent). Some students from Thailand used negative terms like "stupid" (5.5 per cent), and a small proportion described Thailand as "hot" (4.0 per cent). Unsurprisingly, a strong primary term in the responses from Thailand was "home" (17.4 per cent).

VIETNAM

There are two main associations which all ten nations made with reference to Vietnam, which are war/politics and the economy. The concepts of war and politics are grouped together due to both being closely linked and they are often primary or secondary terms except in the case of Vietnamese students: Indonesia (41.3 per cent), the Philippines (34.8 per cent), Malaysia (22.3 per cent), Singapore (21.5 per cent), Brunei (20.3 per cent), Laos (16.4 per cent), Thailand (9.2 per cent), Cambodia (7.4 per cent), Myanmar (6.3 per cent), and Vietnam (2.3 per cent). Notably, these concepts are far less salient among Vietnamese students themselves as compared to their counterparts elsewhere. Students in many countries made reference to Ho Chi Minh: Cambodia (18.6 per cent), Laos (16.4 per cent), Myanmar (15.6 per cent), Thailand (4.3 per cent), Malaysia (4.1 per cent), Indonesia (2.6 per cent), and Vietnam (2.3 per cent); although it is not clear in many cases if the reference was being made to the person or the city.

All ten nations also noted the concept of economic growth in Vietnam, seen in a variety of mostly positive terms used to describe the development and economy: Vietnam (30.8 per cent), Myanmar (18.8 per cent), Malaysia (14.9 per cent), Laos (9.7 per cent), Brunei (7.8 per cent), Thailand (4.3 per cent), Indonesia

(3.6 per cent), Cambodia (3.5 per cent), Singapore (2.3 per cent), and the Philippines (2.3 per cent).

Other significant associations made with reference to Vietnam include agriculture/production, Vietnamese culture, food, and tourism. Vietnam is also well-known for its agriculture, specifically rice production in all ten nations except for students from Vietnam: Myanmar (18.8 per cent), Laos (13.5 per cent), Cambodia (13.0 per cent), Malaysia (12.8 per cent), Brunei (11.8 per cent), Thailand (10.2 per cent), Singapore (7.9 per cent), Indonesia (5.7 per cent), and the Philippines (3.3 per cent). Within this concept of agriculture/production, one interesting thing that caught our attention is that some Thai students viewed Vietnam as its "rice market competitor", which makes up 4.3 per cent out of the 10.2 per cent.

Seven of the ten nations, except for Indonesia, Myanmar, and Singapore, brought up the concept of culture, especially pertaining to Vietnamese culture and traditions: Brunei (15.7 per cent), the Philippines (13.8 per cent), Thailand (12.9 per cent), Cambodia (8.7 per cent), Vietnam (6.9 per cent), Malaysia (4.1 per cent), and Laos (3.4 per cent). Besides the concept of traditional culture, Brunei (2.0 per cent) and the Philippines (3.9 per cent) also brought up the concept of pop culture, as seen in the terms like "movie" and "Miss Saigon".

Respondents from seven nations also associated Vietnam with its cuisine, such as *pho*, and they are often primary or secondary terms: Singapore (31.1 per cent), Thailand (25.8 per cent), the Philippines (21.5 per cent), Brunei (10.5 per cent), Indonesia (6.2 per cent), Cambodia (6.1 per cent), and Laos (8.2 per cent). The concept of tourism was also common among the ten nations except Myanmar, Thailand, and Vietnam. This can be seen in the responses about travelling, shopping, and places within Vietnam: Cambodia (29.0 per cent), Malaysia (12.2 per cent), Laos (11.6 per cent), Brunei (10.4 per cent), Singapore (10.1 per cent), the Philippines (9.9 per cent), and Indonesia (9.8 per cent).

There were also references towards the people and nature of Vietnam. These are often secondary and tertiary terms mentioned in a few nations. Vietnamese referred to both "beautiful" (18.9 per cent) and "good-natured" (6.9 per cent), Bruneians referred to "immigrant" (3.9 per cent), Laotians referred to "diligent" (3.9 per cent), Cambodians referred to "language" (3.0 per cent), while Singaporeans referred to both "bride(s)" (2.3 per cent) and "friend(s)" (2.3 per cent). Four nations, specifically Laos (7.2 per cent), the Philippines (2.8 per cent), Brunei (2.0 per cent), and Malaysia (2.0 per cent) also brought up the concept of nature in Vietnam, and these are seen as secondary or tertiary terms.

There were also nations which talked about the transport in Vietnam and generic terms describing Vietnam. The concept of transport came up as tertiary terms in Laos (4.3 per cent), Vietnam (4.0 per cent), and Thailand (3.2 per cent). Terms that described Vietnam in either positive or negative terms were seen in the responses of Myanmar (17.2 per cent), Vietnam (15.6 per cent), Brunei (3.3 per cent), and Malaysia (2.0 per cent). Myanmar (17.2 per cent) students very frequently used a series of positive words or phrases to describe Vietnam, e.g. "good", "good at football", "imaginative", "beautiful", etc. Yet others from Myanmar (9.4 per cent) made reference to "many problems", "need technology", and other negative references. Responses given by the Vietnamese students also reflected, in a more balanced way, a series of positive and negative terms for their own country.

There were some unique associations by specific nations. Singaporeans referred to their community involvement projects held in Vietnam (2.3 per cent). Bruneians and Indonesians associated the country with ASEAN (9.3 per cent and 4.1 per cent respectively). Malaysia (5.4 per cent) and Thailand (4.3 per cent associated China with Vietnam, with words like "Chinese" and "same culture as China". Lao students also associated the country with hospitals (3.8 per cent), highlighting their perception of Vietnam as a medical tourism destination. Malaysian students were also the only ones who talked about the concept of religion (2.0 per cent).

Notes

1. The survey was taken in all countries several months after the MH370 disappearance (8 March 2014); but in Cambodia, Laos, and Malaysia, before the shooting down of MH17 (17 July 2014). Given the lack of reference to the airline disasters in Cambodia, Laos, and Malaysia, this suggests that these are fleeting rather than lasting associations between news events and a particular country (i.e. Malaysia).
2. There has been a very prominent anti-Malaysian sentiment in Indonesia over the past several years, particularly around the idea that Malaysia has been "stealing" or claiming cultural icons (*batik*, songs, etc.) considered to be "Indonesian".
3. Note that in Thai, Khmer, and Lao, the name for Myanmar has not changed.

7
COGNITIVE MAPS OF ASEAN

In the 2014 survey, we expanded the survey questionnaire to include a set of sixty triad questions. This method is adopted from cultural anthropological semantic domain analysis, and developed by principal investigator Eric C. Thompson in reference to countries generally and ASEAN countries specifically in earlier research. Triad questions ask respondents to judge similarities and differences among items (in this case, countries). The purpose of the method is to solicit and reveal what criteria respondents are using to make their judgements (i.e. to get at their cultural knowledge or understanding of a domain) rather than have the criteria predetermined by the researcher. Responses to the triad questions are used to produce aggregate similarity matrices, showing the relative similarity and difference amongst all items in the domain, as judged by the sample of respondents. These matrices in turn are subjected to correspondence analysis, through which multidimensional, cognitive maps are produced, giving a visual representation of how students from a particular university or sample as a whole think about the relationship among ASEAN nations.

METHODS AND INTERPRETATION

The "cognitive maps" presented in this report (in full, in Appendix F) provide a visual representation of the relationship among ASEAN countries based on the aggregate judgements of similarity and difference among countries within each university sample. They reflect, in a simplified form, the cultural concepts — the learned, shared knowledge — that students from each university have regarding Southeast Asia.

The maps are derived from questions of similarity and difference presented to the respondents in the form of triad questions. A triad question asks respondents to select the most different item from a set of three items. For example, if respondents are presented with "cow", "buffalo", and "rock", they would almost certainly choose "rock" as different from "cow" and "buffalo". In a triad exercise, the items are selected from among a specific domain of items — in our case, that domain is ASEAN members and the domain has ten items.

The triad test is scored by assigning one point to the relationship between the two items *not* selected (i.e. they are being judged as most similar within that triad). The results produce an item-by-item matrix (in our case, a ten-by-ten matrix), within which items with the maximum score (four in our case) are the most similar and those with the minimum score (0) are the least similar. Answers from all respondents in a particular sample are combined into an aggregate similiarity matrix, which converts the scores to a percentage between 0.00 (minimum similarity) and 1.00 (maximum similarity). The diagonal scores are all 1.00, as each country is perfectly similar to itself.

The cognitive maps are produced by applying correspondence analysis (a kind of factor analysis) to the aggregate similiarity matrices. Correspondence analysis works by reducing as much of the complexity of the data to as small a number of dimensions (factors) as possible. A ten-by-ten matrix will be reduced to no more than nine dimensions. Each item is given a score in each dimension (generally between −1 and +1), which shows how it relates to other items (countries) on that dimension. Dimensions are ranked based on how much of the total information in the matrix they contain. The lowest dimensions (first, second, third) will contain most of the overall variation and information in the matrix. Higher dimensions (seventh, eighth, ninth) capture remaining information, resulting from idiosyncratic or random answers to the triad questions. Put simply, the strongest, shared patterns of response from any given sample of respondents are represented in the lower dimensions of the correspondence analysis, while the higher dimensions contain "noise" (e.g. random, uninformed, or idiosyncratic responses to the questionnaire).

The cognitive maps in this report display the first (x-axis) and second (y-axis) dimensions mapped onto each other. This provides a quick view of how, on the whole, respondents from a particular university are differentiating among ASEAN members as well as how certain sets of ASEAN members cluster together in the judgement of those students. The horizontal (x-axis) of each map shows the most significant dimension of similarity and difference, while the vertical (y-axis) shows the next most significant (once the first or lower order of similarities and differences are taken into account). While these give a good, overall view of how the domain of ASEAN members is organized as a whole by the respondents, important information is also often contained in the third, fourth and sometimes fifth dimensions of contrast. These are not represented visually in this report (due to space constraints and the difficulty of visually interpreting a three-, four- or five-dimensional map). The researchers, however, have examined these dimensions and where important, report on their significance. For example, in some instances, the second and third dimensions may be weighted extremely similarly and may be switched between two samples with very similar responses. In such cases, the two maps may look rather different (because the second/third dimensions are being alternately represented), when in fact the results from the two sets of respondents are very similar. We note this below where relevant. For purposes of this report, we present (Appendix F) the first and second dimensional maps from each university sample along with the overall aggregate similarity matrix from which the map is derived.

An additional procedure, which allows us to judge the similarity and difference between university samples is QAP, or Quadratic Assignment Procedure, applied to the aggregate similiarity matrices. QAP correlations measure the extent of similarity or difference between the responses from two samples. QAP results range from +1.00 to –1.00. If the result is 1.00 then the two sets of responses (the aggregate similarity matrices) are exactly the same. The closer the results are to 1.00, the more similar the matrices. If the results are –1.00, then the two matrices would be exact opposites. Results approaching 0.00 indicate that the two sets of responses are not correlated, in other words, there is no more relationship between the two samples' responses than between two sets of random responses. In this study, the QAP correlation results allow us to see which students' responses, from which universities, are most highly correlated (most similar) and from that, to infer how knowledge about ASEAN, about the relationship among its members — particularly similarities and differences between them — is being spread and framed among university students across the region. Do we see evidence of national framings of such knowledge? Is the extent of national framing of knowledge consistent across the region? Are there other patterns or framings of knowledge about ASEAN, such as might be influenced by subregional (Mainland or Maritime), ethnic, or religious cultures?

In the following, we first discuss the cognitive maps derived from each university sample and within each nation, then turn to the results of QAP correlation analysis (see table at the end of Appendix F) to further assess national, transnational, and regional patterns in students' perceptions of the relationship among ASEAN members.

COGNITIVE MAPS:
DESCRIPTION AND INTERPRETATION

In the cognitive map from Brunei — mapping the responses of the students from the Universiti Brunei Darussalam (UBD) — we see Brunei and Singapore closely related. More generally, the Malay-Muslim majority countries of Brunei, Indonesia and Malaysia, along with Singapore, are clustered together on the left-hand side of the figure. On the opposite, right-hand side of the figure, the Mainland Southeast Asian countries of Cambodia, Laos, Myanmar, and Vietnam (CLMV countries) are also closely clustered together. In the lower, right-hand quadrant, the Philippines and Thailand are closely associated. This is the effect of residual categorization. In the first dimension of difference (horizontal), the Philippines and Thailand are judged to be unlike the Brunei–Indonesia–Malaysia–Singapore group. In the second dimension of difference, they are differentiated from both that group and the CLMV countries. Differentiation between the Philippines and Thailand only appears in the fourth dimension of the results. This pattern of thinking about Southeast Asia appears to be a "Malay-Muslim" perception of the region, replicated in several other predominantly Malay-Muslim or Indonesian-Muslim universities around the region.

In Indonesia, a similar pattern to the one in Brunei appears in the results from both the Universitas Indonesia (UI, located in Depok, a suburb of Jakarta) and the Universitas Syiah Kuala (Unsyiah, located in Aceh). Some minor differences appear between these maps and that of the UBD students. In the UI map, for instance, Brunei is more differentiated from Indonesia, Malaysia, and Singapore, which cluster close together in the first two dimensions of contrast. Singapore is differentiated from this group in the third dimension, but a distinction between Indonesia and Malaysia does not appear until the fifth dimension of contrast. Students in the Unsyiah sample cluster Brunei, Indonesia, and Malaysia more closely together and differentiate Singapore from this group more than Brunei. For both UI and Unsyiah students, the greatest similarity within this group is between Indonesia and Malaysia.

The cognitive map produced from responses by students from Universitas Nusa Cendana (Undana, located in Kupang, West Timor) appears very different from those of UI and Unsyiah students. The first dimension of contrast differentiates CLMV countries from other ASEAN members, but they are not closely clustered and they are differentiated in the second (vertical dimension). Neither do we see the Malay-Muslim clustering of Brunei, Indonesia, and Malaysia plus Singapore. Indonesia, Malaysia, and Singapore are loosely clustered in the lower left quadrant, while Brunei, the Philippines, and Thailand form a residual cluster in the upper left quadrant. QAP analysis (discussed below) shows that the overall pattern of answers from Undana is very highly correlated with responses from UI (0.93) and Unsyiah (0.87) despite the strong visual difference between the maps, but to a lesser degree compared with most other within-nation correlations.

The Malay-Muslim pattern of thinking about Southeast Asian countries again appears in the results from the University of Malaya (UM) in Malaysia. In this case, while the overall pattern is similar to that in Brunei and Indonesia, there is a somewhat greater differentiation among the Malay-Muslim countries in the second (vertical) dimension of the map. While Indonesian students tend to cluster the countries more closely together, particularly Indonesia and Malaysia, the Malay students at UM differentiate mainly between Indonesia and the rest of this group of countries.

In Malaysia, the "Malay-Muslim" pattern of perception of ASEAN members also appears in responses from the sample from the Universiti Malaysia Sarawak (Unimas). In this report, we present the results from students in the sample who are non-Malay, but are *Bumiputera* (indigenous ethnic groups; not ethnically Chinese or Indian). Their responses are very similar to those from UBD, UI, and Unsyiah, as well as from UM. Unlike UM students, they do not differentiate Indonesia from the Malay-Muslim cluster. In the aggregate similiarity matrix, they score both Malaysia and Indonesia and Malaysia and Brunei as very similar (as well as Malaysia and Singapore).

The greatest within-nation difference among any of the results is between Chinese-Malaysian students from the Universiti Tunku Abdul Rahman (UTAR) and their Malay and other *Bumiputera* counterparts at UM and Unimas. In the UTAR results, we see a cognitive map in which Singapore is differentiated from all other countries in both the first and second dimensions of contrast. It is differentiated most strongly, in the first dimension, from the CLMV countries. In the second dimension, it is differentiated from Malaysia (as well as Thailand, Indonesia, and the Philippines). While there is some affinity between Singapore and Brunei, these are differentiated strongly in the third dimension of contrast (not shown in the mapping here).

The cognitive map produced by the Chinese-Malaysian students from UTAR is, in fact, very similar to that produced by Singaporean students. From these maps, we see UTAR and Singaporean students sharing a particular view of "Singapore exceptionalism". For these students, the view of the relationship among Southeast Asian countries is dominated by the difference between Singapore and all other countries. Simple visual inspection shows the similarity of the cognitive maps produced by UTAR, National University of Singapore (NUS) and Singapore Polytechnic (SP) students. The robustness of this finding is reflected in earlier work, where this pattern was found among NUS students. It is also found in the analysis of responses of the Chinese-Malaysian students from the UM (both in the current study and in past research). Also, notably, this pattern of perception of Southeast Asia is produced by results from ethnically Malay students at NUS (both in the current study and in past research). Thus, it is worth noting that this is best interpreted not as a Chinese-centric pattern but as a Singapore-centric one.

Results from the Philippines produce a cognitive map rather distinct from either the "Malay-Muslim" or "Singapore exceptionalism" patterns. Responses from both University of the Philippines Diliman (UP Diliman, located in the greater metro-Manila) and University of the Philippines Visayas (UP Visayas, situated in the central Philippines) produce similar maps. In the results from the Philippines, the first order of contrast is between the Mainland CLMV countries and the Maritime countries of Indonesia, Malaysia, the Philippines, and

Singapore, and anchored by both the Philippines and Singapore (at the far left of the map figures reproduced here). Thailand and Brunei are located in an intermediary position between the two Maritime countries and CLMV clusters. The second order of contrast is then between the Philippines and the most affluent, small, Maritime countries of Singapore and Brunei. This contrast is captured in the second (vertical) dimension of the cognitive map produced from the UP Diliman respondents. The UP Visayas map differentiates only Brunei in the second dimension, but Singapore is differentiated in a similar fashion in the third dimension (not shown here).

Results from Mindanao State University (MSU) in the southern Philippines, where the student body and our sample are majority Muslim, exhibits elements of both the Philippine pattern and the Malay-Muslim pattern of responses, though the former appears more influential than the latter. As with responses from UP Diliman and UP Visayas, the MSU results show the first dimension of contrast to be between the CLMV countries (on the right-hand side of the figure) and Maritime countries anchored by the Philippines (on the left). The second dimension of contrast, like the UP Visayas map, differentiates Brunei from the Philippines, and at the same time, shows some clustering of the Malay-Muslim countries of Brunei, Indonesia, and Malaysia in the upper, left quadrant. QAP analysis also supports the interpretation that MSU students have a distinctive perspective on Southeast Asia. Their results have the lowest correlation with counterparts at UP Diliman (0.84) and UP Visayas (0.84) for any within-nation comparisons, other than that between UTAR and other Malaysian students.

Among responses from Mainland Southeast Asian nations, we see a distinctive, shared "Mainland" perspective among responses from Cambodia, Laos, and Thailand. In results from the Royal University of Phnom Penh (RUPP), the National University of Laos (NUOL), and all four Thai universities, we see cognitive maps in which the first dimension of contrast is dominated by a broad, clear distinction between the five Mainland and five Maritime countries. In the results from Cambodia, we see differentiation among Mainland countries in the second (vertical) dimension, which clusters Cambodia with its two powerful neighbours, Thailand and Vietnam, while differentiating Laos and, particularly, Myanmar. The results from Laos differentiate Thailand from other Mainland countries in the second dimension, with Laos as intermediary between Thailand and the other CLMV countries.

Results from Chulalongkorn University (CU) in Thailand, while emphasizing the Mainland-Maritime distinction in the first dimension of contrast, differentiate Maritime rather than Mainland countries in the second dimension of contrast; specifically Singapore and secondarily Brunei are differentiated from Indonesia and the Philippines. Notably, this same distinction is seen in the third dimension of contrast in results from both Cambodia and Laos. Differentiation amongst Mainland countries in the CU cognitive map appears most noticeably in the fourth dimension of contrast, where Thailand is sharply differentiated from the CLMV cluster (this is apparent, to a lesser degree, in both the second and third dimensions of contrast for CU as well). This is similar to results from earlier research, which showed CU students producing a cognitive map which differentiated Mainland from Maritime countries first then secondly differentiating Thailand from all other Mainland countries.

That CU cognitive map from the earlier study is very similar visually to the cognitive map produced by results from Saint John's University (SJU, located in Bangkok) in this study, where

Thailand is differentiated from CLMV countries in the second dimension of contrast. The third and fourth dimensions of the SJU results differentiate Brunei, and secondarily Singapore, from amongst the Maritime countries. In the results from Khon Kaen University (KKU), differentiation amongst both Mainland and Maritime countries is resolved in the second dimension of contrast i.e. Thailand is differentiated from other Mainland countries, particularly Cambodia and Myanmar while, to a lesser extent, Brunei and Singapore are contrasted to Indonesia and the Philippines among Maritime countries.

The results from Walailak University (WU) in southern Thailand also follow the general Mainland pattern of other Thai as well as Cambodian and Lao universities. At the same time, in the second dimension of contrast, we can see that the majority Malay-Muslim countries of Brunei, Indonesia, and Malaysia cluster together. Thus we see some evidence of the Malay-Muslim as well as the Mainland patterns of perception in the WU results, though the correlation with other Mainland respondents is higher than with those from Malay-Muslim majority universities outside of Thailand (see QAP correlation table).

In contrast to the similar views among Cambodian, Lao, and Thai students, those from Myanmar and Vietnam show distinctive, nationally-framed perceptions. In Myanmar, both our Mandalay and Yangon samples show a Mainland-Maritime distinction in the first dimension of contrast, though not as sharp as that found among the other Mainland universities. In the second dimension of contrast, Singapore is differentiated from all other countries, particularly the Brunei–Indonesia–Malaysia cluster. Thus, some elements of Malay-Muslim clustering, Singapore exceptionalism, and the Mainland-Maritime distinction are visually apparent in both cognitive maps from Myanmar, which also have high QAP correlation and visual similarity to each other. But the Myanmar results do not highly correlate overall with any results from elsewhere in the region (see QAP correlation table).

Finally, the results from Vietnam also suggest a distinctive Vietnamese view of the region. Results from the Vietnam National University, Hanoi (VNU-Hanoi) and Vietnam National University, Ho Chi Minh City (VNU-HCMC) both show Vietnam, Laos, and Cambodia contrasted to Maritime countries in the first (horizontal) dimension. Thailand and Myanmar sit in an intermediary position along the first dimension in both cases. The second (vertical) dimension resolves the differentiation of Singapore from all other countries (though less so from Thailand in the VNU-HCMC results). The Vietnamese results overall correlate more highly with Cambodia, Laos, and Thai results than those of Myanmar. But the visual representation makes clear that a distinctive relationship among Vietnam, Laos, and Cambodia (Vietnam's immediate neighbours and traditional sphere of influence in the region) is of significance for Vietnamese students in a way that is not evident elsewhere in the region.

FINDINGS BASED ON QAP CORRELATION

The following terms are used in describing the findings based on QAP correlations between aggregate similiarity matrices produced with the triad data collected from each pair of universities.

Exceptionally High = 1.00 to 0.90 (p average = 0.0000)
Very High = 0.89 to 0.80 (p average = 0.0002)
High = 0.79 to 0.70 (p average = 0.0006)
Moderate = 0.69 to 0.60 (p average = 0.0019)
Low = 0.59 to 0.50 (p average = 0.0047)
Very Low = 0.49 to 0.20 (p average = 0.0123)

Each QAP test generates a unique p value by running random permutations (n=5,000) of the matrix and reporting the percentage of random correlations that were higher than the observed correlation between the two matrices being tested. As the p value may vary slightly from test to test, each QAP test was run approximately ten times and the most commonly occurring (modal) p value was recorded. The p value can also vary somewhat based on the characteristics of the matrices being compared. The average p values within each level of correlation is reported above, to provide a general sense of the strength of correlation. For example, on average, the odds of the "very high" correlations happening by chance is about 2 in 10,000. The odds of even the "very low" correlations happening by chance is only slightly more than 1 in 100. Overall, these suggest that across the region, students generally have a shared, non-random set of ideas about the relationship among Southeast Asian countries. The difference lies in the degree to which these ideas are shared or not within and across nations, as well as evidence that general sensibilities about these relationships are further shaped by local or subregional patterns in students perceptions of the region.

Strong National Frames-of-Reference

The correlations within nations are almost all exceptionally high (>0.90). This supports the hypothesis that perceptions of Southeast Asia are driven by national frames-of-reference (via national media, schooling, etc.). For example, the correlations between UM and Unimas in Malaysia, between NUS and SP in Singapore, and between CU and KKU in Thailand are all extremely high (0.97). Similarly high correlations were observed between CU and WU (0.94), KKU and WU (0.95), UI and Unsyiah in Aceh (0.94), UI and Undana in Kupang (0.93), VNU-Hanoi and VNU-HCMC (0.92), UP Diliman and UP Visayas (0.91), and between KKU and SJU in Bangkok (0.93). The correlation between CU and SJU (0.896), between WU and SJU (0.894), and between University of Yangon (YU) and University of Mandalay (MU) (0.893) were also very high, though just below the 0.90 mark.

Only three within-nation correlations outside the exceptional level by more than 0.01 (1 per cent). The correlation between Unsyiah in Aceh and Undana in Kupang was 0.87; still very high, but when compared to other within-nation correlations, it suggests some divergence in the perceptions of Southeast Asia between students at these two regionally distant and ethno-religiously distinctive Indonesian universities. Correlations of results from MSU in the Philippines with UP Diliman (0.84) and UP Visayas (0.84) similarly suggest regionally and ethno-religiously distinctive views in the southern Philippines.

The most striking, less-than-exceptional within-nation correlation, is that of Chinese-Malaysian students at UTAR with Malay-Malaysian students at UM (0.76) and with non-Malay, *Bumiputera* (indigenous) students from Unimas (0.68). This finding corroborates findings from earlier research (in 2004–6) that found Malay and Chinese students in Malaysia to have the most divergent within-nation perceptions of any groups researched to date. The earlier research compared Malay to Chinese students in Malaysia and Singapore as well as Thai and Sino–Thai students in Thailand; only those in Malaysia were found to have substantially different perceptions of Southeast Asia.

Taken together, the QAP correlations support the hypothesis that national frames-of-reference have a primary influence on perceptions of the relationship among nations in Southeast Asia. But the findings from Malaysia (and to a lesser extent, Indonesia and the Philippines) also show that there is nothing automatic about the national cultivation of these perceptions. Malaysia is a particularly divided society, with citizens going to different Malay- or Chinese-medium schools and experiencing different Malay and Chinese language media environments, which appear to produce different views of the region.

Transnational, Subregional Patterns

The QAP correlations also support the interpretation of transnational, subregional patterns mentioned previously in this chapter; that is to say, patterns of students' ideas about Southeast Asia that transcend national borders and map onto subregional variations within Southeast Asia.

a. Mainland correlation among Cambodia, Laos, and Thailand: Responses from students across Cambodia, Laos, and Thailand are almost as highly correlated cross-nationally as the general extremely high correlation pattern we see for within-nation results above. The responses of students from NUOL correlate exceptionally high with all four universities in Thailand (KKU, 0.93; CU, 0.91; WU, 0.91; St John's, 0.90). Correlations between Cambodian students from RUPP with Thai and Lao students are nearly as high (0.90 with CU; 0.89 with KKU, WU, and NUOL). The correlation between RUPP students and SJU students is somewhat lower, but still within the "very high" range (0.82).

b. Distinctive views of Myanmar and Vietnam amongst Mainland nations:
    In contrast to the exceptionally or near-exceptionally high correlations among Cambodian, Lao, and Thai students, the

correlation of both Myanmar and Vietnamese students' views with other Mainland students is distinctively lower. Among the Vietnamese results, there is a clear pattern in relation to other Mainland nations. Students from VNU-Hanoi and VNU-HCMC have "high" correlation with both RUPP (0.78 and 0.75 respectively) and NUOL (0.78 and 0.75 respectively) students. The correlation between Vietnamese and Thai students generally falls in the "moderate" range (0.69 to 0.62) with the exceptions of a "high" correlation between VNU-Hanoi and CU students (0.75) and a "low" correlation between VNU-HCMC and SJU students (0.56). Based on our MU sample, Myanmar students' results correlate most highly with those from Thailand's major public universities (0.617 to 0.645), then next with responses from Cambodia, Laos and SJU (all 0.55), and least with responses from Vietnam (VNU-Hanoi, 0.421; VNU-HCMC, 0.366).

c.   Malay-Muslim pattern:
      Another set of exceptionally high correlations — as high as those found within-nations — is among several of the majority "Malay-Muslim" universities in the data set: UBD in Brunei, UI and Unsyiah in Indonesia, and UM in Malaysia. Correlations among these universities range from 0.96 between UBD and Unsyiah and 0.91 between UI and UM. Notably, and lending support to the interpretation of this as a "Malay-Muslim" pattern, correlations with the other universities in Indonesia and Malaysia are notably lower. The correlation is 0.85 for UBD and Undana and 0.79 for UM and Undana. Correlations between UBD, UI, and Unsyiah, with UTAR (the predominantly Chinese-Malaysian university) are even lower (0.62, 0.66, and 0.57 respectively).

By contrast, the pattern of answers from respondents from Unimas, specifically non-Malay but *Bumiputera* (indigenous) students, is highly correlated with the Malay-Muslim universities identified here (between 0.94 and 0.99).

Two other universities with predominantly Muslim or Malay-Muslim students show variation amongst such respondents. Responses from WU in Thailand, where our sample was 80 per cent Muslim, have correlations of between 0.85 and 0.76 with UBD, UI, Unsyiah, and UM. For students from MSU in the Philippines, the correlations are lower, between 0.65 and 0.49, with the same four universities. Looking at the cognitive map plotted for WU, we see that Brunei, Indonesia, and Malaysia are closely clustered together. But we also see that the Philippines is associated with other Maritime countries, particularly in the first dimension of contrast, thus conforming to the Mainland-Maritime distinction found elsewhere in Thailand and other Mainland nations.

For the results from Mindanao, visual examination of the two dimensions plotted on the cognitive map provide some insight into the divergence between MSU and other Malay-Muslim students. For MSU students, the Philippines is clearly among the Maritime nations; in fact, it is the most extreme Maritime Southeast Asian country on a map, thus making a clear Mainland-Maritime distinction. However, for Malay-Muslim students in other nations, the Philippines is not part of the "Malay-Muslim" grouping of Brunei, Indonesia, Malaysia, and also Singapore. Rather the Philippines is clustered with Thailand, forming a residual category of neither "Malay-Muslim" countries nor CLMV (less affluent, Mainland) countries.

Taken together, these results demonstrate a "Malay-Muslim" pattern of thinking about the relationship among ASEAN members, though one that is tempered by other factors. In both Thailand (WU) and the Philippines (MSU), it intersects with national framings of the region. Also, notably, the results from Unimas in Malaysia demonstrate that holding this "Malay-Muslim" view of the relationship among Southeast Asian nations does not require that the respondents themselves are Malay-Muslims. Among the indigenous (*Bumiputera*) but non-Malay respondents from Unimas, the overwhelming majority are not Muslim. But they appear to be strongly influenced by the majority Malay-Muslim national framing of perceptions of the region (while their Chinese-Malaysian peers at UTAR are not).

d. "Singapore exceptionalism" pattern:
    Another transnational pattern is the exceptional to very high correlation of UTAR students to Singaporean students (0.92 with SP; 0.88 with NUS). As noted above, the within-nation correlation between UM and UTAR students is only 0.76 (notably low for a within-nation correlation) and in all other cases, transnationally, UTAR students' correlation with others in the region is moderate (two cases), low (four cases) or very low (seven cases). (The same is not the case with Singaporean students in general, whose perceptions are more in line with others in the region than those of Chinese-Malaysian students.) In this case, the perception of Singapore as particularly unique in the region extends beyond Singaporean students to their Chinese-Malaysian peers to the north.

e. Distinctive view of the Philippines amongst Maritime
    nations:
    As with Myanmar and Vietnam on the Mainland, the cross-
    national correlation of Filipino students' perceptions is
    distinctively lower than that of other Maritime countries.
    Students from both UP Diliman and UP Visayas are highly
    to moderately correlated with students from Singapore
    (between 0.76 to 0.65) and with Indonesian students, apart
    from those in Aceh (0.72 and 0.65 with UI; 0.71 and 0.62
    with Undana). Their correlation with the Malay-Muslim
    university students (apart from UI) is generally low (0.62
    and 0.55 with UBD; 0.59 and 0.53 with UM; 0.57 and 0.49
    with Unsyiah) and low to very low (0.52 and 0.47) with
    UTAR students. In fact, the correlation between Filipino
    students and those from Mainland nations is higher than that
    with UBD, UM, Unsyiah, and UTAR in all but four cases,
    and in those, it is comparable. Similarly, MSU students,
    who have relatively low within-nation correlations with
    peers from UP Diliman and UP Visayas, have even lower
    correlations with responses from other Maritime or Malay-
    Muslim nations.

f. Evidence of transnational, centralized, elite knowledge:
    Among all across-nation correlations (n=173), about 40 per
    cent (n=68) are high to extremely high, and about 30 per
    cent each are either moderate (n=51) or low to very low
    (n=54). Analysis of these across-nation correlations yields a
    number of useful findings. With almost 70 per cent correlated
    at 0.60 or above ("moderate" to "extremely high"), they
    suggest that there exists a standard, transnational perception
    of the relationship among Southeast Asian nations across

the entire region. Moreover, and of particular interest, that standard perception is most consistently held by students at the more centralized, elite universities as compared to those at regional or less elite, vocationally-oriented universities (i.e. SP in Singapore and SJU in Bangkok). (Note: Due to the contingencies of the Myanmar data, Myanmar's results are not considered in this cross-national analysis; though if considered they generally support the arguments here.)

The main observation supporting this conclusion is that the "primary" or flagship universities are consistently more highly correlated cross-nationally with other flagship universities as compared to cross-national correlations among additional vocational-technical or regional universities. Observed cross-nation correlations average 0.73 (n=36) among flagship universities, whereas they average 0.60 (n=49) among additional, regional and vocational-technical universities. Cross-national correlations of primary with additional universities fall in between, at 0.67 (n=88). The average within-nation correlation by comparison is 0.89 (n=18).

Parsing the data and results of the analysis, we can argue that at least two things make the cross-national results from additional universities less correlated than those from primary universities. One is the evidence of patterns of knowledge in which additional universities diverge from central, flagship universities in particular instances. The second is evidence that generally, students from flagship universities are more attuned and those at regional or vocational-technical universities are less attuned to "standard" transnational knowledge (within and between nations) of Southeast Asia. So while the nationally-framed view of Southeast Asia is influential everywhere, a standard, shared transnational view is most in evidence at the flagship universities and least in evidence among the additional universities, leading us to label it as a form of "transnational, centralized, elite knowledge" of the region.

We will focus in particular on cross-national correlations across the Mainland-Maritime divide (i.e. Cambodia, Laos, Thailand, Vietnam versus Brunei, Indonesia, Malaysia, the Philippines, and Singapore; leaving results from Myanmar aside). We have previously noted that there are important transnational but subregional patterns (i.e. "Malay-Muslim", "Mainland-Maritime", and "Singapore exceptionalism"). Setting aside the correlations within these subregions provides a better view of the pattern of correlations regarding a "standard" transnational view across the region as a whole.

Focusing on the Mainland-Maritime cross-national correlations, low and very low correlations are dominated by pairings of additional universities with all other universities. The lowest set of correlations are between UTAR and all Mainland universities (0.51 to 0.29; all but one being "very low"). Correlations between SP and all Mainland universities are similarly overwhelmingly "low" or "very low" (0.61 to 0.41), with only one "moderate" correlation with CU. The same pattern holds for correlations between VNU-HCMC and SJU with Maritime nations (0.66 to 0.31; 0.63 to 0.29). In each case, there is one "moderate" correlation but all others are "low" or "very low".

In the case of SJU and SP, both are centrally located (in Bangkok and Singapore respectively) and the student profiles (e.g. in terms of ethnicity and other characteristics) largely match those of the "flagship" universities in each nation (CU and NUS). But both are technical-vocational universities and the students generally have lower educational attainments (i.e. in secondary school results) than their counterparts at the highly-selective, "flagship" universities. SJU and SP have a very low correlation with each other (0.41). By contrast, the correlation between CU and NUS is considerably higher (0.70), while the correlations of CU with SP (0.61) and NUS with SJU (0.48) fall in between. In both cases, within-nation perceptions of the relationship among Southeast Asian countries is exceptionally highly correlated or nearly so (0.97 between SP and NUS; 0.90, rounded up, between SJU and CU).

In the case of UTAR and VNU-HCMC, the relatively low correlation is likely the result of distinctive national or subregional (i.e. "Singapore exceptionalism") patterns of perception as it is a lack of "standardized" or "elite" knowledge about the region. In the case of VNU-HCMC, as noted above, Vietnamese students in general (both from VNU-Hanoi and VNU-HCMC) display a pattern of thinking about Southeast Asia that is distinctive from all other students in the region. Similarly, UTAR students have a view of Southeast Asia that correlates with students from Singapore, but not very highly with students from anywhere else, even their Malay and *Bumiputera* counterparts at UM and Unimas.

Looking further at the correlations across Mainland and Maritime nations, we see one set of "high" correlations between Maritime UBD and UI students on the one hand and those Mainland students from Thailand (CU and KKU; but not SJU), Cambodia (RUPP), and Laos (NUOL). All of these correlations are in the "high" range (0.79 to 0.70). Notably here, a regional university (KKU) is amongst the group; though it consistently correlates with other universities to a slightly lower degree than the "flagship" Thai university (CU).

All three Philippine universities (UP Diliman, UP Visayas, and MSU) correlate at a "high" to "moderate" degree with the "flagship" Mainland universities of CU, VNU-Hanoi, RUPP and NUOL as well as KKU (0.74 to 0.61). CU and KKU correlate with the Maritime universities of UM, NUS, Unsyiah, and Undana to a similar high to moderate degree (0.72 to 0.62). Again, the same pattern holds, in which the "flagship" university (UP Diliman or CU) almost always correlates to a slightly higher degree as compared to the regional universities (UP Visayas, MSU, or KKU).

Exceptions to the pattern of generally higher correlations among flagship universities are seen in two places across the Mainland-Maritime division. The Philippine regional university of MSU correlates slightly higher with RUPP (0.74) and NUOL (0.72) than does UP Diliman (0.71 and 0.66 respectively). More substantially, responses from Unimas all correlate more highly with the four flagship Mainland universities than do the UM results (by an average of +0.10). In this case, visual analysis of the cognitive maps and similarity matrices suggests a reason.

UM students place considerably more distance between Indonesia and others in the Brunei–Indonesia–Malaysia–Singapore group that consistently cluster together in the "Malay-Muslim" pattern of perception (found in both the UM and Unimas results). This places Indonesia in a more intermediate position in the UM cognitive map so overall, there is a less sharp distinction between the left and right side clusters in the first (horizontal) dimension. By contrast, as we have seen, the Mainland-Maritime distinction found especially in Cambodia, Laos, and Thailand has a sharp distinction between clusters in the first dimension of contrast. And this (sharp distinction) is more evident in the Unimas cognitive maps when compared to the UM cognitive maps, providing the likely explanation for the higher correlation between Unimas and the Mainland flagship universities.

Overall, while there are exceptions for particular reasons, the consistent pattern of higher correlation amongst flagship rather than regional or vocational-technical universities supports the idea we have proposed of a standard transnational perception of the region circulating foremost among the ("elite") cohort of students at top national universities. Of course, this needs to be understood as one dimension of culturally-shared knowledge operating in tandem with national and subregional frames-of-reference.

g.   Influence of economic and historical-cultural criteria:
A final procedure we carried out with QAP correlations was to test the hypothesis that economic and historical-cultural criteria play an important role in students' judgements of the similarities and differences among ASEAN members. By historical-cultural criteria, we mean significance of the knowledge that certain countries have shared histories and cultures, particularly through patterns of the spread of Buddhism and Islam. In our visual analysis of the cognitive maps, we have inferred the significance of historical-cultural criteria, such as the division between Mainland and Maritime

countries, or the clustering of Malay-Muslim ones. We also see the significance of economic criteria, as when Singapore and Brunei (the most affluent nations) or CLMV countries (the least affluent) are differentiated from other ASEAN members.

In order to test these hypotheses, we used triad data generated through a ranking of countries by GDP per capita (GDP) and a ranking of countries based on a Muslim-Buddhist Index (MBI), which ranked countries from those with the greatest Muslim majorities to those with the largest Buddhist ones. These provide rough approximations of important economic and historical-cultural criteria that students might employ to answer the triad questions presented to them. As a further test, we also compared results from the twenty-two universities to a set of answers generated by ranking the countries by population (POP). A reasonable person could answer the triad questions based on such criteria (i.e. judging large population countries to be most similar e.g. Indonesia, the Philippines, and Vietnam, in contrast to small population countries e.g. Brunei, Singapore, and Laos). And finally, we also tested the university samples against a combined GDP+MBI set of answers.

The results show mostly low to moderate sets of correlations when university responses are compared to either the GDP or MBI individually. There are some cases where this analysis supports the conclusion that one or the other of these criteria tends to be more important among particular student samples. For example, we see a substantially higher correlation with MBI rather than GDP in Cambodia, Laos, and Thailand, demonstrating the strength of the Mainland-Maritime criteria in those countries.

By contrast, GDP is a stronger factor among Singaporean students and Chinese-Malaysian students at UTAR. In all cases, correlations are higher or at least equivalent when GDP and MBI are combined, suggesting that throughout the region, particular combinations of these criteria are playing an important role in how university students think about the ASEAN region and the relationship among ASEAN members and likely feed into the "standard" but also "elite" transnational view of the region we have proposed above. By contrast, nowhere does the population (POP) criteria have even a low correlation (>0.50) with actual university responses. In almost all cases, the correlation is extremely low (<0.10).

8
CONCLUSIONS AND RECOMMENDATIONS

What do young people in ASEAN expect of the ASEAN Community? Do they have a sense of regional identity in the way the Association has cultivated the "ASEAN Way" at policymaking levels in its member states? Do young people know ASEAN?

The two ten-nation surveys — the first in 2007 and the 2014 expanded update — both confirm that, among the young undergraduates in this region, there continues to be an emerging sense of identification with the region of Southeast Asia, and with ASEAN as the representative grouping for regional cooperation. Indeed, all forms of ASEAN cooperation, especially those initiated without government prodding, are what will ultimately glue the ASEAN Community together. The more often the people of Southeast Asia get together — to exchange views, help each other, or work together — the stronger the community will become, despite the diversity of culture, ethnicity, and politics. Yet, challenges remain. Young people in the region have correctly identified some of the most important: bridging the development gaps that still exist between and within the ASEAN members, and entrenching a sense of regional identity.

We can expect that as the ASEAN Community project, especially the ASEAN Economic Community (AEC), becomes a more concrete reality, there may be more dissension over the value of ASEAN. The increase in the number of Thai students being more critical of ASEAN in 2014–15 serves as a good illustration of how more information and discussion of ASEAN within the national context can bring about more critical thinking. At the same time, the Myanmar findings for 2014–15 provide exactly the reverse; with the country's chairing of ASEAN in 2014, sentiments of the students in Myanmar now track the ASEAN-enthusiast tendencies in Vietnam, Laos, and Cambodia.

ASEAN stakeholders should thus be prepared for this, i.e. not to see contention of ASEAN's usefulness or value as a "failure" but rather see the increasing importance of ASEAN on people's future and the contention as a measure of the students' heightened knowledge of and interest in regional integration issues. At the same time, substantial attention is needed to alleviate the unintended consequences of integration.

The ranking of the importance of different aspects of integration indicates priority areas for ASEAN to focus its regional cooperation measures in the post-2015 years. These pertain more to people-to-people issues. Despite higher levels of awareness and the "we-feeling" demonstrated by purposeful samplings such as this survey, regional identity still ranks low in the list of priorities. On the other hand, the Internet, as an increasingly important information source, will be a powerful communication medium to engage young people in the region on integration issues that affect them the most. The interest in greater people-to-people interaction is also evidenced in the students' ranking of tourism as the most important aspect of regional integration in the 2014 survey update. This, and the prevailing preferences on travel and work destinations should also be taken into account when formulating regional initiatives for people-to-people connectivity.

Thus, the survey findings suggest that:

- For the most part, there is stability in various aspects of perceptions and attitudes.
- But there are particular shifts that are important to note (e.g. in Thailand and in Myanmar, especially over the 2007 to 2014 period).
- This reminds us that while radical shifts in perceptions may be rare or unlikely, they *do* occur and need to be monitored.

The following broad recommendations are offered for further consideration by policymakers and educators in ASEAN member states.

Continuing the Research

1. Further research or future surveys should look at measuring objective knowledge about the region and ASEAN, particularly the perceptions of how regional integration has affected people's lives, especially the AEC and its impact on people in the different member states. The continued upward trend of ASEAN citizenship notions and the interest to learn more about ASEAN provide a useful springboard for more purposeful research and discussion among the policy, business, and academic communities dealing with ASEAN integration issues and impacts.

Leveraging on Existing Networks

2.   ASEAN currently has several formal programmes for student and youth exchanges under sectoral cooperation mechanisms for education, youth, and culture. In addition, youth model ASEAN meetings are emerging more and more in ASEAN countries, most notably Singapore. However, networks forged at these meetings are usually not sustained over the long run. Using the survey findings as a starting or rallying point, these ASEAN bodies can consider initiating focused discussions or dialogues on the future of ASEAN among the youth participating in the various activities and projects, and thus build up a sustained network in the ASEAN member states.

3.   Most countries of ASEAN have an association facilitating preparations for young people to participate in model United Nations (UN) conferences. At the time of writing, we have learned that the ASEAN Foundation has embarked on an initiative to develop guidelines to facilitate a realistic simulation of modelling ASEAN meetings. Model ASEAN meetings may be a good way for young people to explore practical pathways for their aspirations for regional integration to be realized in one form or another. Model ASEAN associations/leagues, similar to those formed for model UN conferences, can further network among themselves and, with ASEAN organs involved in further promoting awareness of ASEAN such as the ASEAN Foundation and ASEAN Secretariat, exchange information and experiences as well as develop opportunities for youth participating in the model ASEAN meetings to meet with ASEAN decision makers at the annual ASEAN Summits.

Developing More Targeted Outreach and Communication on ASEAN

4.   The survey data can also be useful inputs for programmes and activities that communicate ASEAN integration issues to wider audiences, including the youth. Building on the findings of the 2007 and 2014 surveys, and under the overall framework of the ASEAN Communications Master Plan adopted in November 2014, officials (and researchers) involved in promoting ASEAN integration to the public could further discuss how country-specific findings will feed into respective national programmes, activities, and discussions on ASEAN, relevant to the next phases of regional integration and specific to particular audiences (e.g. students, young leaders, young professionals, practitioners, businesses).

5.   With the next phase of the ASEAN Community project, i.e. the Post-2015 Vision for ASEAN Community, to start implementation in 2016 and run through to 2025, the impact of economic globalization, open regionalism, and the global challenges of climate change and its attendant consequences will feature more largely as concerns for Southeast Asian citizens. It is timely for future surveys to focus on these aspects.

6.   Greater use of the ASEAN Curriculum Sourcebook — not just in schools but as a resource for educators at any level — to discuss relevant aspects of ASEAN integration will also help create more in-depth interest and discussion on ASEAN. Almost all of the survey respondents (in both 2007 and 2014) have expressed an interest to learn more of the region and the Association. ASEAN member countries — individually and collectively — have a rich store of information and intellectual resources on ASEAN to put to use.

Ultimately, community-building in ASEAN is people-driven. People-driven communities can work only if there is sufficient awareness and knowledge of the region, its aspirations, and the realities facing the achievement of these aspirations.

APPENDICES

Appendix A

ASEAN SURVEY 2014
RESEARCHERS AND ASSISTANTS

ASEAN Survey 2014 Researchers and Assistants

Name	Institution
Principal Investigators	
Eric C. Thompson	National University of Singapore
Chulanee Thianthai	Chulalongkorn University, Thailand
Moe Thuzar	ISEAS – Yusof Ishak Institute, Singapore

Research Assistants from ISEAS – Yusof Ishak Institute and National University of Singapore

Ms Pham Thi Phuong Thao	Research Officer
Ms Catherine James	Research Officer
Ms Sakunika Wewalaarichchi	Research Assistant
Mr Raymund Vitorio	Research Assistant
Ms Rachel Howard	Statistical Analyst

Undergraduate Research Opportunities Programme (UROP) Students from the National University of Singapore

Ms Kung Xin Ni	Ms Sylvia Oh
Ms Ong Lin Hui	Ms Teshura Nair
Ms Poon Yee Suan	

Research Coordinators	*Nation (University)*
Dr Rommel Curaming	Brunei (Universiti Brunei Darussalam)
Mr Men Prachvuthy	Cambodia (Royal University of Phnom Penh)
Dr Stefani Nugroho	Indonesia (Universitas Indonesia, Universitas Syiah Kuala, Universitas Nusa Cendana)
Mr Bounnhot Boupha	Laos (National University of Laos)
Dr Seyed Yasin Yazdi	Malaysia (University of Malaya)
Dr Chou Wen Loong	Malaysia (Universiti Tunku Abdul Rahman)
Mr Kuan Chee Wah	Malaysia (Universiti Tunku Abdul Rahman)
Dr Nurul Huda bt Marwan	Malaysia (Universiti Malaysia Sarawak)
Mr Ye Myat Thu	Myanmar (University of Yangon, University of Mandalay)
Dr Manuel Sapitula	The Philippines (University of the Philippines Diliman)
Dr Cristabel Parcon	The Philippines (University of the Philippines Visayas)
Dr Acram Latiph	The Philippines (Mindanao State University)
Mr Nattapon Meekaew	Thailand (Khon Kaen University)
Mr Manawat Promrat	Thailand (Walailak University)
Mr Dinh Quang Hung	Vietnam (Vietnam National University, Hanoi)
Dr Truong Thu Thi Hang	Vietnam (Vietnam National University, Ho Chi Minh City)

Appendix B

ASEAN SURVEY 2014
SURVEY QUESTIONNAIRE SAMPLES
(LIST AND MAP)

SAMPLE QUESTIONNAIRE

The sample questionnaire on the following pages shows the standard questions asked at all the selected universities in ASEAN member nations. All of the substantive questions were asked in all nations. Citizenship, sex, age, year in university, and main subject of study were included in all questionnaires. Other demographic questions were included to fit local conditions in each nation. Subjects of study in most cases were Social Sciences and Humanities (Subject 1), Sciences (Subject 2), Engineering (Subject 3) and Other (Subject 4). However, in some cases, such as the vocational-technical universities (Singapore Polytechnic, Saint John's University), a different distribution of subjects was used as relevant to that university; the purpose of the question was for enumerators to collect a diversity of responses, with no one subject representing more than 50 per cent of the sample.

Two versions of the questionnaire, a List and a Map version were administered at each university. The only difference between the two versions was the second substantive question (Q2). Half of the respondents were given the List version of Q2 and the other half the Map version.

The 2014 Questionnaire replicated all questions from the 2007 Questionnaire, except that Q13 was new, replacing a poorly worded question from the 2007 Questionnaire. Question 19, one word descriptions, and Question 20, sixty randomized triads, were newly added for the 2014 Questionnaire.

At each university, the questionnaire was administered in the main language of instruction at that university, as follows:

Nation, University	*Language*
Brunei, University Brunei Darussalam	Bahasa Melayu
Cambodia, Royal University of Phnom Penh	Khmer
Indonesia, University of Indonesia	Bahasa Indonesia
Laos, National University of Laos	Lao
Malaysia, University of Malaya	Bahasa Malaysia
Mynamar, Distance education students	Burmese
Philippines, University of the Philippines	English
Singapore, National University of Singapore	English
Thailand, Chulalongkorn University	Thai
Vietnam, Vietnam National University (Hanoi)	Vietnamese

ASEAN SURVEY

The purpose of this survey is to assess awareness and opinions about the Association of Southeast Asian Nations (ASEAN). The survey is sponsored by the ASEAN Foundation. Please ANSWER ALL of the questions. If you are not sure about an answer, please give your BEST GUESS. Thank you for your participation.

***** **Please complete this information about yourself** *****

Are you a citizen of Singapore?   1. Yes   2. No

Sex: 1. Male   2. Female

Age: _____

Year in University: 1. First Year
                                    2. Second Year
                                    3. Third Year
                                    4. Fourth Year
                                    5. Other: _____

Main subject of study: 1. Social Science and Humanities
                                    2. Sciences
                                    3. Engineering
                                    4. Other: _____

Where were you born: _____

What is your ethnicity: 1. Chinese
                                    2. Malay
                                    3. Indian
                                    4. Other: _____

What is your religion:

1. Buddhism
2. Christian/Catholic
3. Hindu
4. Islam
5. Taoist/Chinese
6. Other: _____

When speaking with
friends and
family, what language
do you use
MOST OFTEN: _____

***** PLEASE COMPLETE THE FOLLOWING QUESTIONS*****
PLEASE CIRCLE YOUR ANSWERS.
IF YOU ARE NOT SURE, GIVE YOUR BEST GUESS.

Q1.   In general, how familiar are you with ASEAN?
        A.   Very Familiar
        B.   Somewhat Familiar
        C.   A Little Familiar
        D.   Not at All Familiar

Q2(L): List the Ten Countries in the Association of Southeast Asian
        Nations (ASEAN). (If you are not sure, give your BEST
        GUESS.)

        1.   _____

        2.   _____

        3.   _____

        4.   _____

        5.   _____

        6.   _____

        7.   _____

        8.   _____

        9.   _____

        10. _____

Q2(M): List the names of the ASEAN Countries according to the map below.

(If you are not sure, give your BEST GUESS.)

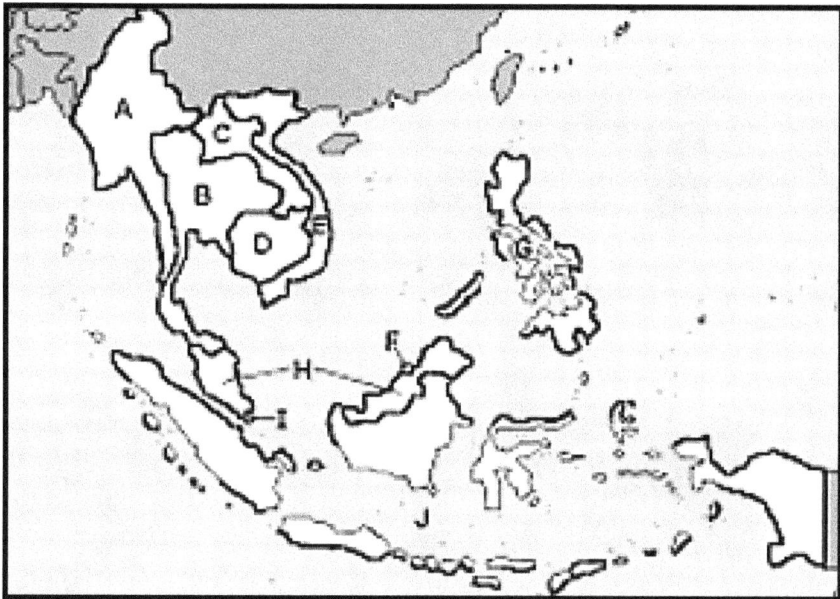

A. _____   B. _____

C. _____   D. _____

E. _____   F. _____

G. _____   H. _____

I. _____   J. _____

Q3.   Which of the following is the flag of ASEAN?
       (Circle the letter above the correct flag; if you are not sure,
       give your BEST GUESS.)

A

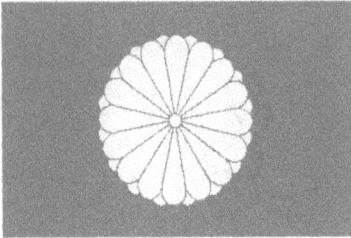

B

C

D

E

F

Q4.   What year was ASEAN founded?
      (Circle your answer; if you are not sure, give your BEST
      GUESS.)

      1947   1957   1967   1977   1987   1997

Q5.   ASEAN countries are similar culturally.
      A.   Strongly Agree
      B.   Somewhat Agree
      C.   Somewhat Disagree
      D.   Strongly Disagree

Q6.   ASEAN countries are similar economically.
      A.   Strongly Agree
      B.   Somewhat Agree
      C.   Somewhat Disagree
      D.   Strongly Disagree

Q7.   ASEAN countries are similar politically.
      A.   Strongly Agree
      B.   Somewhat Agree
      C.   Somewhat Disagree
      D.   Strongly Disagree

Q8.   Membership in ASEAN is beneficial to my country.
      A.   Strongly Agree
      B.   Somewhat Agree
      C.   Somewhat Disagree
      D.   Strongly Disagree

Q9.   My country's membership in ASEAN is beneficial to me
      personally.
      A.   Strongly Agree
      B.   Somewhat Agree
      C.   Somewhat Disagree
      D.   Strongly Disagree

Q10. In what ways have you learned about ASEAN?
      (Circle ALL that apply)

      A.   Advertising   B.   Books
      C.   Television   D.   Radio
      E.   Newspaper   F.   Internet
      G.   Movies   H.   Music
      I.   Sports   J.   Family Members
      K.   Friends   L.   School
      M.   Travelling   N.   Work Experiences
      O.   Other: _____   P.   None of the Above

Q11. Please give your opinion of the importance of the following
      aspects of integration and cooperation among ASEAN
      countries:

      a.   Cultural Exchanges among ASEAN countries are
           important.
           A.   Strongly Agree
           B.   Somewhat Agree
           C.   Somewhat Disagree
           D.   Strongly Disagree

b. Economic Cooperation among ASEAN countries is
    important.
    A. Strongly Agree
    B. Somewhat Agree
    C. Somewhat Disagree
    D. Strongly Disagree

c. Development Assistance among ASEAN countries is
    important.
    A. Strongly Agree
    B. Somewhat Agree
    C. Somewhat Disagree
    D. Strongly Disagree

d. Educational Exchanges among ASEAN countries are
    important.
    A. Strongly Agree
    B. Somewhat Agree
    C. Somewhat Disagree
    D. Strongly Disagree

e. Security and Military Cooperation among ASEAN
    countries is important.
    A. Strongly Agree
    B. Somewhat Agree
    C. Somewhat Disagree
    D. Strongly Disagree

f.   Political Cooperation among ASEAN countries is important.
    A.   Strongly Agree
    B.   Somewhat Agree
    C.   Somewhat Disagree
    D. Strongly Disagree

g.   Sports Competitions among ASEAN countries are important.
    A.   Strongly Agree
    B.   Somewhat Agree
    C.   Somewhat Disagree
    D.   Strongly Disagree

h.   Tourism among ASEAN countries is important.
    A.   Strongly Agree
    B.   Somewhat Agree
    C.   Somewhat Disagree
    D.   Strongly Disagree

Q12. I feel that I am a citizen of ASEAN.
    A.   Strongly Agree
    B.   Somewhat Agree
    C.   Somewhat Disagree
    D.   Strongly Disagree

Q13. The future of ASEAN is important.
    A.   Strongly Agree
    B.   Somewhat Agree
    C.   Somewhat Disagree
    D.   Strongly Disagree

Q14. Besides my own country, I am most familiar with the following three ASEAN countries (please list three countries):

Country 1: _____

Country 2: _____

Country 3: _____

Q15. If I could travel to another country in ASEAN, I would most like to travel to:

Name of Country: _____

Q16. If I could work in another country in ASEAN, I would most like to work in:

Name of Country: _____

Q17. I would like to know more about other ASEAN countries.
A. Strongly Agree
B. Somewhat Agree
C. Somewhat Disagree
D. Strongly Disagree

Q18. Please circle the issues that you feel are most crucial for ASEAN to enhance cooperation and awareness:
A. Health maintenance and disease control
B. Natural resources and environmental management
C. Disaster prevention, relief, and recovery assistance
D. Educational improvements and exchanges
E. Reduction of poverty and economic disparities
F. Science and technology development and applications
G. Cultural, literary, and artistic preservation and promotion
H. Regional identity and solidarity enhancement
I. Others (please specify): _____

Q19. Write ONE word for each of the following countries or regions.
       Write the first word that comes to mind.

Africa _____   America _____

ASEAN _____   Brunei _____

Cambodia _____   China _____

Europe _____   Indonesia _____

India _____   Japan _____

Korea _____   Laos _____

Malaysia _____   Mexico _____

Myanmar _____   Philippines _____

Saudi Arabia _____   Singapore _____

Thailand _____   Vietnam _____

Q20. For each SET OF THREE of countries below, CIRCLE the country MOST DIFFERENT from the other two.

For example, in the set: HORSE   ROCK   COW
You would circle ROCK.

DO NOT SKIP ANY SETS. If you are not sure, just circle one.

BRUNEI	MALAYSIA	INDONESIA
VIETNAM	THAILAND	MALAYSIA
MALAYSIA	BRUNEI	SINGAPORE
CAMBODIA	MALAYSIA	THAILAND
PHILIPPINES	VIETNAM	INDONESIA
PHILIPPINES	BRUNEI	VIETNAM
VIETNAM	THAILAND	BRUNEI
CAMBODIA	SINGAPORE	VIETNAM
CAMBODIA	VIETNAM	MALAYSIA
MALAYSIA	MYANMAR	LAOS
LAOS	PHILIPPINES	BRUNEI
CAMBODIA	BRUNEI	PHILIPPINES
VIETNAM	MYANMAR	SINGAPORE
INDONESIA	LAOS	THAILAND
PHILIPPINES	LAOS	SINGAPORE
INDONESIA	LAOS	MALAYSIA
PHILIPPINES	VIETNAM	MALAYSIA
MALAYSIA	SINGAPORE	THAILAND
BRUNEI	CAMBODIA	SINGAPORE
THAILAND	BRUNEI	INDONESIA
LAOS	THAILAND	BRUNEI
MYANMAR	PHILIPPINES	SINGAPORE
MYANMAR	INDONESIA	BRUNEI
SINGAPORE	MYANMAR	BRUNEI
MALAYSIA	INDONESIA	SINGAPORE
VIETNAM	PHILIPPINES	LAOS
VIETNAM	MYANMAR	BRUNEI
LAOS	MALAYSIA	VIETNAM

Continue on next page.

Q20 (continued).

PHILIPPINES	SINGAPORE	INDONESIA
LAOS	THAILAND	SINGAPORE
INDONESIA	LAOS	CAMBODIA
THAILAND	SINGAPORE	PHILIPPINES
LAOS	PHILIPPINES	CAMBODIA
THAILAND	PHILIPPINES	BRUNEI
SINGAPORE	LAOS	MYANMAR
VIETNAM	SINGAPORE	INDONESIA
INDONESIA	MYANMAR	PHILIPPINES
MYANMAR	CAMBODIA	PHILIPPINES
VIETNAM	SINGAPORE	THAILAND
CAMBODIA	VIETNAM	LAOS
LAOS	THAILAND	MYANMAR
PHILIPPINES	CAMBODIA	THAILAND
MYANMAR	MALAYSIA	CAMBODIA
INDONESIA	CAMBODIA	BRUNEI
CAMBODIA	SINGAPORE	INDONESIA
VIETNAM	INDONESIA	MYANMAR
CAMBODIA	BRUNEI	VIETNAM
MALAYSIA	MYANMAR	BRUNEI
BRUNEI	SINGAPORE	LAOS
INDONESIA	MALAYSIA	PHILIPPINES
THAILAND	CAMBODIA	MYANMAR
CAMBODIA	MALAYSIA	SINGAPORE
VIETNAM	MYANMAR	THAILAND
INDONESIA	THAILAND	MYANMAR
CAMBODIA	INDONESIA	THAILAND
LAOS	BRUNEI	MALAYSIA
PHILIPPINES	MALAYSIA	THAILAND
PHILIPPINES	MYANMAR	MALAYSIA
MYANMAR	CAMBODIA	LAOS
LAOS	INDONESIA	VIETNAM

END

Appendix C

DEMOGRAPHICS OF RESPONDENTS

Number of Respondents by Gender

Primary Universities	Male	Female	No Response	Total
Brunei (B1)	100	100	0	200
Cambodia (C1)	116	124	1	240
Indonesia (I1)	103	102	0	205
Laos (L1)	112	108	0	220
Malaysia (M1)	103	100	0	203
Myanmar (N2)	98	109	2	209
Philippines (P1)	103	115	2	220
Singapore (S1)	104	108	0	212
Thailand (T1)	104	104	0	208
Vietnam (V1)	110	109	1	220
Total Primary	**1,053**	**1,079**	**6**	**2,137**
Additional Universities				
Unsyiah (I2)	98	102	0	200
Undana (I3)	101	100	0	201
UTAR (M2)	98	111	1	210
Unimas (M3)	102	118	0	220
YU (N1)	55	116	6	177
UP Visayas (P2)	103	105	0	208
MSU (P3)	92	127	0	219
SP (S2)	109	131	0	240
KKU (T2)	66	146	1	213
WU (T3)	79	127	0	206
SJU (T4)	100	78	0	178
VNU-HCMC (V2)	106	106	0	214
Total Additional	**1,109**	**1,367**	**8**	**2,486**
Total	**2,162**	**2,446**	**14**	**4,623**

Percentage of Respondents by Gender

Primary Universities	Male	Female	No Response
Brunei (B1)	50.0%	50.0%	0.0%
Cambodia (C1)	48.3%	51.7%	0.0%
Indonesia (I1)	50.2%	49.8%	0.0%
Laos (L1)	50.9%	49.1%	0.0%
Malaysia (M1)	50.7%	49.3%	0.0%
Myanmar (N2)	46.9%	52.2%	1.0%
Philippines (P1)	46.8%	52.3%	0.9%
Singapore (S1)	49.1%	50.9%	0.0%
Thailand (T1)	50.0%	50.0%	0.0%
Vietnam (V1)	50.0%	49.5%	0.5%
Average Primary	**49.3%**	**50.5%**	**0.2%**
Additional Universities			
Unsyiah (I2)	49.0%	50.0%	0.0%
Undana (I3)	50.3%	49.8%	0.0%
UTAR (M2)	46.7%	52.9%	0.5%
Unimas (M3)	46.4%	53.6%	0.0%
YU (N1)	31.1%	65.5%	3.4%
UP Visayas (P2)	49.5%	50.5%	0.0%
MSU (P3)	42.0%	58.0%	0.0%
SP (S2)	45.4%	54.6%	0.0%
KKU (T2)	31.0%	68.5%	0.5%
WU (T3)	38.4%	61.7%	0.0%
SJU (T4)	56.2%	43.8%	0.0%
VNU-HCMC (V2)	49.5%	50.5%	0.0%
Average Additional	**44.6%**	**54.9%**	**0.4%**
Average Total	**46.7%**	**52.9%**	**0.3%**

Age of Respondents

Primary Universities	Mean Age	Minimum Age	Maximum Age
Brunei (B1)	21	17	30
Cambodia (C1)	21	18	30
Indonesia (I1)	20	17	25
Laos (L1)	22	18	30
Malaysia (M1)	22	18	25
Myanmar (N2)	20	15	43
Philippines (P1)	19	16	25
Singapore (S1)	22	18	31
Thailand (T1)	19	17	23
Vietnam (V1)	19	18	23
Average Primary	**20.5**	**17.2**	**28.5**
Additional Universities			
Unsyiah (I2)	21	18	25
Undana (I3)	21	17	30
UTAR (M2)	21	17	28
Unimas (M3)	22	19	30
YU (N1)	29	19	57
UP Visayas (P2)	18	15	22
MSU (P3)	20	16	27
SP (S2)	18	16	24
KKU (T2)	21	14	53
WU (T3)	19	18	23
SJU (T4)	18	16	23
VNU-HCMC (V2)	19	18	25
Average Additional	**20.6**	**16.7**	**30.1**
Average Total	**20.5**	**17.0**	**29.6**

Year in University (n)

Primary Universities	First Year	Second Year	Third Year	Fourth Year	Others	No Response	Total
Brunei (B1)	111	51	5	16	17	0	200
Cambodia (C1)	47	69	88	36	0	0	240
Indonesia (I1)	13	82	62	25	22	0	204
Laos (L1)	1	46	109	33	31	0	220
Malaysia (M1)	61	68	59	14	1	0	203
Myanmar (N2)	31	54	47	22	51	4	209
Philippines (P1)	35	46	57	57	25	0	220
Singapore (S1)	30	53	56	62	10	1	212
Thailand (T1)	92	39	27	49	1	0	208
Vietnam (V1)	77	45	69	24	3	2	220
Total Primary	**498**	**553**	**579**	**338**	**161**	**7**	**2,136**
Additional Universities							
Unsyiah (I2)	17	38	58	76	11	0	200
Undana (I3)	42	26	62	56	15	0	201
UTAR (M2)	88	75	38	8	1	0	210
Unimas (M3)	50	70	92	8	0	0	220
YU (N1)	8	0	0	22	137	10	177
UP Visayas (P2)	45	43	60	58	2	0	208
MSU (P3)	20	45	60	60	21	2	208
SP (S2)	117	57	45	1	0	20	240
KKU (T2)	89	21	45	47	3	8	213
WU (T3)	128	40	30	6	1	1	206
SJU (T4)	7	44	105	0	22	0	178
VNU-HCMC (V2)	81	73	32	26	2	0	214
Total Additional	**692**	**532**	**627**	**368**	**215**	**41**	**2,475**
Total	**1,190**	**1,085**	**1,206**	**706**	**376**	**48**	**4,611**

Year in University (%)

Primary Universities	First Year	Second Year	Third Year	Fourth Year	Others	No Response
Brunei (B1)	55.5%	25.5%	2.5%	8.0%	8.5%	0.0%
Cambodia (C1)	19.6%	28.8%	36.7%	15.0%	0.0%	0.0%
Indonesia (I1)	6.4%	40.2%	30.4%	12.3%	10.8%	0.0%
Laos (L1)	0.5%	20.9%	49.6%	15.0%	14.1%	0.0%
Malaysia (M1)	30.1%	33.5%	29.1%	6.9%	0.5%	0.0%
Myanmar (N2)	14.8%	25.8%	22.5%	10.5%	24.4%	1.9%
Philippines (P1)	15.9%	20.9%	25.9%	25.9%	11.4%	0.0%
Singapore (S1)	14.2%	25.0%	26.4%	29.3%	4.7%	0.5%
Thailand (T1)	44.2%	18.8%	13.0%	23.6%	0.5%	0.0%
Vietnam (V1)	35.0%	20.5%	31.4%	10.9%	1.4%	0.9%
Average Primary	**23.6%**	**26.0%**	**26.7%**	**15.7%**	**7.6%**	**0.3%**
Additional Universities						
Unsyiah (I2)	8.5%	19.0%	29.0%	38.0%	5.5%	0.0%
Undana (I3)	20.9%	12.9%	30.9%	27.9%	7.5%	0.0%
UTAR (M2)	41.9%	35.7%	18.1%	3.8%	0.5%	0.9%
Unimas (M3)	22.7%	31.8%	41.8%	3.6%	0.0%	0.0%
YU (N1)	4.5%	0.0%	0.0%	12.4%	77.4%	5.7%
UP Visayas (P2)	21.6%	20.7%	28.9%	27.9%	1.0%	0.0%
MSU (P3)	9.6%	21.6%	28.8%	28.8%	10.1%	1.0%
SP (S2)	48.8%	23.8%	18.8%	0.4%	0.0%	8.3%
KKU (T2)	41.8%	9.9%	21.1%	22.1%	1.4%	3.8%
WU (T3)	61.1%	19.4%	14.6%	2.9%	0.5%	0.5%
SJU (T4)	3.9%	24.7%	59.0%	0.0%	12.4%	0.0%
VNU-HCMC (V2)	37.9%	34.1%	15.0%	12.2%	0.9%	0.0%
Average Additional	**26.9%**	**21.1%**	**25.5%**	**15.0%**	**9.8%**	**1.7%**
Average Total	**25.4%**	**23.3%**	**26.1%**	**15.3%**	**8.8%**	**1.1%**

Subject of Study (n)

Primary Universities	Subject 1	Subject 2	Subject 3	Others	No Response	Total
Brunei (B1)	80	57	9	54	0	200
Cambodia (C1)	115	124	0	1	0	240
Indonesia (I1)	103	7	70	25	0	205
Laos (L1)	51	0	1	168	0	220
Malaysia (M1)	101	34	20	48	0	203
Myanmar (N2)	82	66	33	20	8	209
Philippines (P1)	68	37	32	81	2	220
Singapore (S1)	94	41	48	29	0	212
Thailand (T1)	102	81	25	0	0	208
Vietnam (V1)	103	59	53	2	3	220
Total Primary	**899**	**506**	**291**	**428**	**13**	**2,137**
Additional Universities						
Unsyiah (I2)	83	25	29	63	0	200
Undana (I3)	100	8	21	72	0	201
UTAR (M2)	94	82	17	17	0	210
Unimas (M3)	115	42	11	35	16	219
YU (N1)	57	7	2	95	16	177
UP Visayas (P2)	103	95	6	4	0	208
MSU (P3)	53	21	33	106	6	219
SP (S2)	47	27	58	107	1	240
KKU (T2)	101	62	27	18	5	213
WU (T3)	41	6	11	147	1	206
SJU (T4)	77	26	54	21	0	178
VNU-HCMC (V2)	109	46	54	5	0	214
Total Additional	**980**	**447**	**323**	**690**	**45**	**2,485**
Total	**1,879**	**953**	**614**	**1,118**	**58**	**4,622**

Subject of Study (%)

Primary Universities	Subject 1	Subject 2	Subject 3	Others	No Response
Brunei (B1)	40.0%	28.5%	4.5%	27.0%	0.0%
Cambodia (C1)	47.9%	51.7%	0.0%	0.4%	0.0%
Indonesia (I1)	50.2%	3.4%	34.2%	12.2%	0.0%
Laos (L1)	23.3%	0.0%	0.5%	76.4%	0.0%
Malaysia (M1)	49.8%	16.8%	9.9%	23.7%	0.0%
Myanmar (N2)	39.2%	31.6%	15.8%	9.6%	3.8%
Philippines (P1)	30.9%	16.8%	14.6%	36.8%	0.9%
Singapore (S1)	44.3%	19.3%	22.6%	13.7%	0.0%
Thailand (T1)	49.0%	38.9%	12.0%	0.0%	0.0%
Vietnam (V1)	46.8%	26.8%	24.1%	0.9%	1.4%
Average Primary	**42.1%**	**23.4%**	**13.8%**	**20.1%**	**0.6%**
Additional Universities					
Unsyiah (I2)	41.5%	12.5%	14.5%	31.5%	0.0%
Undana (I3)	49.8%	4.0%	10.5%	35.8%	0.0%
UTAR (M2)	44.8%	39.1%	8.1%	8.1%	0.0%
Unimas (M3)	52.5%	19.2%	5.0%	15.9%	7.3%
YU (N1)	32.2%	4.0%	1.1%	53.7%	9.0%
UP Visayas (P2)	49.5%	45.7%	2.9%	1.9%	0.0%
MSU (P3)	24.2%	9.6%	15.1%	48.4%	2.7%
SP (S2)	19.6%	11.3%	24.2%	44.6%	0.4%
KKU (T2)	47.4%	29.1%	12.7%	8.5%	2.4%
WU (T3)	19.9%	2.9%	5.3%	71.4%	0.5%
SJU (T4)	43.3%	14.6%	30.3%	11.8%	0.0%
VNU-HCMC (V2)	50.9%	21.5%	25.2%	2.3%	0.0%
Average Additional	**39.6%**	**17.8%**	**12.9%**	**27.8%**	**1.9%**
Average Total	**40.8%**	**20.3%**	**13.3%**	**24.3%**	**1.3%**

Appendix D

SALIENCE TABLES BASED ON LISTING ASEAN COUNTRIES

SALIENCE TABLES

The following tables are based on responses to Q2 List Question ("List the Ten Countries in the Association of Southeast Asian Nations (ASEAN)"). The first table shows the rank by salience of each country (item, in rows) at each primary university (columns) along with the average rank (Avg Rank) across all primary universities. Subsequent tables record the detailed results from each primary university.

Countries are ordered (ranked) by Smith's Salience Index (Smith's S), a measure of salience that combines frequency (how often a country was listed) and priority (did respondents tend to list the country earlier or later in the list). Smith's S gives a score of between one and zero to each country listed, based on frequency (how often a country was listed) and priority (how close to the top of each list a country appears). A score of 1.0 would mean that the country was listed first on every list by every student. As the score approaches zero, it indicates that the country is only listed by a few or just one student and that it comes to mind (at the end of the list) only after students have thought of all other countries.

TABLE D1
Average Salience Rank Regionally

Country	University										Avg Rank
	B1	C1	I1	L1	M1	N2	P1	S1	T1	V1	
Thailand	4	1	4	1	2	2	4	5	1	3	2.7
Malaysia	2	9	2	6	1	4	2	2	5	7	4
Singapore	5	5	3	5	4	6	6	1	7	6	4.8
Indonesia	3	8	1	8	3	7	3	3	8	5	4.9
Vietnam	7	4	6	3	5	8	5	4	6	1	4.9
Laos	9	3	8	2	9	3	7	6	2	2	5.1
Cambodia	8	2	9	4	10	5	8	7	4	4	6.1
Myanmar	10	6	10	7	8	1	9	10	3	8	7.2
Philippines	6	7	7	10	6	9	1	8	10	9	7.3
Brunei	1	10	5	9	7	10	10	9	9	10	8

TABLE D2
Brunei (B1), University of Brunei Darussalam, n=100

Country	Frequency	Per Cent	Avg Rank	Smith's S
Brunei	99	99	1.758	0.914
Malaysia	100	100	2.89	0.808
Indonesia	99	99	5.212	0.566
Thailand	98	98	5.265	0.556
Singapore	97	97	5.351	0.54
Philippines	92	92	6.272	0.426
Vietnam	95	95	6.442	0.424
Cambodia	89	89	6.36	0.407
Laos	85	85	7.247	0.314
Myanmar	79	79	7.304	0.288
China	12	12	6.083	0.059
Timor Leste	15	15	8.4	0.039
Japan	7	7	7.714	0.022
Korea	6	6	7.833	0.019
Taiwan	3	3	8.667	0.007
India	4	4	9.5	0.006
Hanoi	1	1	9	0.002

TABLE D3
Cambodia (C1), Royal University Phnom Pehn, n=110

Country	Frequency	Per Cent	Avg Rank	Smith's S
Thailand	110	100	2.4	0.857
Cambodia	110	100	3.009	0.793
Laos	109	99	4.339	0.651
Vietnam	107	97	4.804	0.594
Singapore	106	96	6.075	0.463
Myanmar	108	98	6.213	0.457
Philippines	100	91	6.58	0.39
Indonesia	98	89	6.633	0.38
Malaysia	95	86	6.937	0.342
Brunei	99	90	7.101	0.337
China	10	9	6.5	0.04
America	4	4	5	0.021
India	3	3	8.333	0.007
Japan	4	4	9	0.006
Korea	2	2	7.5	0.006
Timor Leste	1	1	6	0.005
Sri Lanka	1	1	7	0.004
Canada	1	1	8	0.003
Tibet	1	1	9	0.002

TABLE D4
Indonesia (I1), Universitas Indonesia, n=103

Country	Frequency	Per Cent	Avg Rank	Smith's S
Indonesia	103	100	1.728	0.927
Malaysia	103	100	2.699	0.829
Singapore	102	99	4.157	0.676
Thailand	101	98	4.911	0.595
Brunei	100	97	6.47	0.439
Vietnam	100	97	6.55	0.43
Philippines	100	97	6.88	0.399
Laos	102	99	7.059	0.387
Cambodia	96	93	6.969	0.374
Myanmar	98	95	7.255	0.353
Timor Leste	10	10	7.7	0.031
Japan	3	3	6.333	0.014
Papua New Guinea	2	2	9.5	0.002
Hong Kong	1	1	9	0.002
Sri Lanka	1	1	10	0.001
Korea	1	1	10	0.001

TABLE D5
Indonesia (I2), Universitas Syiah Kuala, Aceh, n=99

Country	Frequency	Per Cent	Avg Rank	Smith's S
Indonesia	97	98	1.412	0.939
Malaysia	98	99	3.122	0.761
Thailand	95	96	4.926	0.566
Singapore	92	93	5.424	0.506
Brunei	92	93	5.783	0.47
Vietnam	94	95	6.351	0.425
Philippines	84	85	6.512	0.374
Laos	88	89	6.716	0.372
Myanmar	85	86	6.741	0.353
Cambodia	85	86	6.976	0.335
China	9	9	4.889	0.056
Japan	5	5	4	0.035
Timor Leste	8	8	8.75	0.013
India	2	2	5.5	0.009
America	1	1	5	0.006
Chile	2	2	8.5	0.005
Bangladesh	1	1	6	0.005
Korea	1	1	7	0.004
Sri Lanka	1	1	8	0.003

TABLE D6
Indonesia (I3), Universitas Nusa Cendana, Kupang, n=100

Country	Frequency	Per Cent	Avg Rank	Smith's S
Indonesia	99	99	1.646	0.925
Malaysia	95	95	4.063	0.657
Singapore	97	97	4.887	0.589
Thailand	94	94	5.904	0.476
Philippines	91	91	6	0.449
Brunei	88	88	6.045	0.434
Cambodia	90	90	6.311	0.418
Laos	93	93	6.473	0.416
Myanmar	85	85	6.294	0.397
Vietnam	77	77	6.299	0.36
Timor Leste	31	31	7.871	0.094
Japan	9	9	6	0.045
Korea	6	6	4.667	0.038
China	9	9	8.222	0.025
India	4	4	6	0.02
Australia	4	4	6.25	0.019
Saudi Arabia	2	2	3	0.016
America	1	1	1	0.01
Bangladesh	1	1	2	0.009
Kuala Lumpur	1	1	2	0.009
Bangkok	1	1	2	0.009
Chile	1	1	5	0.006
Papua New Guinea	2	2	8	0.006
Iraq	2	2	9	0.004
Iran	2	2	9	0.004
Maladewa	1	1	8	0.003
Africa	3	3	10	0.003

TABLE D7
Laos (L1), National University of Laos, n=110

Country	Frequency	Per Cent	Avg Rank	Smith's S
Thailand	110	100	2.755	0.824
Laos	105	95	2.619	0.799
Vietnam	110	100	4.2	0.678
Cambodia	106	96	5.283	0.55
Singapore	106	96	5.811	0.498
Malaysia	107	97	6.131	0.47
Myanmar	107	97	6.234	0.463
Indonesia	106	96	6.745	0.407
Brunei	105	95	7.352	0.344
Philippines	99	90	7.333	0.328
China	10	9	5.4	0.051
Japan	4	4	5.5	0.019
India	3	3	6	0.014
Timor Leste	8	7	9.875	0.008
America	2	2	8	0.005
France	1	1	8	0.003
Taiwan	2	2	10	0.002
Mexico	1	1	10	0.001

TABLE D8
Malaysia (M1), University of Malaya, n=103

Country	Frequency	Per Cent	Avg Rank	Smith's S
Malaysia	97	94	1.794	0.861
Thailand	99	96	3.909	0.663
Indonesia	98	95	3.98	0.647
Singapore	89	86	4.596	0.533
Vietnam	90	87	5.578	0.449
Philippines	87	84	5.678	0.425
Brunei	79	77	6.127	0.355
Myanmar	82	80	6.378	0.344
Laos	71	69	6.775	0.281
Cambodia	70	68	7.214	0.241
China	22	21	5.909	0.104
Japan	19	18	6.579	0.074
Korea	11	11	6.636	0.043
Timor Leste	14	14	8.143	0.036
India	10	10	7.9	0.025
Sri Lanka	3	3	7.333	0.011
Taiwan	2	2	7	0.008
England	1	1	4	0.007
Australia	3	3	8	0.006
Riau	1	1	7	0.003
Papua New Guinea	1	1	8	0.003
Turkey	1	1	8	0.003
Sumatera	1	1	8	0.003
Jawa Timur	1	1	9	0.002
Saudi Arabia	1	1	7	0.001
Bangladesh	1	1	10	0.001

TABLE D9
Malaysia (M2), Universiti Tunku Abdul Rahman (UTAR), n=97

Country	Frequency	Per Cent	Avg Rank	Smith's S
Malaysia	90	93	2.256	0.811
Thailand	89	92	4.539	0.589
Singapore	83	86	4.398	0.565
Indonesia	86	89	5.151	0.518
Vietnam	80	82	5.613	0.441
Philippines	66	68	6.045	0.336
Brunei	64	66	6.609	0.29
Cambodia	55	57	6.4	0.26
China	45	46	5.6	0.25
Japan	41	42	5.61	0.227
Myanmar	52	54	6.885	0.219
Korea	34	35	5.706	0.184
Laos	48	49	7.417	0.177
America	19	20	5.947	0.098
India	17	18	6.765	0.074
Taiwan	13	13	6	0.066
Australia	10	10	5.5	0.057
Hong Kong	11	11	5.636	0.056
Africa	6	6	6.667	0.027
England	8	8	7.75	0.027
Germany	5	5	6.2	0.025
Europe	3	3	4.667	0.02
Portugal	2	2	2.5	0.018
Columbia	2	2	3	0.016
Russia	3	3	7	0.012
Brazil	3	3	7	0.012
Saudi Arabia	3	3	7.667	0.01
Uruguay	1	1	3	0.008
South Africa	1	1	4	0.007
Bangladesh	1	1	4	0.007
Iraq	1	1	5	0.006
Nepal	2	2	8	0.006
Dubai	2	2	8.5	0.005
New Zealand	2	2	9	0.004

TABLE D9 (continued)

Country	Frequency	Per Cent	Avg Rank	Smith's S
France	3	3	10	0.003
Seoul	1	1	8	0.003
Sumatera	1	1	8	0.003
Ivory	1	1	8	0.003
Ghana	1	1	9	0.002
Iran	1	1	10	0.001
Manila	1	1	10	0.001
Asgard	1	1	10	0.001
Macau	1	1	10	0.001
Pakistan	1	1	10	0.001

TABLE D10
Malaysia (M3), Universiti Malaysia Sarawak (Unimas), n=44

Country	Frequency	Per Cent	Avg Rank	Smith's S
Malaysia	43	98	2.093	0.87
Thailand	44	100	4.386	0.657
Singapore	44	100	4.705	0.626
Indonesia	41	93	4.415	0.611
Philippines	41	93	5.439	0.515
Brunei	39	89	5.282	0.504
Vietnam	40	91	6.25	0.429
Myanmar	36	82	7.056	0.319
Cambodia	32	73	6.906	0.293
Laos	36	82	7.417	0.289
China	15	34	6.267	0.16
Japan	8	18	6.625	0.08
Korea	7	16	8.714	0.036
Netherlands	1	2	5	0.014
England	1	2	8	0.007
Timor Leste	3	7	10	0.007
India	1	2	8	0.007
Papua New Guinea	1	2	9	0.005
Denmark	1	2	9	0.005
America	1	2	10	0.002

TABLE D11
Myanmar (N2), University of Mandalay, n=106

Country	Frequency	Per Cent	Avg Rank	Smith's S
Myanmar	104	98	2.875	0.796
Thailand	105	99	3.019	0.789
Laos	105	99	4.648	0.628
Malaysia	103	97	5.718	0.511
Cambodia	99	93	5.525	0.509
Singapore	104	98	5.894	0.501
Indonesia	99	93	6.253	0.443
Vietnam	100	94	6.34	0.437
Philippines	95	90	7.232	0.334
Brunei	91	86	7.462	0.3
China	21	20	5	0.118
Timor Leste	8	8	7.625	0.025
India	6	6	7.167	0.022
Bangladesh	4	4	5.75	0.02
Japan	4	4	8.25	0.01
Bhutan	1	1	10	0.001
Hong Kong	1	1	10	0.001

TABLE D12
Myanmar (N1), University of Yangon (YU), n=35

Country	Frequency	Per Cent	Avg Rank	Smith's S
Myanmar	34	97	2.059	0.869
Thailand	35	100	3.686	0.724
Singapore	35	100	5.114	0.573
Laos	34	97	5.235	0.557
Malaysia	34	97	5.353	0.543
Indonesia	34	97	5.971	0.482
Cambodia	33	94	6.333	0.438
Philippines	34	97	6.765	0.405
Vietnam	31	89	6.645	0.384
Brunei	32	91	7.094	0.354
China	1	3	6	0.014
East Timor	2	6	9	0.011
Korea	1	3	10	0.003

TABLE D13
Philippines (P1), University of the Philippines Diliman, n=109

Country	Frequency	Per Cent	Avg Rank	Smith's S
Philippines	108	99	1.731	0.915
Malaysia	101	93	4.178	0.621
Indonesia	102	94	4.853	0.564
Thailand	97	89	4.969	0.524
Vietnam	99	91	5.313	0.507
Singapore	96	88	5.531	0.477
Laos	91	83	6.374	0.381
Cambodia	94	86	6.66	0.37
Myanmar	83	76	7.542	0.258
Brunei	75	69	7.6	0.232
Taiwan	19	17	5.579	0.085
Japan	16	15	5.563	0.077
Korea	10	9	3.6	0.066
China	11	10	5.636	0.049
Timor Leste	9	8	7.667	0.028
Hong Kong	8	7	7.625	0.025
Sri Lanka	4	4	7.5	0.012
India	1	1	5	0.006
Papua New Guinea	2	2	8	0.006
Iran	1	1	6	0.003
Nepal	1	1	9	0.002
Jordan	1	1	7	0.001
Borneo	1	1	10	0.001

TABLE D14
Philippines (P2), University of the Philippines Visayas (UP Visayas),
n=103

Country	Frequency	Per Cent	Avg Rank	Smith's S
Philippines	103	100	2	0.899
Malaysia	98	95	4.796	0.585
Singapore	92	89	5.185	0.514
Thailand	89	86	5.258	0.494
Vietnam	91	88	5.462	0.484
Indonesia	87	84	5.299	0.475
Cambodia	76	74	6.066	0.358
Laos	68	66	6.279	0.306
Myanmar	65	63	6.631	0.272
Brunei	66	64	7.152	0.243
China	29	28	4.517	0.182
Japan	29	28	5.31	0.158
South Korea	25	24	6.08	0.118
Taiwan	25	24	6.52	0.106
East Timor	15	15	8.2	0.04
Hong Kong	13	13	8.077	0.036
India	8	8	6.75	0.033
North Korea	6	6	7.5	0.02
Sri Lanka	4	4	7.75	0.013
Papua New Guinea	4	4	8	0.012
Germany	1	1	2	0.009
Bangladesh	1	1	5	0.006
Mongolia	3	3	9	0.006
Colombia	1	1	6	0.005
Macau	1	1	7	0.004
Saudi Arabia	1	1	9	0.002
Egypt	1	1	10	0.001
Jakarta	1	1	10	0.001
Australia	1	1	10	0.001
Kuwait	1	1	10	0.001
Iran	1	1	10	0.001
Uk	1	1	10	0.001
Borneo	1	1	10	0.001

TABLE D15
Philippines (P3), Mindanao State University (MSU), n=108

Country	Frequency	Per Cent	Avg Rank	Smith's S
Philippines	103	95	2.291	0.83
Malaysia	105	97	3.99	0.676
Indonesia	95	88	4.968	0.528
Singapore	89	82	5.584	0.444
Thailand	83	77	5.88	0.391
Vietnam	82	76	6.085	0.367
Brunei	78	72	6.641	0.312
Myanmar	69	64	6.449	0.288
Laos	71	66	6.606	0.288
Cambodia	67	62	6.537	0.276
Japan	42	39	4.833	0.24
China	42	39	5.024	0.232
Korea	29	27	5.448	0.149
Taiwan	21	19	5.476	0.106
Hong Kong	15	14	7	0.056
Saudi Arabia	12	11	6.75	0.047
America	9	8	5.333	0.047
India	14	13	8.214	0.036
North Korea	4	4	7.25	0.014
Russia	2	2	4.5	0.012
Sri Lanka	4	4	7.75	0.01
Egypt	2	2	5.5	0.01
Qatar	3	3	7.667	0.009
Australia	1	1	1	0.009
United Arab Emirates	2	2	7	0.007
Europe	3	3	8.667	0.006
Pakistan	1	1	4	0.006
Israel	1	1	6	0.005
New York	1	1	7	0.004
Borneo	1	1	7	0.004
Kuwait	1	1	7	0.004
Bangladesh	1	1	8	0.003
Iran	2	2	9.5	0.003
East Timor	2	2	9.5	0.002

TABLE D15 (continued)

Country	Frequency	Per Cent	Avg Rank	Smith's S
Bhutan	1	1	9	0.002
Zimbabwe	1	1	9	0.002
Dubai	1	1	9	0.002
Iraq	2	2	10	0.002
Guam	1	1	10	0.001
Mexico	1	1	10	0.001
Kuala Lumpur	1	1	10	0.001
Binidayan	1	1	10	0.001

TABLE D16
Singapore (S1), National University of Singapore, n=105

Country	Frequency	Per Cent	Avg Rank	Smith's S
Singapore	104	99	1.577	0.927
Malaysia	102	97	3.02	0.759
Indonesia	100	95	5.16	0.527
Vietnam	95	90	5.326	0.493
Thailand	93	89	5.559	0.46
Laos	84	80	5.821	0.407
Cambodia	90	86	6.144	0.403
Philippines	86	82	6.605	0.343
Brunei	81	77	6.667	0.322
Myanmar	82	78	7.463	0.265
China	13	12	5.385	0.066
India	7	7	5.714	0.03
Timor Leste	8	8	8.125	0.022
Japan	6	6	5.833	0.019
Korea	6	6	7.667	0.014
Hong Kong	2	2	6.5	0.007
Papau New Guinea	1	1	5	0.006
Mongolia	1	1	9	0.002

TABLE D17
Singapore (S2), Singapore Polytechnic (SP), n=118

Country	Frequency	Per Cent	Avg Rank	Smith's S
Singapore	113	96	1.938	0.862
Malaysia	114	97	3.509	0.708
Indonesia	107	91	4.944	0.53
Thailand	107	91	5.178	0.513
Vietnam	102	86	6.088	0.407
Laos	94	80	5.862	0.398
Philippines	101	86	6.475	0.364
Brunei	92	78	6.326	0.353
Cambodia	89	75	6.562	0.326
Myanmar	93	79	6.731	0.323
China	24	20	4.667	0.123
Japan	15	13	6.533	0.054
India	11	9	5.818	0.045
South Korea	10	8	5.7	0.043
East Timor	4	3	5.5	0.019
Australia	5	4	7.4	0.013
Hong Kong	4	3	8	0.01
New Zealand	1	1	1	0.008
Brazil	1	1	1	0.008
Netherlands	1	1	2	0.007
Germany	1	1	3	0.006
United Nations	1	1	5	0.005
Italy	1	1	6	0.004
North Korea	2	2	9.5	0.002
Taiwan	1	1	9	0.002
Russia	1	1	9	0.002
Bangkok	1	1	8	0.001

TABLE D18
Thailand (T1), Chulalongkorn University, n=106

Country	Frequency	Per Cent	Avg Rank	Smith's S
Thailand	104	98	1.606	0.921
Laos	104	98	3.798	0.705
Myanmar	104	98	3.981	0.687
Cambodia	104	98	4.894	0.598
Malaysia	101	95	5.198	0.551
Vietnam	104	98	6.24	0.463
Singapore	104	98	6.606	0.427
Indonesia	100	94	6.8	0.392
Brunei	97	92	7.515	0.319
Philippines	101	95	7.842	0.298
China	7	7	8	0.019
India	4	4	8.5	0.009
Korea	3	3	8.667	0.007
Japan	2	2	8	0.006
Timor Leste	4	4	10	0.005
Sri Lanka	1	1	8	0.003
America	1	1	10	0.001

TABLE D19
Thailand (T2), Khon Kaen University (KKU), n=108

Country	Frequency	Per Cent	Avg Rank	Smith's S
Thailand	107	99	1.336	0.957
Laos	106	98	2.915	0.79
Myanmar	106	98	3.962	0.689
Cambodia	103	95	5.204	0.549
Vietnam	105	97	5.705	0.511
Malaysia	105	97	6.219	0.462
Singapore	104	96	6.577	0.416
Indonesia	102	94	7.049	0.37
Philippines	102	94	7.716	0.308
Brunei	103	95	7.796	0.302
China	7	6	7.143	0.025
Kaew	1	1	3	0.006
Timor Leste	5	5	9.8	0.006
America	1	1	4	0.005
Khonkaen	1	1	5	0.003
Udon	1	1	6	0.002

TABLE D20
Thailand (T3), Walailak University (WU), n=99

Country	Frequency	Per Cent	Avg Rank	Smith's S
Thailand	99	100	2.22	0.877
Malaysia	99	100	3.80	0.716
Laos	99	100	5.10	0.586
Myanmar	98	99	5.15	0.575
Indonesia	97	98	5.60	0.526
Cambodia	97	98	5.94	0.492
Singapore	97	98	6.07	0.477
Brunei	97	98	6.35	0.451
Vietnam	97	98	6.54	0.429
Philippines	93	94	7.871	0.291
Japan	1	1	6	0.005
China	2	2	9.5	0.003
England	1	1	8	0.003

TABLE D21
Thailand (T4), Saint John's University (SJU), n=78

Country	Frequency	Per Cent	Avg Rank	Smith's S
Thailand	78	100	1.821	0.918
Myanmar	77	99	4.494	0.642
Laos	75	96	4.627	0.613
Cambodia	76	97	5.316	0.554
Malaysia	76	97	5.566	0.529
Brunei	75	96	6.413	0.441
Singapore	74	95	6.351	0.441
Vietnam	73	94	6.37	0.433
Indonesia	71	91	6.775	0.385
Philippines	74	95	7.135	0.367
India	6	8	8.5	0.019
America	1	1	1	0.013
Italy	2	3	6	0.013
Germany	2	3	6.5	0.012
Mexico	1	1	2	0.012
England	1	1	2	0.012
Brazil	3	4	8.333	0.01
France	2	3	7.5	0.009
Spain	1	1	4	0.009
China	1	1	4	0.009
Peru	1	1	4	0.009
Japan	1	1	5	0.008
German	1	1	6	0.006
New Zealand	1	1	6	0.006
Alaska	1	1	7	0.005
Argentina	1	1	7	0.005
Arab	1	1	8	0.004
Congo	1	1	8	0.004
Madagasgar	1	1	9	0.003
Holland	1	1	10	0.001

TABLE D22
Vietnam (V1), Vietnam National University, Hanoi, n=109

Country	Frequency	Per Cent	Avg Rank	Smith's S
Vietnam	107	98	1.981	0.885
Laos	108	99	4.111	0.681
Thailand	105	96	4.39	0.634
Cambodia	107	98	5.159	0.571
Indonesia	99	91	5.707	0.48
Singapore	105	96	6.076	0.473
Malaysia	105	96	6.514	0.428
Myanmar	104	95	6.5	0.426
Philippines	104	95	6.596	0.418
Brunei	101	93	7.465	0.327
Timor Leste	23	21	7.609	0.072
China	3	3	2.333	0.024
England	1	1	3	0.006
Japan	2	2	9	0.004
Turkey	1	1	4	0.004
Germany	1	1	5	0.002

TABLE D23
Vietnam (V2), Vietnam National University, Ho Chi Minh City, n=110

Country	Frequency	Per Cent	Avg Rank	Smith's S
Vietnam	110	100	1.936	0.905
Laos	106	96	3.5	0.716
Cambodia	108	98	4.556	0.627
Thailand	106	96	4.783	0.594
Malaysia	106	96	5.736	0.494
Indonesia	101	92	5.941	0.458
Philippines	98	89	6.327	0.41
Singapore	100	91	6.51	0.4
Myanmar	96	87	6.938	0.345
Brunei	99	90	7.758	0.284
East Timor	37	34	7.784	0.107
China	4	4	4.75	0.023
Korea	2	2	3.5	0.014
India	1	1	2	0.008
Japan	1	1	7	0.004
Taiwan	1	1	7	0.004

Appendix E

ATTITUDES TOWARD ASPECTS OF INTEGRATION AND COOPERATION

Cultural Exchange is Important.

Primary Universities	Strongly Agree	Somewhat Agree	Somewhat Disagree	Strongly Disagree	Total Agree	Total Disagree
Brunei (B1)	58.5%	36.5%	4.5%	0.5%	95.0%	5.0%
Cambodia (C1)	44.2%	42.9%	8.8%	4.2%	87.1%	13.0%
Indonesia (I1)	52.7%	37.6%	7.3%	2.4%	90.3%	9.7%
Laos (L1)	55.0%	42.3%	1.8%	0.9%	97.3%	2.7%
Malaysia (M1)	24.6%	63.6%	10.8%	1.0%	88.2%	11.8%
Myanmar (N2)	50.7%	43.1%	4.3%	1.9%	93.8%	6.2%
Philippines (P1)	50.5%	45.0%	4.6%	0.0%	95.5%	4.6%
Singapore (S1)	41.5%	50.5%	3.8%	4.3%	92.0%	8.1%
Thailand (T1)	26.0%	61.5%	9.6%	2.9%	87.5%	12.5%
Vietnam (V1)	65.0%	29.0%	3.7%	2.3%	94.0%	6.0%
Average Primary	**46.9%**	**45.2%**	**5.9%**	**2.0%**	**92.1%**	**8.0%**
Additional Universities						
Unsyiah (I2)	65.0%	25.5%	6.5%	3.0%	90.5%	9.5%
Undana (I3)	53.2%	25.9%	10.0%	11.0%	79.1%	20.9%
UTAR (M2)	44.8%	48.6%	4.8%	1.9%	93.3%	6.7%
Unimas (M3)	29.8%	56.0%	12.4%	1.8%	85.8%	14.2%
YU (N1)	37.9%	47.7%	8.6%	5.8%	85.6%	14.4%
UP Visayas (P2)	44.7%	47.6%	6.7%	1.0%	92.3%	7.7%
MSU (P3)	47.0%	40.6%	9.6%	2.7%	87.7%	12.3%
SP (S2)	46.7%	51.3%	2.1%	0.0%	97.9%	2.1%
KKU (T2)	42.3%	53.1%	4.7%	0.0%	95.3%	4.7%
WU (T3)	42.7%	51.0%	5.8%	0.5%	93.7%	6.3%
SJU (T4)	38.8%	44.4%	15.2%	1.7%	83.1%	16.9%
VNU-HCMC (V2)	68.7%	27.6%	1.9%	1.9%	96.3%	3.7%
Average Additional	**46.8%**	**43.3%**	**7.3%**	**2.6%**	**90.1%**	**9.9%**
Average Total	**46.8%**	**44.1%**	**6.7%**	**2.3%**	**91.0%**	**9.0%**

Economic Cooperation is Important.

Primary Universities	Strongly Agree	Somewhat Agree	Somewhat Disagree	Strongly Disagree	Total Agree	Total Disagree
Brunei (B1)	63.0%	35.0%	2.0%	0.0%	98.0%	2.0%
Cambodia (C1)	69.2%	28.3%	2.1%	0.4%	97.5%	2.5%
Indonesia (I1)	62.4%	35.1%	2.4%	0.0%	97.5%	2.4%
Laos (L1)	62.7%	35.9%	1.4%	0.0%	98.6%	1.4%
Malaysia (M1)	47.3%	52.2%	0.0%	0.5%	99.5%	0.5%
Myanmar (N2)	74.2%	24.9%	1.0%	0.0%	99.0%	1.0%
Philippines (P1)	64.1%	30.0%	5.5%	0.5%	94.1%	6.0%
Singapore (S1)	55.7%	38.7%	1.9%	3.8%	94.4%	5.7%
Thailand (T1)	49.0%	46.6%	3.9%	0.5%	95.7%	4.3%
Vietnam (V1)	79.7%	16.6%	1.8%	1.8%	96.3%	3.7%
Average Primary	**62.7%**	**34.3%**	**2.2%**	**0.8%**	**97.1%**	**2.9%**
Additional Universities						
Unsyiah (I2)	81.0%	19.0%	0.0%	0.0%	100.0%	0.0%
Undana (I3)	83.1%	14.4%	1.0%	1.5%	97.5%	2.5%
UTAR (M2)	51.4%	45.7%	2.4%	0.5%	97.1%	2.9%
Unimas (M3)	49.5%	48.6%	0.9%	0.9%	98.2%	1.8%
YU (N1)	62.1%	34.5%	2.3%	1.2%	96.6%	3.5%
UP Visayas (P2)	72.6%	24.0%	1.9%	1.4%	96.6%	3.4%
MSU (P3)	69.0%	28.3%	2.7%	0.0%	97.3%	2.7%
SP (S2)	50.0%	47.5%	2.1%	0.4%	97.5%	2.5%
KKU (T2)	52.1%	46.0%	1.4%	0.5%	98.1%	1.9%
WU (T3)	52.9%	44.7%	2.4%	0.0%	97.6%	2.4%
SIU (T4)	46.1%	47.8%	5.1%	1.1%	93.8%	6.2%
VNU-HCMC (V2)	82.2%	16.4%	1.4%	0.0%	98.6%	1.4%
Average Additional	**62.7%**	**34.7%**	**2.0%**	**0.6%**	**97.4%**	**2.6%**
Average Total	**62.7%**	**34.6%**	**2.1%**	**0.7%**	**97.2%**	**2.8%**

Development Assistance is Important.

Primary Universities	Strongly Agree	Somewhat Agree	Somewhat Disagree	Strongly Disagree	Total Agree	Total Disagree
Brunei (B1)	59.0%	40.0%	1.0%	0.0%	99.0%	1.0%
Cambodia (C1)	64.6%	32.5%	2.9%	0.0%	97.1%	2.9%
Indonesia (I1)	65.4%	32.2%	2.4%	0.0%	97.6%	2.4%
Laos (L1)	69.1%	30.0%	0.9%	0.0%	99.1%	0.9%
Malaysia (M1)	43.8%	55.2%	0.0%	1.0%	99.0%	1.0%
Myanmar (N2)	79.9%	19.1%	0.5%	0.5%	99.0%	1.0%
Philippines (P1)	66.4%	29.1%	4.1%	0.5%	95.5%	4.6%
Singapore (S1)	46.2%	45.3%	3.8%	4.7%	91.5%	8.5%
Thailand (T1)	51.4%	44.7%	3.9%	0.0%	96.2%	3.9%
Vietnam (V1)	87.5%	10.7%	4.6%	1.4%	98.2%	6.0%
Average Primary	**63.3%**	**33.9%**	**2.4%**	**0.8%**	**97.2%**	**3.2%**
Additional Universities						
Unsyiah (I2)	78.5%	20.0%	1.5%	0.0%	98.5%	1.5%
Undana (I3)	80.1%	15.9%	3.5%	0.5%	96.0%	4.0%
UTAR (M2)	45.5%	45.9%	8.1%	0.5%	91.4%	8.6%
Unimas (M3)	51.4%	46.8%	1.4%	0.5%	98.2%	1.9%
YU (N1)	77.8%	21.6%	0.6%	0.0%	99.4%	0.6%
UP Visayas (P2)	73.6%	25.5%	1.0%	0.0%	99.0%	1.0%
MSU (P3)	74.0%	24.2%	1.8%	0.0%	98.2%	1.8%
SP (S2)	49.5%	47.5%	2.9%	0.0%	97.0%	2.9%
KKU (T2)	54.5%	42.3%	2.8%	0.5%	96.7%	3.3%
WU (T3)	55.3%	44.2%	0.0%	0.5%	99.5%	0.5%
SIU (T4)	47.8%	44.9%	5.1%	2.3%	92.7%	7.3%
VNU-HCMC (V2)	87.4%	10.3%	1.4%	0.9%	97.7%	2.3%
Average Additional	**64.6%**	**32.4%**	**2.5%**	**0.5%**	**97.0%**	**3.0%**
Average Total	**64.0%**	**33.1%**	**2.5%**	**0.6%**	**97.1%**	**3.1%**

Educational Exchange is Important.

Primary Universities	Strongly Agree	Somewhat Agree	Somewhat Disagree	Strongly Disagree	Total Agree	Total Disagree
Brunei (B1)	69.5%	29.0%	1.5%	0.0%	98.5%	1.5%
Cambodia (C1)	72.9%	25.4%	1.7%	0.0%	98.3%	1.7%
Indonesia (I1)	65.9%	31.7%	1.5%	1.0%	97.6%	2.5%
Laos (L1)	71.8%	28.2%	0.0%	0.0%	100.0%	0.0%
Malaysia (M1)	36.5%	61.6%	2.0%	0.0%	98.1%	2.0%
Myanmar (N2)	85.1%	13.0%	1.4%	0.5%	98.1%	1.9%
Philippines (P1)	60.0%	33.2%	5.0%	1.8%	93.2%	6.8%
Singapore (S1)	34.6%	53.1%	5.7%	6.6%	87.7%	12.3%
Thailand (T1)	37.0%	57.2%	4.8%	1.0%	94.2%	5.8%
Vietnam (V1)	69.6%	26.7%	2.3%	1.4%	96.3%	3.7%
Average Primary	**60.3%**	**35.9%**	**2.6%**	**1.2%**	**96.2%**	**3.8%**
Additional Universities						
Unsyiah (I2)	86.5%	12.5%	0.0%	1.0%	99.0%	1.0%
Undana (I3)	82.1%	14.4%	2.0%	1.5%	96.5%	3.5%
UTAR (M2)	47.1%	43.8%	8.1%	1.0%	91.0%	9.1%
Unimas (M3)	38.5%	54.6%	6.4%	0.5%	93.1%	6.9%
YU (N1)	76.0%	22.9%	0.6%	0.6%	98.9%	1.1%
UP Visayas (P2)	65.9%	32.2%	1.9%	0.0%	98.1%	1.9%
MSU (P3)	64.8%	30.6%	4.1%	0.5%	95.4%	4.6%
SP (S2)	43.3%	51.3%	3.3%	2.1%	94.6%	5.4%
KKU (T2)	49.5%	44.8%	5.2%	0.5%	94.3%	5.7%
WU (T3)	66.5%	30.5%	3.0%	0.0%	97.0%	3.0%
SJU (T4)	52.8%	38.8%	6.2%	2.3%	91.6%	8.4%
VNU-HCMC (V2)	72.0%	24.8%	2.3%	0.9%	96.7%	3.3%
Average Additional	**62.1%**	**33.4%**	**3.6%**	**0.9%**	**95.5%**	**4.5%**
Average Total	**61.3%**	**34.6%**	**3.1%**	**1.1%**	**95.8%**	**4.2%**

Security Cooperation is Important.

Primary Universities	Strongly Agree	Somewhat Agree	Somewhat Disagree	Strongly Disagree	Total Agree	Total Disagree
Brunei (B1)	62.5%	32.5%	4.5%	0.5%	95.0%	5.0%
Cambodia (C1)	52.1%	38.8%	8.3%	0.8%	90.9%	9.1%
Indonesia (I1)	54.2%	41.5%	4.4%	0.0%	95.7%	4.4%
Laos (L1)	29.1%	55.0%	13.2%	2.7%	84.1%	15.9%
Malaysia (M1)	52.7%	43.4%	3.9%	0.0%	96.1%	3.9%
Myanmar (N2)	55.5%	36.4%	6.2%	1.9%	91.9%	8.1%
Philippines (P1)	53.0%	33.3%	9.6%	4.1%	86.3%	13.7%
Singapore (S1)	55.9%	33.2%	6.2%	4.7%	89.1%	10.9%
Thailand (T1)	22.1%	45.2%	26.0%	6.7%	67.3%	32.7%
Vietnam (V1)	80.1%	16.2%	2.3%	1.4%	96.3%	3.7%
Average Primary	**51.7%**	**37.5%**	**8.5%**	**2.3%**	**89.3%**	**10.7%**
Additional Universities						
Unsyiah (I2)	74.0%	22.0%	2.0%	2.0%	96.0%	4.0%
Undana (I3)	79.1%	15.4%	3.5%	2.0%	94.5%	5.5%
UTAR (M2)	46.7%	44.3%	8.1%	1.0%	91.0%	9.1%
Unimas (M3)	56.9%	40.4%	2.3%	0.5%	97.3%	2.8%
YU (N1)	48.0%	40.6%	5.1%	6.3%	88.6%	11.4%
UP Visayas (P2)	63.0%	28.9%	6.3%	1.9%	91.8%	8.2%
MSU (P3)	63.9%	26.5%	7.3%	2.3%	90.4%	9.6%
SP (S2)	57.1%	38.8%	2.5%	1.7%	95.8%	4.2%
KKU (T2)	35.6%	46.5%	15.6%	2.4%	82.0%	18.0%
WU (T3)	38.4%	41.9%	18.2%	1.5%	80.3%	19.7%
SJU (T4)	39.9%	43.8%	12.4%	3.9%	83.7%	16.3%
VNU-HCMC (V2)	74.8%	22.4%	1.9%	0.9%	97.2%	2.8%
Average Additional	**56.4%**	**34.3%**	**7.1%**	**2.2%**	**90.7%**	**9.3%**
Average Total	**54.3%**	**35.8%**	**7.7%**	**2.3%**	**90.1%**	**10.0%**

Political Cooperation is Important.

Primary Universities	Strongly Agree	Somewhat Agree	Somewhat Disagree	Strongly Disagree	Total Agree	Total Disagree
Brunei (B1)	38.5%	46.0%	12.5%	3.0%	84.5%	15.5%
Cambodia (C1)	44.6%	44.6%	9.6%	1.3%	89.2%	10.9%
Indonesia (I1)	47.8%	46.3%	5.9%	0.0%	94.1%	5.9%
Laos (L1)	23.2%	49.1%	25.5%	2.3%	72.3%	27.8%
Malaysia (M1)	39.4%	51.7%	8.4%	0.5%	91.1%	8.9%
Myanmar (N2)	43.5%	44.5%	9.1%	2.9%	88.0%	12.0%
Philippines (P1)	40.0%	44.1%	14.1%	1.9%	84.1%	16.0%
Singapore (S1)	47.4%	44.6%	4.7%	3.3%	92.0%	8.0%
Thailand (T1)	20.2%	41.4%	29.8%	8.7%	61.5%	38.5%
Vietnam (V1)	68.5%	25.5%	4.6%	1.4%	94.0%	6.0%
Average Primary	**41.3%**	**43.8%**	**12.4%**	**2.5%**	**85.1%**	**14.9%**
Additional Universities						
Unsyiah (I2)	65.5%	28.0%	4.5%	2.0%	93.5%	6.5%
Undana (I3)	60.7%	30.9%	6.0%	2.5%	91.6%	8.5%
UTAR (M2)	36.4%	45.5%	15.3%	2.9%	81.8%	18.2%
Unimas (M3)	41.7%	51.4%	5.5%	1.4%	93.1%	6.9%
YU (N1)	30.6%	53.2%	9.8%	6.4%	83.8%	16.2%
UP Visayas (P2)	49.0%	42.8%	8.2%	0.0%	91.8%	8.2%
MSU (P3)	49.8%	38.8%	9.1%	2.3%	88.6%	11.4%
SP (S2)	50.8%	43.3%	5.0%	0.8%	94.2%	5.8%
KKU (T2)	30.7%	50.5%	16.0%	2.8%	81.1%	18.9%
WU (T3)	35.5%	52.7%	11.8%	0.0%	88.2%	11.8%
SJU (T4)	27.0%	48.9%	21.4%	2.8%	75.9%	24.2%
VNU-HCMC (V2)	59.8%	33.6%	4.7%	1.9%	93.4%	6.5%
Average Additional	**44.8%**	**43.3%**	**9.8%**	**2.1%**	**88.1%**	**11.9%**
Average Total	**43.2%**	**43.5%**	**11.0%**	**2.3%**	**86.7%**	**13.3%**

Sports Competitions are Important.

Primary Universities	Strongly Agree	Somewhat Agree	Somewhat Disagree	Strongly Disagree	Total Agree	Total Disagree
Brunei (B1)	55.5%	41.0%	2.5%	1.0%	96.5%	3.5%
Cambodia (C1)	47.5%	43.3%	8.3%	0.8%	90.8%	9.1%
Indonesia (I1)	69.3%	28.3%	2.0%	0.5%	97.6%	2.5%
Laos (L1)	60.5%	39.1%	0.5%	0.0%	99.6%	0.5%
Malaysia (M1)	50.3%	44.8%	4.4%	0.5%	95.1%	4.9%
Myanmar (N2)	70.8%	26.3%	1.4%	1.4%	97.1%	2.9%
Philippines (P1)	50.9%	41.4%	6.8%	0.9%	92.3%	7.7%
Singapore (S1)	23.7%	46.9%	20.4%	9.0%	70.6%	29.4%
Thailand (T1)	24.5%	51.0%	22.6%	1.9%	75.5%	24.5%
Vietnam (V1)	69.1%	25.8%	3.7%	1.4%	94.9%	5.1%
Average Primary	**52.2%**	**38.8%**	**7.3%**	**1.7%**	**91.0%**	**9.0%**
Additional Universities						
Unsyiah (I2)	81.5%	16.5%	2.0%	0.0%	98.0%	2.0%
Undana (I3)	90.1%	7.5%	1.0%	1.5%	97.5%	2.5%
UTAR (M2)	38.6%	49.1%	11.9%	0.5%	87.6%	12.4%
Unimas (M3)	57.8%	40.4%	1.4%	0.5%	98.2%	1.9%
YU (N1)	60.2%	38.1%	1.7%	0.0%	98.3%	1.7%
UP Visayas (P2)	48.1%	42.8%	8.7%	0.5%	90.9%	9.1%
MSU (P3)	60.7%	32.9%	5%	0.9%	93.6%	5.9%
SP (S2)	35.6%	54.8%	8.0%	1.7%	90.4%	9.6%
KKU (T2)	47.2%	44.3%	7.5%	0.9%	91.5%	8.5%
WU (T3)	48.8%	41.9%	8.9%	0.5%	90.6%	9.4%
SJU (T4)	53.9%	38.8%	5.1%	2.3%	92.7%	7.3%
VNU-HCMC (V2)	68.2%	28.0%	1.9%	1.9%	96.3%	3.7%
Average Additional	**57.6%**	**36.2%**	**5.3%**	**0.9%**	**93.8%**	**6.2%**
Average Total	**55.1%**	**37.4%**	**6.2%**	**1.3%**	**92.5%**	**7.5%**

Tourism is Important.

Primary Universities	Strongly Agree	Somewhat Agree	Somewhat Disagree	Strongly Disagree	Total Agree	Total Disagree
Brunei (B1)	78.0%	21.5%	0.5%	0.0%	99.5%	0.5%
Cambodia (C1)	78.3%	20.4%	1.3%	0.0%	98.7%	1.3%
Indonesia (I1)	70.7%	28.3%	1.0%	0.0%	99.0%	1.0%
Laos (L1)	60.9%	38.2%	0.9%	0.0%	99.1%	0.9%
Malaysia (M1)	53.7%	44.3%	1.5%	0.5%	98.0%	2.0%
Myanmar (N2)	64.1%	31.6%	1.9%	2.4%	95.7%	4.3%
Philippines (P1)	71.4%	24.6%	3.6%	0.5%	96.0%	4.1%
Singapore (S1)	47.4%	44.6%	2.8%	5.2%	92.0%	8.0%
Thailand (T1)	51.0%	41.4%	5.8%	1.9%	92.3%	7.7%
Vietnam (V1)	74.7%	22.6%	1.8%	0.9%	97.2%	2.8%
Average Primary	**65.0%**	**31.7%**	**2.1%**	**1.1%**	**96.8%**	**3.3%**
Additional Universities						
Unsyiah (I2)	79.5%	18.5%	2.0%	0.0%	98.0%	2.0%
Undana (I3)	82.1%	14.4%	2.5%	1.0%	96.5%	3.5%
UTAR (M2)	63.8%	34.3%	1.9%	0.0%	98.1%	1.9%
Unimas (M3)	46.8%	49.5%	2.8%	0.9%	96.3%	3.7%
YU (N1)	61.5%	36.2%	1.7%	0.6%	97.7%	2.3%
UP Visayas (P2)	77.4%	19.7%	2.9%	0.0%	97.1%	2.9%
MSU (P3)	74.0%	23.7%	2.3%	0.0%	97.7%	2.3%
SP (S2)	49.2%	47.9%	2.1%	0.8%	97.1%	2.9%
KKU (T2)	67.0%	31.6%	1.4%	0.0%	98.6%	1.4%
WU (T3)	63.1%	32.5%	4.4%	0.0%	95.6%	4.4%
SJU (T4)	68.5%	28.1%	2.3%	1.1%	96.6%	3.4%
VNU-HCMC (V2)	77.6%	20.6%	0.9%	0.9%	98.1%	1.9%
Average Additional	**67.5%**	**29.8%**	**2.3%**	**0.4%**	**97.3%**	**2.7%**
Average Total	**66.4%**	**30.7%**	**2.2%**	**0.8%**	**97.0%**	**3.0%**

Appendix F

COGNITIVE MAPS AND TABLES

COGNITIVE MAPS AND AGGREGATE SIMILARITY MATRICES

The following maps and tables show the results of the Triad Test (Q20) aggregated across respondents from each university. In the triad test, for each respondent, each pair of countries (items) is given a score of 1 for each triad in which the pair are not circled (i.e. the third country is judged most different; thus, within that triad, the pair not selected are judged most similar). The maximum score from each respondent is 4, as each pair occurs four times across the sixty triads. The judgements of all students in each sample are combined and represented as a percentage in the Aggregate Similarity Matrix for each university. A score of 1.00 would indicate that the pair of countries is judged most similar every time it appears together in a triad. Conversely, a score of 0.00 would indicate that the pair was never chosen as most similar within any triad. The diagonal of the matrix is 1.00 because each country is assumed to be perfectly similar to itself.

The Cognitive Maps for each university are a visual representation of the results of correspondence analysis applied to each university's Aggregate Similarity Matrix. Correspondence analysis, a type of factor analysis, reduces the complexity of the data into ranked dimensions of similarity and difference. In this case, with ten items (countries), correspondence analysis produces no more than nine dimensions. Each country is given a score (generally between about +1.0 and −1.0) in each dimension, indicating how close (similar) or far (different) the country is from others on that dimension. The lowest (first, second, third) dimensions contain most of the information within the responses, and represent the most common ways in which judgements are being made within the sample. Higher dimensions (ninth, eighth, seventh) account for idiosyncratic (e.g. random or uninformed) answers within the data.

The Cognitive Maps visually represent the first (x-axis) and second (y-axis) dimensions of difference, mapped onto each other. Countries judged most similar appear close to one another; those judged most different appear farther from one another. The procedure allows us to see visually how countries are clustered or differentiated based on different university samples. In some cases, important information is also contained in the third, fourth and possibly fifth dimensions of contrast. For example, if three or four countries cluster closely together in the first and second dimensions, the third through fifth dimensions provide information on which countries within the cluster differentiate from the others. These were examined by the researchers, but are difficult to interpret when represented visually.

The size of the circle representing each country in the cognitive maps is based on the Smith's S (salience) derived from the List Question from each university. Thus the maps also provide a visual representation to the relative salience of each country within ASEAN for students at each university.

Finally, at the end of the appendix is a QAP Correlation Table. QAP Correlation is a measure of similarity between every two aggregate similarity matrices. In other words, these figures demonstrate how highly each university's responses correlate with one another. A score of 1.00 would mean that the two matrices are exactly the same while a score of 0.00 would mean that there is no similarity between the matrices. Tests were also done to examine how highly each university's responses correlate with judgements of similarity and difference based on each country's Gross Domestic Product (GDP), the relative size of the Muslim versus Buddhist population of each country based on a Muslim-Buddhist Index (MBI), a combination (GDP+MBI) of the economic (GDP) and cultural (MBI) criteria, and the size of the country's population (POP).

Further detailed discussion of the findings represented in these maps and tables is found in Chapter 7.

Brunei, Universiti Brunei Darussalam (B1)

Cognitive Map of ASEAN, Universiti Brunei Darussalam, n=200

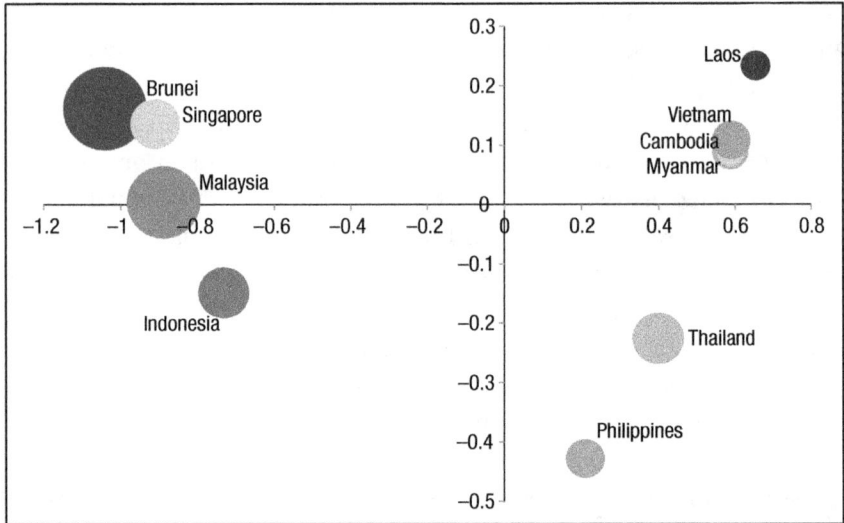

Aggregate Similiarity Matrix, Universiti Brunei Darussalam, n=200

	BRUN	CAMB	INDO	LAOS	MSIA	MYAN	PHIL	SING	THAI	VIET
BRUN	1	0.06	0.55	0.06	0.68	0.05	0.17	0.65	0.11	0.07
CAMB	0.06	1	0.17	0.65	0.09	0.68	0.4	0.1	0.56	0.69
INDO	0.55	0.17	1	0.09	0.71	0.14	0.31	0.48	0.22	0.14
LAOS	0.06	0.65	0.09	1	0.06	0.64	0.34	0.08	0.43	0.71
MSIA	0.68	0.09	0.71	0.06	1	0.13	0.22	0.64	0.21	0.1
MYAN	0.05	0.68	0.14	0.64	0.13	1	0.41	0.08	0.52	0.65
PHIL	0.17	0.4	0.31	0.34	0.22	0.41	1	0.22	0.51	0.42
SING	0.65	0.1	0.48	0.08	0.64	0.08	0.22	1	0.14	0.11
THAI	0.11	0.56	0.22	0.43	0.21	0.52	0.51	0.14	1	0.54
VIET	0.07	0.69	0.14	0.71	0.1	0.65	0.42	0.11	0.54	1

Cambodia, Royal University of Phnom Penh (C1)

Cognitive Map of ASEAN, Royal University of Phnom Penh, n=240

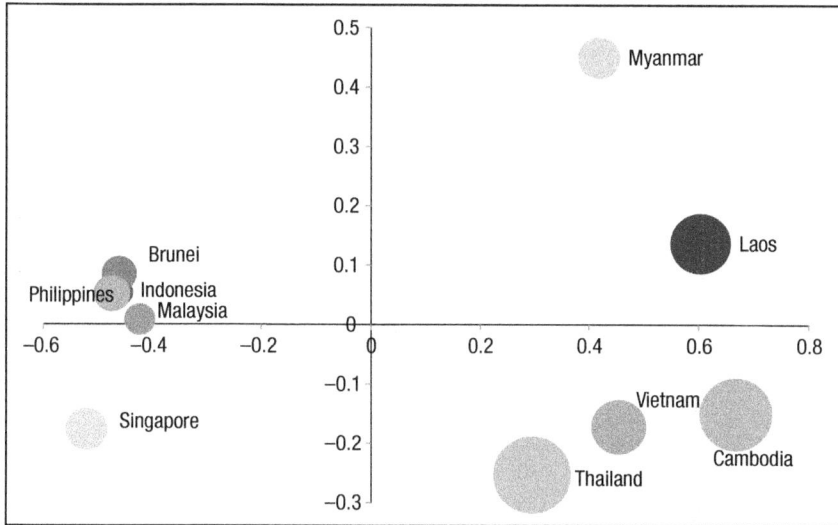

Aggregate Similiarity Matrix, Royal University of Phnom Penh, n=200

	BRUN	CAMB	INDO	LAOS	MSIA	MYAN	PHIL	SING	THAI	VIET
BRUN	1	0.15	0.5	0.19	0.42	0.23	0.46	0.49	0.25	0.21
CAMB	0.15	1	0.16	0.53	0.16	0.43	0.14	0.12	0.58	0.49
INDO	0.5	0.16	1	0.18	0.64	0.26	0.54	0.46	0.28	0.23
LAOS	0.19	0.53	0.18	1	0.19	0.51	0.17	0.14	0.43	0.51
MSIA	0.42	0.16	0.64	0.19	1	0.24	0.49	0.49	0.33	0.25
MYAN	0.23	0.43	0.26	0.51	0.24	1	0.24	0.15	0.36	0.36
PHIL	0.46	0.14	0.54	0.17	0.49	0.24	1	0.5	0.28	0.21
SING	0.49	0.12	0.46	0.14	0.49	0.15	0.5	1	0.34	0.2
THAI	0.25	0.58	0.28	0.43	0.33	0.36	0.28	0.34	1	0.49
VIET	0.21	0.49	0.23	0.51	0.25	0.36	0.21	0.2	0.49	1

Indonesia, University of Indonesia (I1)

Cognitive Map of ASEAN, Universitas Indonesia, n=194

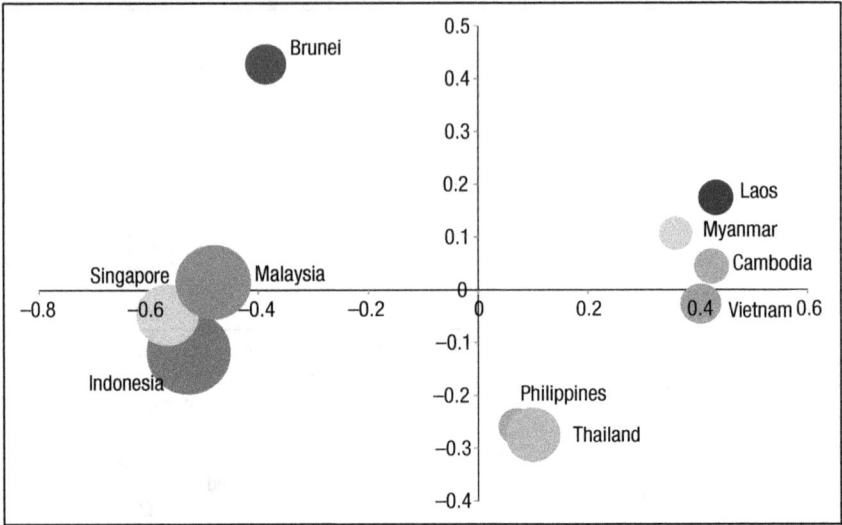

Aggregate Similiarity Matrix, Universitas Indonesia, n=194

	BRUN	CAMB	INDO	LAOS	MSIA	MYAN	PHIL	SING	THAI	VIET
BRUN	1	0.23	0.39	0.23	0.44	0.25	0.27	0.34	0.26	0.24
CAMB	0.23	1	0.22	0.5	0.22	0.51	0.35	0.15	0.41	0.53
INDO	0.39	0.22	1	0.15	0.61	0.21	0.36	0.39	0.31	0.2
LAOS	0.23	0.5	0.15	1	0.23	0.51	0.35	0.2	0.32	0.49
MSIA	0.44	0.22	0.61	0.23	1	0.29	0.3	0.49	0.34	0.24
MYAN	0.25	0.51	0.21	0.51	0.29	1	0.37	0.2	0.36	0.52
PHIL	0.27	0.35	0.36	0.35	0.3	0.37	1	0.29	0.43	0.43
SING	0.34	0.15	0.39	0.2	0.49	0.2	0.29	1	0.27	0.17
THAI	0.26	0.41	0.31	0.32	0.34	0.36	0.43	0.27	1	0.44
VIET	0.24	0.53	0.2	0.49	0.24	0.52	0.43	0.17	0.44	1

Indonesia, Universitas Syiah Kuala (I2)

Cognitive Map of ASEAN, Universitas Syiah Kuala (Aceh), n=200

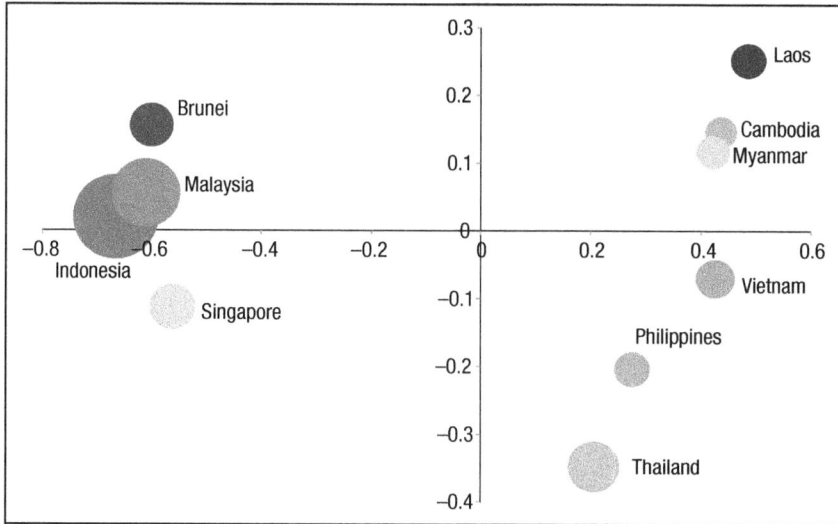

Aggregate Similiarity Matrix, Universitas Syiah Kuala (Aceh), n=200

	BRUN	CAMB	INDO	LAOS	MSIA	MYAN	PHIL	SING	THAI	VIET
BRUN	1	0.19	0.5	0.17	0.59	0.22	0.22	0.47	0.22	0.2
CAMB	0.19	1	0.19	0.54	0.21	0.54	0.41	0.18	0.41	0.53
INDO	0.5	0.19	1	0.12	0.62	0.17	0.24	0.43	0.25	0.16
LAOS	0.17	0.54	0.12	1	0.19	0.5	0.4	0.17	0.34	0.5
MSIA	0.59	0.21	0.62	0.19	1	0.2	0.24	0.54	0.28	0.19
MYAN	0.22	0.54	0.17	0.5	0.2	1	0.43	0.18	0.41	0.51
PHIL	0.22	0.41	0.24	0.4	0.24	0.43	1	0.25	0.41	0.5
SING	0.47	0.18	0.43	0.17	0.54	0.18	0.25	1	0.28	0.21
THAI	0.22	0.41	0.25	0.34	0.28	0.41	0.41	0.28	1	0.47
VIET	0.2	0.53	0.16	0.5	0.19	0.51	0.5	0.21	0.47	1

Indonesia, Universitas Nusa Cendana (I3)

Cognitive Map of ASEAN, Universitas Nusa Cendana (Kupang), n=201

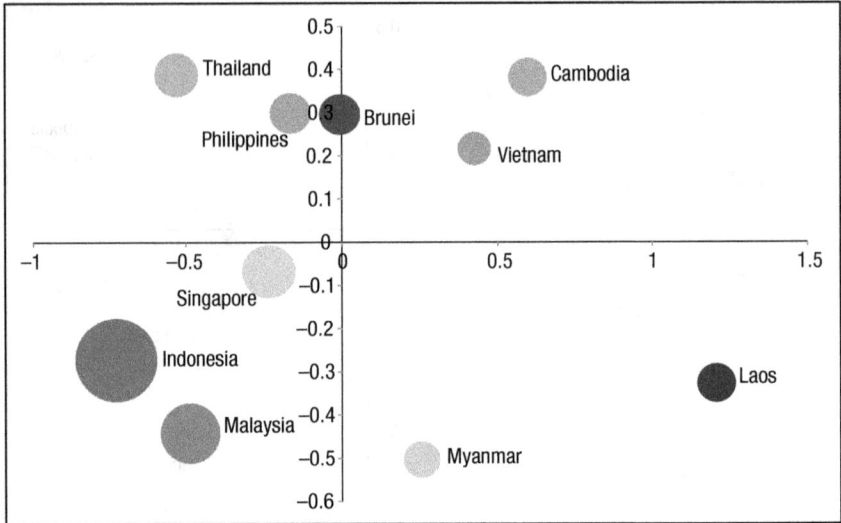

Aggregate Similiarity Matrix, Universitas Nusa Cendana (Kupang), n=201

	BRUN	CAMB	INDO	LAOS	MSIA	MYAN	PHIL	SING	THAI	VIET
BRUN	1	0.31	0.33	0.33	0.38	0.31	0.25	0.33	0.27	0.29
CAMB	0.31	1	0.24	0.45	0.3	0.47	0.35	0.23	0.39	0.44
INDO	0.33	0.24	1	0.18	0.5	0.25	0.28	0.37	0.26	0.23
LAOS	0.33	0.45	0.18	1	0.25	0.45	0.33	0.25	0.34	0.43
MSIA	0.38	0.3	0.5	0.25	1	0.38	0.33	0.44	0.32	0.3
MYAN	0.31	0.47	0.25	0.45	0.38	1	0.34	0.25	0.36	0.45
PHIL	0.25	0.35	0.28	0.33	0.33	0.34	1	0.33	0.41	0.37
SING	0.33	0.23	0.37	0.25	0.44	0.25	0.33	1	0.27	0.26
THAI	0.27	0.39	0.26	0.34	0.32	0.36	0.41	0.27	1	0.41
VIET	0.29	0.44	0.23	0.43	0.3	0.45	0.37	0.26	0.41	1

Lao PDR, National University of Laos (L1)

Cognitive Map of ASEAN, National University of Laos, n=200

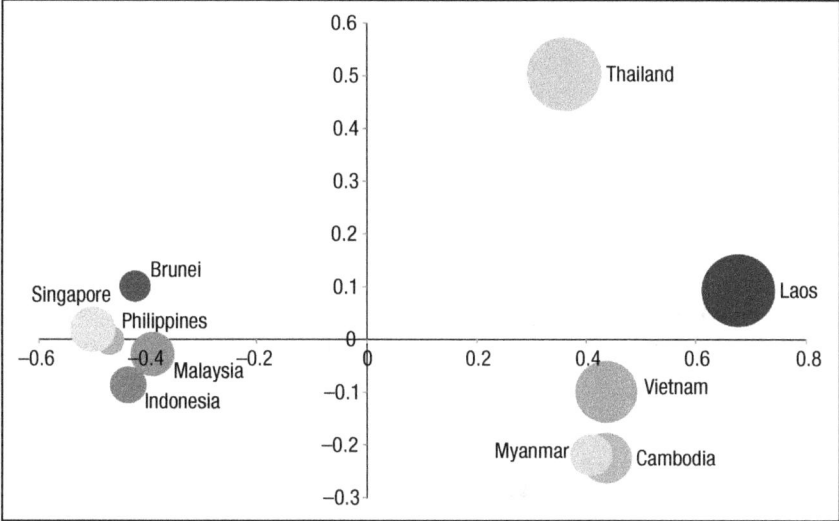

Aggregate Similiarity Matrix, National University of Laos, n=200

	BRUN	CAMB	INDO	LAOS	MSIA	MYAN	PHIL	SING	THAI	VIET
BRUN	1	0.21	0.44	0.14	0.36	0.24	0.44	0.44	0.24	0.2
CAMB	0.21	1	0.28	0.5	0.26	0.51	0.23	0.19	0.34	0.52
INDO	0.44	0.28	1	0.15	0.66	0.26	0.52	0.5	0.22	0.24
LAOS	0.14	0.5	0.15	1	0.16	0.42	0.15	0.15	0.48	0.61
MSIA	0.36	0.26	0.66	0.16	1	0.25	0.5	0.55	0.29	0.31
MYAN	0.24	0.51	0.26	0.42	0.25	1	0.21	0.19	0.35	0.44
PHIL	0.44	0.23	0.52	0.15	0.5	0.21	1	0.54	0.22	0.24
SING	0.44	0.19	0.5	0.15	0.55	0.19	0.54	1	0.21	0.25
THAI	0.24	0.34	0.22	0.48	0.29	0.35	0.22	0.21	1	0.36
VIET	0.2	0.52	0.24	0.61	0.31	0.44	0.24	0.25	0.36	1

Malaysia, University of Malaya (M1)

Cognitive Map of ASEAN, University of Malaya (Malay Respondents), n=142

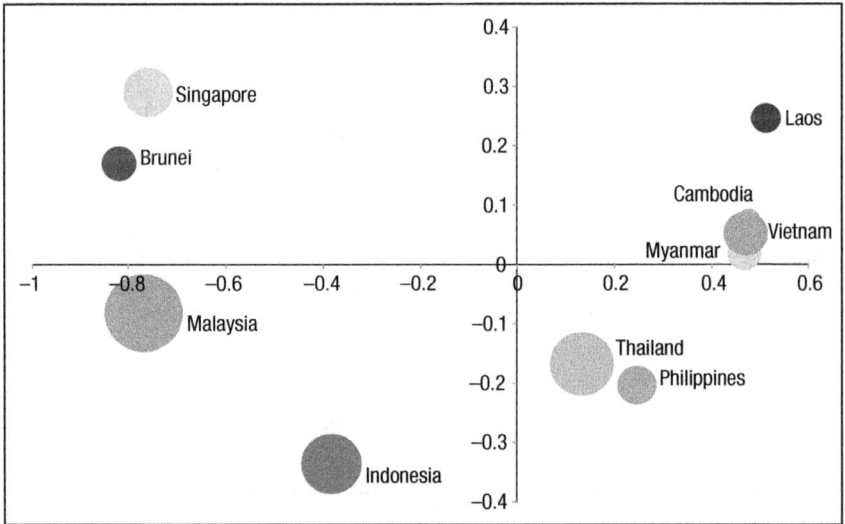

Aggregate Similiarity Matrix, University of Malaya (Malay Respondents), n=142

	BRUN	CAMB	INDO	LAOS	MSIA	MYAN	PHIL	SING	THAI	VIET
BRUN	1	0.14	0.41	0.12	0.58	0.13	0.22	0.53	0.2	0.13
CAMB	0.14	1	0.27	0.56	0.12	0.61	0.45	0.14	0.4	0.63
INDO	0.41	0.27	1	0.19	0.54	0.26	0.33	0.36	0.36	0.24
LAOS	0.12	0.56	0.19	1	0.11	0.54	0.35	0.14	0.36	0.57
MSIA	0.58	0.12	0.54	0.11	1	0.16	0.2	0.54	0.31	0.15
MYAN	0.13	0.61	0.26	0.54	0.16	1	0.48	0.13	0.45	0.64
PHIL	0.22	0.45	0.33	0.35	0.2	0.48	1	0.19	0.41	0.47
SING	0.53	0.14	0.36	0.14	0.54	0.13	0.19	1	0.27	0.15
THAI	0.2	0.4	0.36	0.36	0.31	0.45	0.41	0.27	1	0.48
VIET	0.13	0.63	0.24	0.57	0.15	0.64	0.47	0.15	0.48	1

Malaysia, Universiti Tunku Abdul Rahman (M2)

Cognitive Map of ASEAN, Universiti Tunku Abdul Rahman (Chinese Respondents), n=173

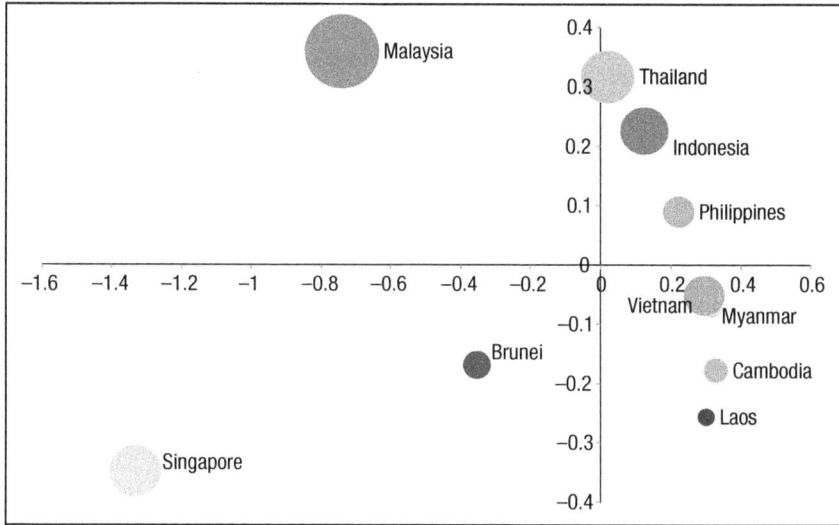

Aggregate Similiarity Matrix, Universiti Tunku Abdul Rahman (Chinese Respondents), n=173

	BRUN	CAMB	INDO	LAOS	MSIA	MYAN	PHIL	SING	THAI	VIET
BRUN	1	0.23	0.27	0.26	0.32	0.27	0.29	0.3	0.26	0.25
CAMB	0.23	1	0.43	0.55	0.14	0.6	0.44	0.11	0.34	0.56
INDO	0.27	0.43	1	0.32	0.32	0.45	0.57	0.13	0.42	0.44
LAOS	0.26	0.55	0.32	1	0.17	0.49	0.39	0.1	0.29	0.53
MSIA	0.32	0.14	0.32	0.17	1	0.18	0.2	0.45	0.37	0.18
MYAN	0.27	0.6	0.45	0.49	0.18	1	0.51	0.08	0.4	0.59
PHIL	0.29	0.44	0.57	0.39	0.2	0.51	1	0.12	0.42	0.53
SING	0.3	0.11	0.13	0.1	0.45	0.08	0.12	1	0.17	0.11
THAI	0.26	0.34	0.42	0.29	0.37	0.4	0.42	0.17	1	0.46
VIET	0.25	0.56	0.44	0.53	0.18	0.59	0.53	0.11	0.46	1

Malaysia, Universiti Malaysia Sarawak (M3)

Cognitive Map of ASEAN, Universiti Malaysia Sarawak (non-Malay, Bumiputera Respondents), n=79

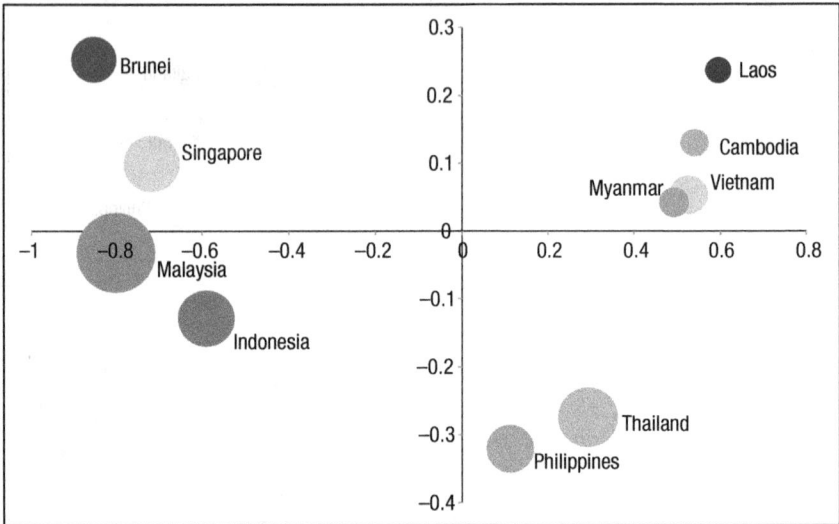

Aggregate Similiarity Matrix, Universiti Malaysia Sarawak (non-Malay, Bumiputera Respondents), n=79

	BRUN	CAMB	INDO	LAOS	MSIA	MYAN	PHIL	SING	THAI	VIET
BRUN	1	0.1	0.52	0.11	0.58	0.09	0.22	0.5	0.14	0.13
CAMB	0.1	1	0.2	0.62	0.1	0.65	0.39	0.15	0.43	0.64
INDO	0.52	0.2	1	0.14	0.67	0.19	0.38	0.41	0.27	0.19
LAOS	0.11	0.62	0.14	1	0.08	0.56	0.34	0.1	0.39	0.59
MSIA	0.58	0.1	0.67	0.08	1	0.14	0.25	0.57	0.25	0.14
MYAN	0.09	0.65	0.19	0.56	0.14	1	0.41	0.14	0.48	0.64
PHIL	0.22	0.39	0.38	0.34	0.25	0.41	1	0.29	0.46	0.44
SING	0.5	0.15	0.41	0.1	0.57	0.14	0.29	1	0.2	0.16
THAI	0.14	0.43	0.27	0.39	0.25	0.48	0.46	0.2	1	0.53
VIET	0.13	0.64	0.19	0.59	0.14	0.64	0.44	0.16	0.53	1

Myanmar, University of Yangon (N1)

Cognitive Map of ASEAN, University of Yangon, n=35

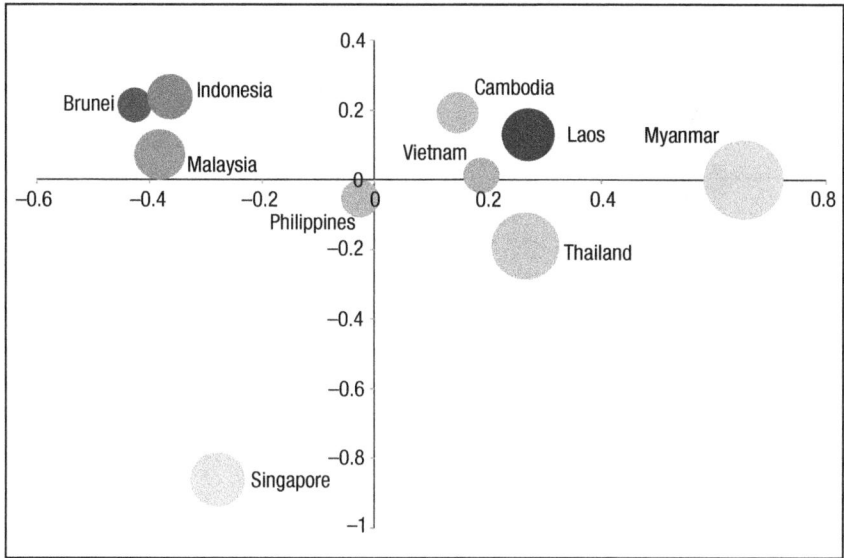

Aggregate Similiarity Matrix, University of Yangon, n=35

	BRUN	CAMB	INDO	LAOS	MSIA	MYAN	PHIL	SING	THAI	VIET
BRUN	1	0.36	0.55	0.29	0.5	0.13	0.33	0.23	0.23	0.29
CAMB	0.36	1	0.48	0.58	0.33	0.36	0.38	0.18	0.37	0.54
INDO	0.55	0.48	1	0.31	0.65	0.18	0.42	0.21	0.26	0.26
LAOS	0.29	0.58	0.31	1	0.28	0.4	0.39	0.19	0.32	0.46
MSIA	0.5	0.33	0.65	0.28	1	0.21	0.34	0.32	0.31	0.26
MYAN	0.13	0.36	0.18	0.4	0.21	1	0.25	0.14	0.42	0.26
PHIL	0.33	0.38	0.42	0.39	0.34	0.25	1	0.31	0.32	0.47
SING	0.23	0.18	0.21	0.19	0.32	0.14	0.31	1	0.29	0.25
THAI	0.23	0.37	0.26	0.32	0.31	0.42	0.32	0.29	1	0.36
VIET	0.29	0.54	0.26	0.46	0.26	0.26	0.47	0.25	0.36	1

Myanmar, University of Mandalay (N2)

Cognitive Map of ASEAN, University of Mandalay, n=106

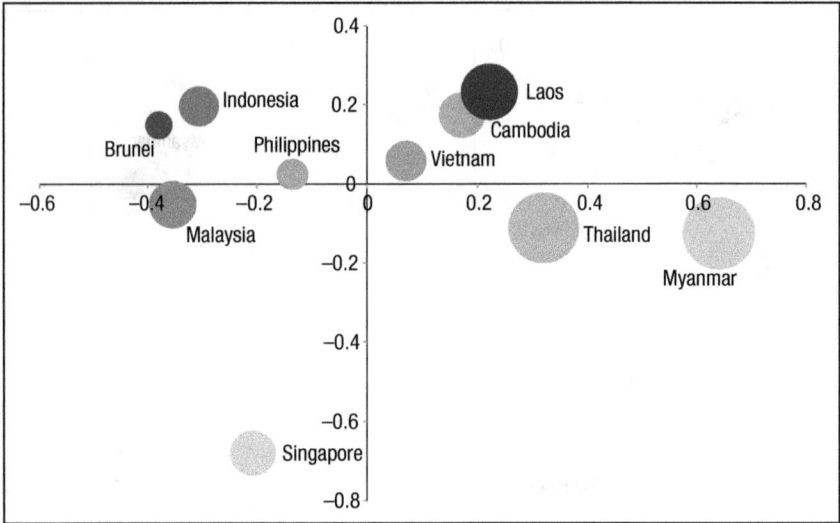

Aggregate Similiarity Matrix, University of Mandalay, n=106

	BRUN	CAMB	INDO	LAOS	MSIA	MYAN	PHIL	SING	THAI	VIET
BRUN	1	0.37	0.47	0.31	0.42	0.13	0.31	0.29	0.26	0.32
CAMB	0.37	1	0.4	0.46	0.33	0.41	0.36	0.21	0.44	0.44
INDO	0.47	0.4	1	0.35	0.57	0.21	0.39	0.24	0.25	0.39
LAOS	0.31	0.46	0.35	1	0.29	0.37	0.29	0.19	0.36	0.42
MSIA	0.42	0.33	0.57	0.29	1	0.17	0.36	0.39	0.35	0.28
MYAN	0.13	0.41	0.21	0.37	0.17	1	0.24	0.24	0.45	0.31
PHIL	0.31	0.36	0.39	0.29	0.36	0.24	1	0.3	0.25	0.45
SING	0.29	0.21	0.24	0.19	0.39	0.24	0.3	1	0.29	0.31
THAI	0.26	0.44	0.25	0.36	0.35	0.45	0.25	0.29	1	0.37
VIET	0.32	0.44	0.39	0.42	0.28	0.31	0.45	0.31	0.37	1

The Philippines, University of the Philippines Diliman (P1)

Cognitive Map of ASEAN, University of the Philippines Diliman, n=184

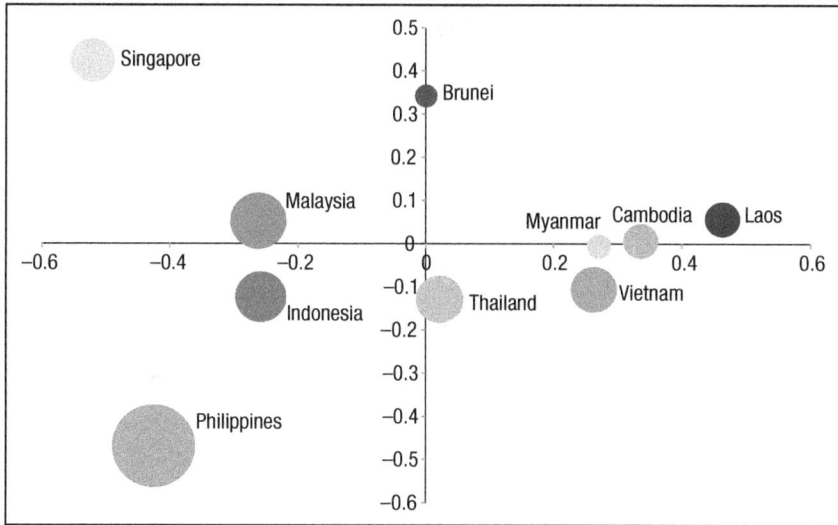

Aggregate Similiarity Matrix, University of the Philippines Diliman, n=184

	BRUN	CAMB	INDO	LAOS	MSIA	MYAN	PHIL	SING	THAI	VIET
BRUN	1	0.34	0.37	0.34	0.39	0.34	0.22	0.29	0.25	0.27
CAMB	0.34	1	0.34	0.47	0.32	0.45	0.2	0.21	0.43	0.52
INDO	0.37	0.34	1	0.22	0.57	0.31	0.44	0.29	0.35	0.35
LAOS	0.34	0.47	0.22	1	0.24	0.41	0.21	0.17	0.31	0.43
MSIA	0.39	0.32	0.57	0.24	1	0.37	0.36	0.42	0.39	0.35
MYAN	0.34	0.45	0.31	0.41	0.37	1	0.24	0.19	0.37	0.4
PHIL	0.22	0.2	0.44	0.21	0.36	0.24	1	0.28	0.34	0.25
SING	0.29	0.21	0.29	0.17	0.42	0.19	0.28	1	0.32	0.22
THAI	0.25	0.43	0.35	0.31	0.39	0.37	0.34	0.32	1	0.48
VIET	0.27	0.52	0.35	0.43	0.35	0.4	0.25	0.22	0.48	1

The Philippines, University of the Philippines Visayas (P2)

Cognitive Map of ASEAN, University of the Philippines Visayas, n=183

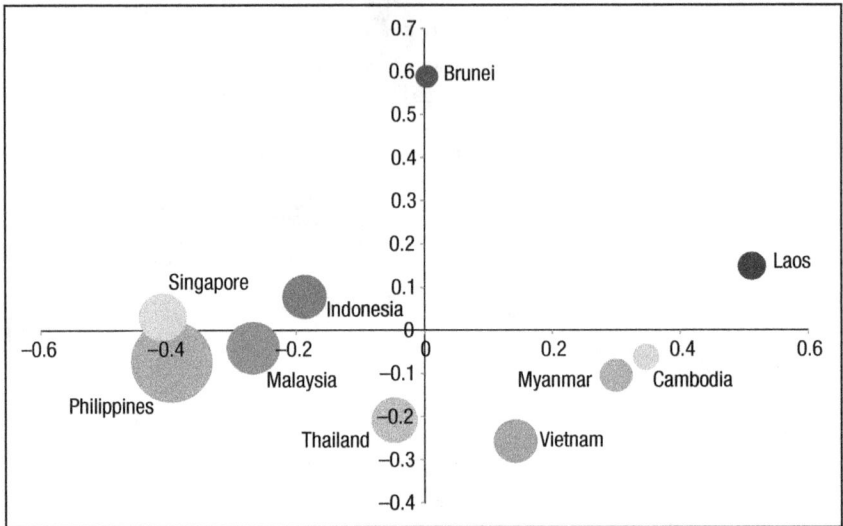

Aggregate Similiarity Matrix, University of the Philippines Visayas, n=183

	BRUN	CAMB	INDO	LAOS	MSIA	MYAN	PHIL	SING	THAI	VIET
BRUN	1	0.31	0.36	0.31	0.31	0.29	0.26	0.3	0.28	0.24
CAMB	0.31	1	0.36	0.4	0.34	0.44	0.22	0.22	0.42	0.47
INDO	0.36	0.36	1	0.27	0.55	0.33	0.43	0.3	0.37	0.31
LAOS	0.31	0.4	0.27	1	0.23	0.42	0.2	0.18	0.26	0.36
MSIA	0.31	0.34	0.55	0.23	1	0.32	0.41	0.44	0.45	0.36
MYAN	0.29	0.44	0.33	0.42	0.32	1	0.21	0.22	0.39	0.39
PHIL	0.26	0.22	0.43	0.2	0.41	0.21	1	0.3	0.36	0.32
SING	0.3	0.22	0.3	0.18	0.44	0.22	0.3	1	0.35	0.31
THAI	0.28	0.42	0.37	0.26	0.45	0.39	0.36	0.35	1	0.45
VIET	0.24	0.47	0.31	0.36	0.36	0.39	0.32	0.31	0.45	1

The Philippines, Mindanao State University (P3)

Cognitive Map of ASEAN, Mindanao State University, n=176

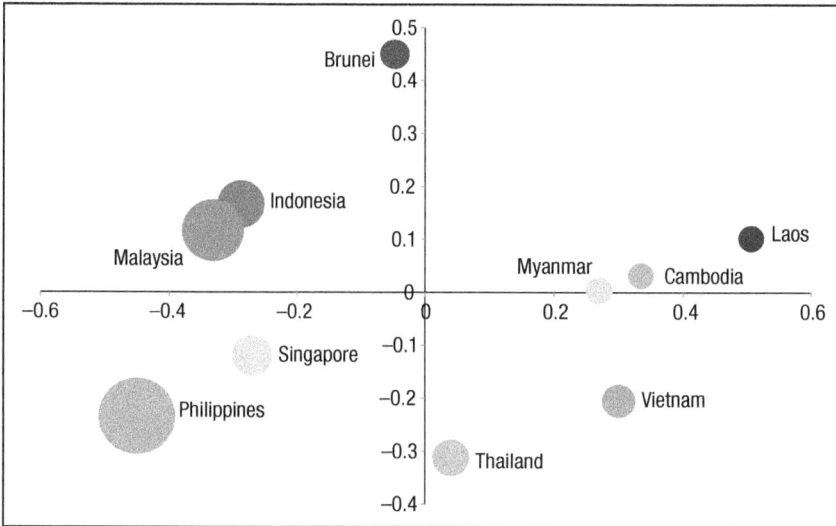

Aggregate Similiarity Matrix, Mindanao State University, n=176

	BRUN	CAMB	INDO	LAOS	MSIA	MYAN	PHIL	SING	THAI	VIET
BRUN	1	0.33	0.42	0.3	0.39	0.31	0.26	0.31	0.25	0.28
CAMB	0.33	1	0.29	0.38	0.29	0.47	0.2	0.28	0.37	0.39
INDO	0.42	0.29	1	0.2	0.65	0.35	0.39	0.32	0.36	0.31
LAOS	0.3	0.38	0.2	1	0.23	0.39	0.19	0.23	0.27	0.37
MSIA	0.39	0.29	0.65	0.23	1	0.33	0.45	0.43	0.35	0.28
MYAN	0.31	0.47	0.35	0.39	0.33	1	0.22	0.3	0.38	0.4
PHIL	0.26	0.2	0.39	0.19	0.45	0.22	1	0.41	0.36	0.24
SING	0.31	0.28	0.32	0.23	0.43	0.3	0.41	1	0.34	0.26
THAI	0.25	0.37	0.36	0.27	0.35	0.38	0.36	0.34	1	0.45
VIET	0.28	0.39	0.31	0.37	0.28	0.4	0.24	0.26	0.45	1

Singapore, National University of Singapore (S1)

Cognitive Map of ASEAN, National University of Singapore, n=210

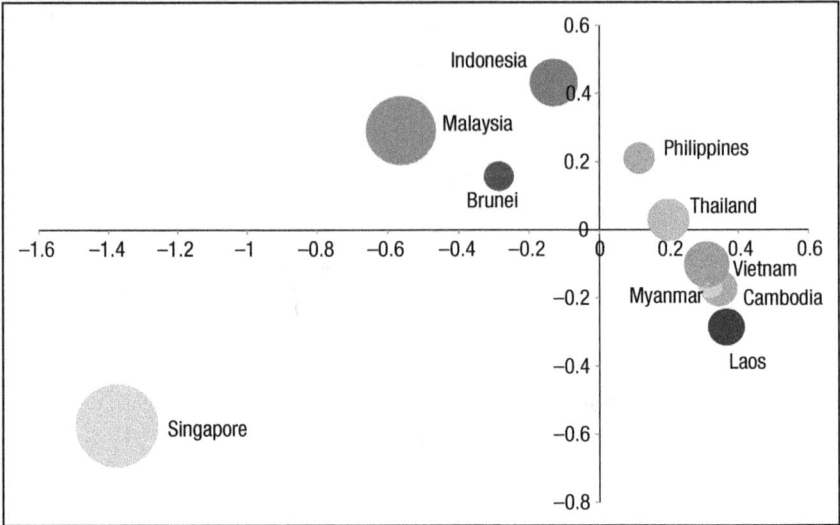

Aggregate Similiarity Matrix, National University of Singapore, n=210

	BRUN	CAMB	INDO	LAOS	MSIA	MYAN	PHIL	SING	THAI	VIET
BRUN	1	0.27	0.4	0.28	0.38	0.3	0.29	0.27	0.24	0.25
CAMB	0.27	1	0.34	0.56	0.18	0.61	0.39	0.09	0.5	0.6
INDO	0.4	0.34	1	0.22	0.57	0.3	0.5	0.15	0.37	0.35
LAOS	0.28	0.56	0.22	1	0.17	0.5	0.29	0.08	0.36	0.49
MSIA	0.38	0.18	0.57	0.17	1	0.2	0.29	0.42	0.32	0.22
MYAN	0.3	0.61	0.3	0.5	0.2	1	0.39	0.09	0.44	0.52
PHIL	0.29	0.39	0.5	0.29	0.29	0.39	1	0.13	0.46	0.46
SING	0.27	0.09	0.15	0.08	0.42	0.09	0.13	1	0.12	0.1
THAI	0.24	0.5	0.37	0.36	0.32	0.44	0.46	0.12	1	0.52
VIET	0.25	0.6	0.35	0.49	0.22	0.52	0.46	0.1	0.52	1

Singapore, Singapore Polytechnic (S2)

Cognitive Map of ASEAN, Singapore Polytechnic, n=231

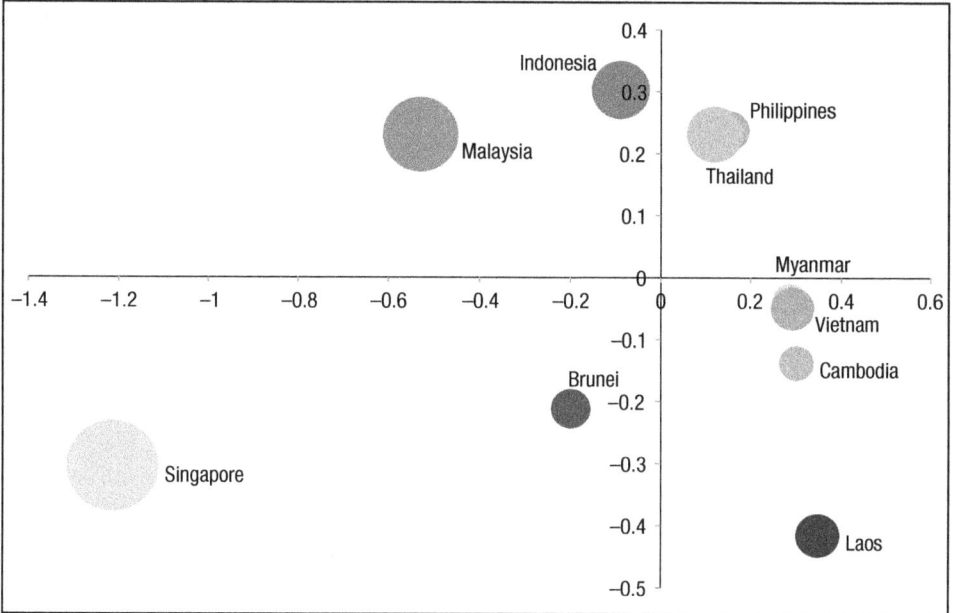

Aggregate Similiarity Matrix, Singapore Polytechnic, n=231

	BRUN	CAMB	INDO	LAOS	MSIA	MYAN	PHIL	SING	THAI	VIET
BRUN	1	0.31	0.36	0.31	0.33	0.28	0.29	0.28	0.23	0.3
CAMB	0.31	1	0.36	0.49	0.21	0.55	0.42	0.11	0.39	0.52
INDO	0.36	0.36	1	0.23	0.5	0.37	0.5	0.21	0.39	0.36
LAOS	0.31	0.49	0.23	1	0.16	0.45	0.29	0.1	0.3	0.46
MSIA	0.33	0.21	0.5	0.16	1	0.27	0.27	0.45	0.36	0.23
MYAN	0.28	0.55	0.37	0.45	0.27	1	0.42	0.1	0.45	0.54
PHIL	0.29	0.42	0.5	0.29	0.27	0.42	1	0.14	0.49	0.45
SING	0.28	0.11	0.21	0.1	0.45	0.1	0.14	1	0.16	0.11
THAI	0.23	0.39	0.39	0.3	0.36	0.45	0.49	0.16	1	0.46
VIET	0.3	0.52	0.36	0.46	0.23	0.54	0.45	0.11	0.46	1

Thailand, Chulalongkorn University (T1)

Cognitive Map of ASEAN, Chulalongkorn University, n=199

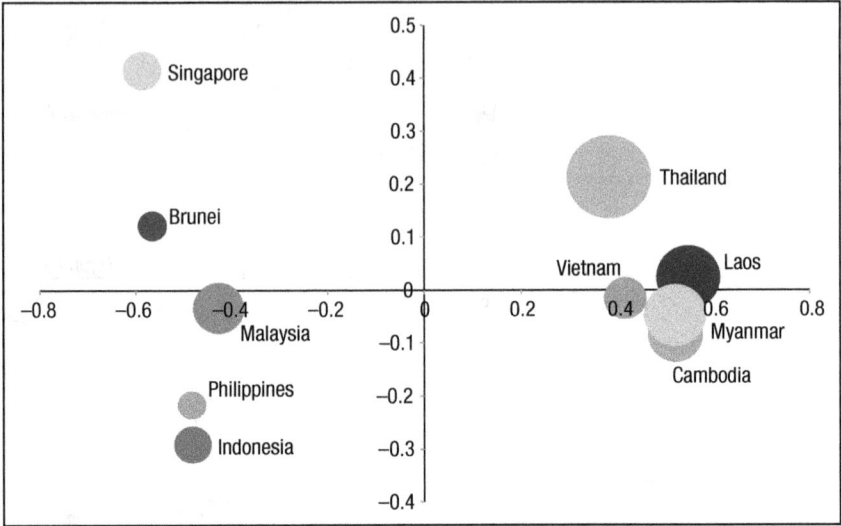

Aggregate Similiarity Matrix, Chulalongkorn University, n=199

	BRUN	CAMB	INDO	LAOS	MSIA	MYAN	PHIL	SING	THAI	VIET
BRUN	1	0.18	0.48	0.16	0.39	0.16	0.38	0.44	0.17	0.19
CAMB	0.18	1	0.24	0.6	0.2	0.61	0.22	0.13	0.43	0.55
INDO	0.48	0.24	1	0.18	0.58	0.22	0.62	0.35	0.21	0.25
LAOS	0.16	0.6	0.18	1	0.24	0.62	0.2	0.15	0.49	0.58
MSIA	0.39	0.2	0.58	0.24	1	0.24	0.47	0.49	0.25	0.27
MYAN	0.16	0.61	0.22	0.62	0.24	1	0.2	0.15	0.43	0.5
PHIL	0.38	0.22	0.62	0.2	0.47	0.2	1	0.45	0.22	0.24
SING	0.44	0.13	0.35	0.15	0.49	0.15	0.45	1	0.22	0.19
THAI	0.17	0.43	0.21	0.49	0.25	0.43	0.22	0.22	1	0.42
VIET	0.19	0.55	0.25	0.58	0.27	0.5	0.24	0.19	0.42	1

Thailand, Khon Kaen University (T2)

Cognitive Map of ASEAN, Khon Kaen University, n=196

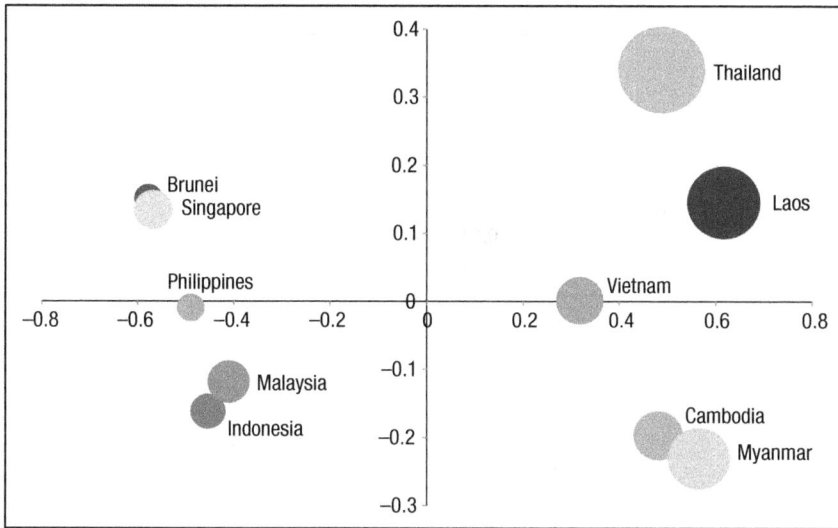

Aggregate Similiarity Matrix, Khon Kaen University, n=196

	BRUN	CAMB	INDO	LAOS	MSIA	MYAN	PHIL	SING	THAI	VIET
BRUN	1	0.15	0.48	0.13	0.41	0.15	0.44	0.49	0.17	0.23
CAMB	0.15	1	0.26	0.52	0.24	0.63	0.22	0.19	0.44	0.5
INDO	0.48	0.26	1	0.16	0.58	0.22	0.57	0.41	0.2	0.28
LAOS	0.13	0.52	0.16	1	0.18	0.57	0.18	0.16	0.58	0.5
MSIA	0.41	0.24	0.58	0.18	1	0.24	0.5	0.48	0.24	0.29
MYAN	0.15	0.63	0.22	0.57	0.24	1	0.16	0.13	0.41	0.45
PHIL	0.44	0.22	0.57	0.18	0.5	0.16	1	0.53	0.21	0.3
SING	0.49	0.19	0.41	0.16	0.48	0.13	0.53	1	0.16	0.23
THAI	0.17	0.44	0.2	0.58	0.24	0.41	0.21	0.16	1	0.43
VIET	0.23	0.5	0.28	0.5	0.29	0.45	0.3	0.23	0.43	1

Thailand, Walailak University (T3)

Cognitive Map of ASEAN, Walailak University (Muslim Respondents), n=178

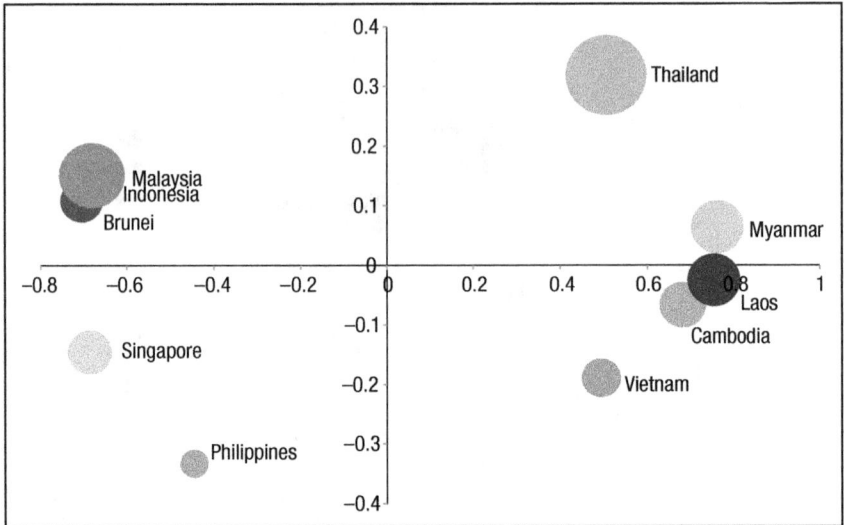

Aggregate Similiarity Matrix, Walailak University (Muslim Respondents), n=178

	BRUN	CAMB	INDO	LAOS	MSIA	MYAN	PHIL	SING	THAI	VIET
BRUN	1	0.12	0.64	0.08	0.63	0.08	0.42	0.57	0.14	0.2
CAMB	0.12	1	0.14	0.68	0.11	0.69	0.22	0.11	0.45	0.61
INDO	0.64	0.14	1	0.09	0.72	0.11	0.47	0.53	0.17	0.17
LAOS	0.08	0.68	0.09	1	0.1	0.72	0.16	0.11	0.48	0.61
MSIA	0.63	0.11	0.72	0.1	1	0.11	0.45	0.64	0.21	0.16
MYAN	0.08	0.69	0.11	0.72	0.11	1	0.14	0.08	0.5	0.51
PHIL	0.42	0.22	0.47	0.16	0.45	0.14	1	0.6	0.21	0.31
SING	0.57	0.11	0.53	0.11	0.64	0.08	0.6	1	0.14	0.19
THAI	0.14	0.45	0.17	0.48	0.21	0.5	0.21	0.14	1	0.4
VIET	0.2	0.61	0.17	0.61	0.16	0.51	0.31	0.19	0.4	1

Thailand, Saint John's University (T4)

Cognitive Map of ASEAN, Saint John's University, n=165

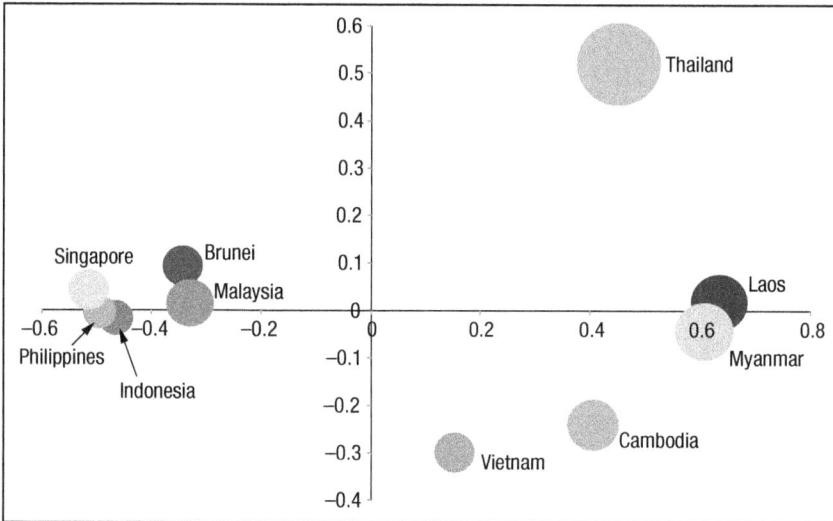

Aggregate Similiarity Matrix, Saint John's University, n=165

	BRUN	CAMB	INDO	LAOS	MSIA	MYAN	PHIL	SING	THAI	VIET
BRUN	1	0.24	0.44	0.2	0.34	0.22	0.4	0.45	0.21	0.28
CAMB	0.24	1	0.24	0.5	0.29	0.53	0.24	0.21	0.34	0.51
INDO	0.44	0.24	1	0.13	0.51	0.21	0.58	0.48	0.19	0.33
LAOS	0.2	0.5	0.13	1	0.2	0.63	0.17	0.16	0.48	0.44
MSIA	0.34	0.29	0.51	0.2	1	0.21	0.52	0.51	0.28	0.38
MYAN	0.22	0.53	0.21	0.63	0.21	1	0.15	0.13	0.41	0.38
PHIL	0.4	0.24	0.58	0.17	0.52	0.15	1	0.59	0.19	0.32
SING	0.45	0.21	0.48	0.16	0.51	0.13	0.59	1	0.19	0.31
THAI	0.21	0.34	0.19	0.48	0.28	0.41	0.19	0.19	1	0.27
VIET	0.28	0.51	0.33	0.44	0.38	0.38	0.32	0.31	0.27	1

Vietnam, Vietnam National University, Hanoi (V1)

Cognitive Map of ASEAN, Vietnam National University, Hanoi, n=153

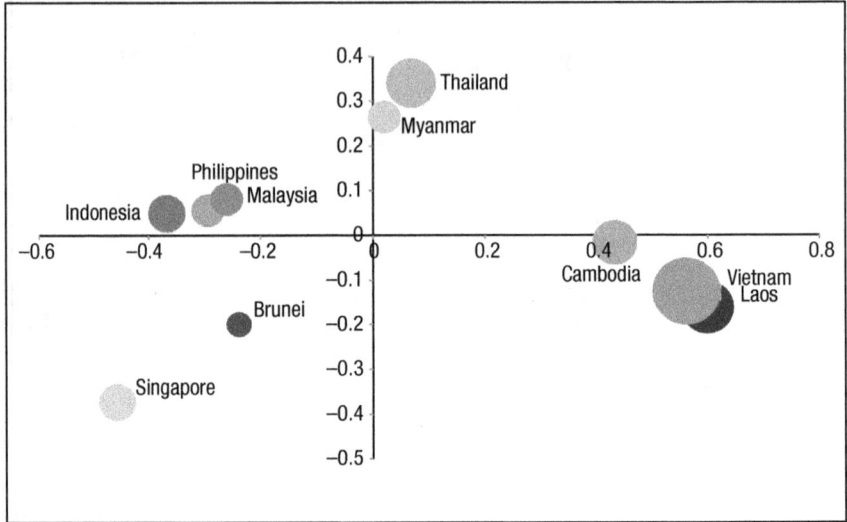

Aggregate Similiarity Matrix, Vietnam National University, Hanoi, n=153

	BRUN	CAMB	INDO	LAOS	MSIA	MYAN	PHIL	SING	THAI	VIET
BRUN	1	0.29	0.42	0.27	0.39	0.35	0.37	0.35	0.25	0.19
CAMB	0.29	1	0.24	0.56	0.28	0.4	0.3	0.19	0.36	0.47
INDO	0.42	0.24	1	0.18	0.54	0.4	0.51	0.41	0.32	0.21
LAOS	0.27	0.56	0.18	1	0.24	0.36	0.2	0.16	0.28	0.54
MSIA	0.39	0.28	0.54	0.24	1	0.41	0.51	0.37	0.35	0.27
MYAN	0.35	0.4	0.4	0.36	0.41	1	0.38	0.23	0.41	0.27
PHIL	0.37	0.3	0.51	0.2	0.51	0.38	1	0.39	0.33	0.24
SING	0.35	0.19	0.41	0.16	0.37	0.23	0.39	1	0.27	0.17
THAI	0.25	0.36	0.32	0.28	0.35	0.41	0.33	0.27	1	0.34
VIET	0.19	0.47	0.21	0.54	0.27	0.27	0.24	0.17	0.34	1

Vietnam, Vietnam National University, Ho Chi Minh City (V2)

Cognitive Map of ASEAN, Vietnam National University, Ho Chi Minh City, n=168

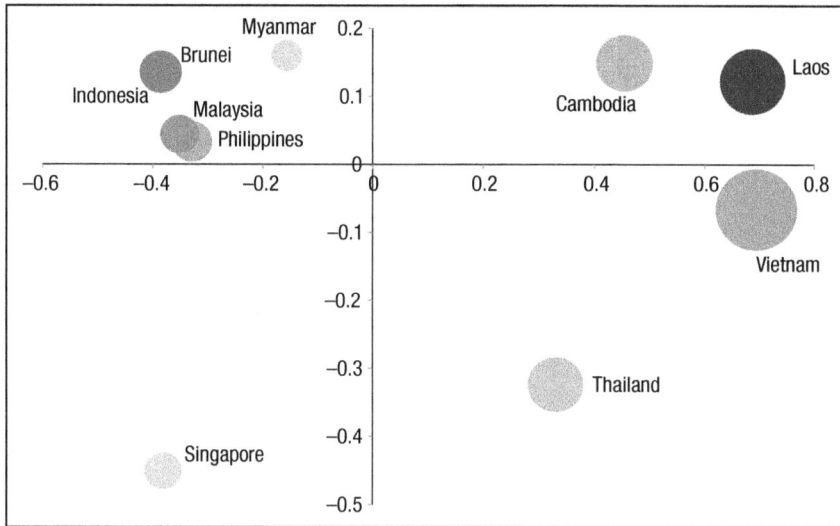

Aggregate Similiarity Matrix, Vietnam National University, Ho Chi Minh City, n=168

	BRUN	CAMB	INDO	LAOS	MSIA	MYAN	PHIL	SING	THAI	VIET
BRUN	1	0.23	0.43	0.17	0.39	0.37	0.35	0.37	0.19	0.15
CAMB	0.23	1	0.29	0.58	0.28	0.37	0.28	0.19	0.4	0.51
INDO	0.43	0.29	1	0.16	0.63	0.48	0.55	0.38	0.25	0.17
LAOS	0.17	0.58	0.16	1	0.2	0.28	0.19	0.13	0.41	0.52
MSIA	0.39	0.28	0.63	0.2	1	0.48	0.55	0.43	0.3	0.18
MYAN	0.37	0.37	0.48	0.28	0.48	1	0.45	0.31	0.34	0.22
PHIL	0.35	0.28	0.55	0.19	0.55	0.45	1	0.43	0.26	0.21
SING	0.37	0.19	0.38	0.13	0.43	0.31	0.43	1	0.32	0.16
THAI	0.19	0.4	0.25	0.41	0.3	0.34	0.26	0.32	1	0.44
VIET	0.15	0.51	0.17	0.52	0.18	0.22	0.21	0.16	0.44	1

QAP Correlation Table

	B1	C1	I1	I2	I3	L1	M1	M2	M3	N1	N2	P1	P2	P3
B1	1.00	0.73	0.93	0.96	0.85	0.71	0.96	0.62	0.99	0.61	0.60	0.62	0.55	0.57
C1	0.73	1.00	0.73	0.65	0.63	0.89	0.62	0.34	0.73	0.52	0.55	0.71	0.68	0.74
I1	0.93	0.73	1.00	0.94	0.93	0.70	0.91	0.66	0.94	0.64	0.58	0.72	0.65	0.65
I2	0.96	0.65	0.94	1.00	0.87	0.62	0.94	0.57	0.96	0.63	0.58	0.57	0.49	0.53
I3	0.85	0.63	0.93	0.87	1.00	0.64	0.79	0.51	0.84	0.53	0.48	0.71	0.62	0.65
L1	0.71	0.89	0.70	0.62	0.64	1.00	0.61	0.34	0.72	0.52	0.55	0.66	0.64	0.72
M1	0.96	0.62	0.91	0.94	0.79	0.61	1.00	0.76	0.97	0.58	0.57	0.59	0.53	0.49
M2	0.62	0.34	0.66	0.57	0.51	0.34	0.76	1.00	0.68	0.47	0.46	0.52	0.47	0.26
M3	0.99	0.73	0.94	0.96	0.84	0.72	0.97	0.68	1.00	0.64	0.63	0.65	0.58	0.60
N1	0.61	0.52	0.64	0.63	0.53	0.52	0.58	0.47	0.64	1.00	0.89	0.60	0.55	0.47
N2	0.60	0.55	0.58	0.58	0.48	0.55	0.57	0.46	0.63	0.89	1.00	0.60	0.61	0.52
P1	0.62	0.71	0.72	0.57	0.71	0.66	0.59	0.52	0.65	0.60	0.60	1.00	0.91	0.84
P2	0.55	0.68	0.65	0.49	0.62	0.64	0.53	0.47	0.58	0.55	0.61	0.91	1.00	0.84
P3	0.57	0.74	0.65	0.53	0.65	0.72	0.49	0.26	0.60	0.47	0.52	0.84	0.84	1.00
S1	0.78	0.59	0.84	0.74	0.74	0.54	0.82	0.88	0.82	0.67	0.67	0.76	0.68	0.55
S2	0.72	0.49	0.79	0.68	0.70	0.47	0.80	0.92	0.77	0.59	0.58	0.71	0.65	0.51
T1	0.79	0.90	0.78	0.69	0.70	0.91	0.72	0.51	0.81	0.61	0.64	0.73	0.67	0.70
T2	0.75	0.89	0.71	0.65	0.65	0.93	0.65	0.41	0.76	0.55	0.62	0.64	0.61	0.67
T3	0.85	0.89	0.80	0.79	0.73	0.91	0.76	0.42	0.86	0.61	0.65	0.63	0.59	0.68
T4	0.61	0.82	0.60	0.53	0.57	0.90	0.50	0.29	0.63	0.49	0.55	0.57	0.58	0.61
V1	0.60	0.78	0.66	0.54	0.61	0.78	0.53	0.39	0.61	0.52	0.42	0.71	0.63	0.69
V2	0.54	0.75	0.57	0.49	0.53	0.75	0.47	0.31	0.56	0.45	0.37	0.64	0.55	0.66
xGDP	0.58	0.39	0.60	0.56	0.41	0.36	0.68	0.67	0.61	0.42	0.38	0.41	0.41	0.28
xMBI	0.66	0.77	0.56	0.58	0.53	0.73	0.54	0.24	0.65	0.52	0.57	0.48	0.45	0.60
xPOP	0.02	-0.14	0.02	0.00	0.07	-0.19	0.04	0.16	0.01	-0.02	0.01	0.09	0.07	-0.01
xGDP+MBI	0.80	0.75	0.75	0.74	0.62	0.71	0.79	0.57	0.82	0.61	0.62	0.58	0.56	0.57

QAP Correlation Table   (continued)

	S1	S2	T1	T2	T3	T4	V1	V2	GDP	MBI	POP	GDP+MBI
BI	0.78	0.72	0.79	0.75	0.85	0.61	0.60	0.54	0.58	0.66	0.02	0.80
CI	0.59	0.49	0.90	0.89	0.89	0.82	0.78	0.75	0.39	0.77	-0.14	0.75
I1	0.84	0.79	0.78	0.71	0.80	0.60	0.66	0.57	0.60	0.56	0.02	0.75
I2	0.74	0.68	0.69	0.65	0.79	0.53	0.54	0.49	0.56	0.58	0.00	0.74
I3	0.74	0.70	0.70	0.65	0.73	0.57	0.61	0.53	0.41	0.53	0.07	0.62
L1	0.54	0.47	0.91	0.93	0.91	0.90	0.78	0.75	0.36	0.73	-0.19	0.71
M1	0.82	0.80	0.72	0.65	0.76	0.50	0.53	0.47	0.68	0.54	0.04	0.79
M2	0.88	0.92	0.51	0.41	0.42	0.29	0.39	0.31	0.67	0.24	0.16	0.57
M3	0.82	0.77	0.81	0.76	0.86	0.63	0.61	0.56	0.61	0.65	0.01	0.82
N1	0.67	0.59	0.61	0.55	0.61	0.49	0.52	0.45	0.42	0.52	-0.02	0.61
N2	0.67	0.58	0.64	0.62	0.65	0.55	0.42	0.37	0.38	0.57	0.01	0.62
P1	0.76	0.71	0.73	0.64	0.63	0.57	0.71	0.64	0.41	0.48	0.09	0.58
P2	0.68	0.65	0.67	0.61	0.59	0.58	0.63	0.55	0.41	0.45	0.07	0.56
P3	0.55	0.51	0.70	0.67	0.68	0.61	0.69	0.66	0.28	0.60	-0.01	0.57
S1	1.00	0.97	0.70	0.62	0.63	0.48	0.58	0.49	0.59	0.46	0.11	0.68
S2	0.97	1.00	0.61	0.52	0.54	0.41	0.56	0.44	0.59	0.32	0.17	0.59
T1	0.70	0.61	1.00	0.97	0.94	0.90	0.75	0.69	0.48	0.79	-0.03	0.82
T2	0.62	0.52	0.97	1.00	0.95	0.93	0.68	0.65	0.39	0.80	-0.06	0.78
T3	0.63	0.54	0.94	0.95	1.00	0.89	0.69	0.62	0.46	0.83	-0.09	0.84
T4	0.48	0.41	0.90	0.93	0.89	1.00	0.64	0.56	0.36	0.69	-0.07	0.69
V1	0.58	0.56	0.75	0.68	0.69	0.64	1.00	0.92	0.38	0.55	-0.03	0.60
V2	0.49	0.44	0.69	0.65	0.62	0.56	0.92	1.00	0.24	0.52	-0.01	0.49
xGDP	0.59	0.59	0.48	0.59	0.46	0.36	0.38	0.24	1.00	0.19	0.20	0.76
xMBI	0.46	0.32	0.79	0.80	0.83	0.69	0.55	0.52	0.19	1.00	-0.09	0.78
xPOP	0.11	0.17	-0.03	0.17	-0.09	-0.07	-0.03	-0.01	0.20	-0.09	1.00	0.07
xGDP+MBI	0.68	0.59	0.82	0.59	0.84	0.69	0.60	0.49	0.76	0.78	0.07	1.00

ABOUT THE AUTHORS

Eric C. Thompson is Associate Professor in the Department of Sociology at the National University of Singapore (NUS). Before joining NUS, he completed a PhD in Sociocultural Anthropology at the University of Washington and was a Postdoctoral Fellow at the Center for Southeast Asian Studies, University of California, Los Angeles.

He teaches anthropology, gender studies, urban studies and research methods. He has conducted research for over two decades throughout Southeast Asia, primarily in Malaysia, Singapore, Thailand, and Indonesia. His research interests include transnational networking, gender studies, urbanism, culture theory, and ASEAN regionalism.

His work has appeared in the journals *American Ethnologist, Asian Studies Review, Citizenship Studies, Contemporary Sociology, Contemporary Southeast Asia, Field Methods, Gender Place and Culture, Global Networks, Political Geography, Urban Studies,* and *Women's Studies International Forum,* among others. He is the author of *Unsettling Absences: Urbanism in Rural Malaysia* (2007) and *Attitudes and Awareness Towards ASEAN: Findings of a Ten-Nation Survey* (co-authored with Chulanee Thianthai, 2008). In 2014–15, he served as lead investigator for the update of this ASEAN Awareness Survey.

Chulanee Thianthai is a tenure track Associate Professor at the Department of Sociology and Anthropology, Faculty of Political Science, Chulalongkorn University. She received a PhD in Biocultural Anthropology in 2003. Her specialization and research interests cover business anthropology, medical anthropology, gender differences, and youth culture, particularly among urban population in Thailand and ASEAN countries. Her diverse interests have led her to many research publications, such as *Attitudes and Awareness Towards ASEAN: Findings of a Ten-Nation Survey* (2008) conducted among undergraduate university students in the ASEAN countries and "Thai Perceptions of the ASEAN Region: Southeast Asia as *Prathet Phuean Ban*" (2007) in *Asian Studies Review*, both of which she co-authored with Eric C. Thompson; "Gender and Class Differences in Young People's Sexuality and HIV/AIDS Risk-taking Behaviours in Thailand" (2004) in *Culture, Health, and Sexuality*; "A Glance into the Life of a Computerized Generation: A Case Study on Thai Teenagers Living in Bangkok" (2007) in *Computing and Philosophy in Asia*; "Do Male and Female Adolescents View Their Dissatisfaction with Body Parts in the Same Way?" (2008) and "Influential Sources Affecting Bangkok Adolescent Body Image Perceptions" (2006) in the *International Journal of Adolescence Medicine and Health*. Currently, she teaches and consults on anthropological research methodology, medical anthropology, business anthropology, organizational anthropology, and cross-cultural management.

Moe Thuzar is Lead Researcher (socio-cultural) at the ASEAN Studies Centre (ASC) at ISEAS – Yusof Ishak Institute. Since July 2012, she has been appointed an ISEAS Fellow with the Regional Social and Cultural Studies Programme. She is also a key member of the Institute's Myanmar Studies Programme, and served as first coordinator of the programme from July 2012 to October 2013. Since joining the ASC at ISEAS in 2008, Moe has assessed the implementation of regional priorities in the areas under the ASEAN Socio-Cultural Community. Prior to joining ISEAS, Moe headed the Human Development Unit at the ASEAN Secretariat, which coordinated regional cooperation in eight main areas: youth, labour, education, health, social welfare and development, rural development and poverty eradication, women, and civil service matters. Moe is the co-author of *Myanmar: Life After Nargis* (with Pavin Chachavalpongpun, 2009), and co-editor of *Urbanization in Southeast Asia: Issues and Impacts* (with Yap Kioe Sheng, 2012). She has also contributed to several compendia/volumes on ASEAN and Myanmar. Moe is also a resident analyst for Channel NewsAsia's news analyses on ASEAN matters, and on Myanmar. In addition to monitoring Myanmar's reforms and democratization, her research interests include ASEAN integration issues and ASEAN's dialogue relations, disaster management and humanitarian assistance, human security, and migration. Moe was a Temasek scholar for the Master in Public Policy Programme at the National University of Singapore.

www.ingramcontent.com/pod-product-compliance
Lightning Source LLC
Chambersburg PA
CBHW060152280326
41932CB00012B/1726